P9-DSZ-112

DATE DUE

NO 3 08			
DE 19 08			

DEMCO 38-296

ELECTRONIC AND COMPUTER MUSIC

**Recent Titles in
the Music Reference Collection**

Rock Stars/Pop Stars: A Comprehensive Bibliography, 1955–1994
Brady J. Leyser, compiler

The Johnny Cash Record Catalog
John L. Smith, compiler

Thesaurus of Abstract Musical Properties: A Theoretical and
Compositional Resource
Jeffrey Johnson

Song Finder: A Title Index to 32,000 Popular Songs in Collections, 1854–1992
Gary Lynn Ferguson, compiler

Musical Anthologies for Analytical Study: A Bibliography
James E. Perone, compiler

A Guide to Popular Music Reference Books: An Annotated Bibliography
Gary Haggerty

Rock Music Scholarship: An Interdisciplinary Bibliography
Jeffrey N. Gatten

Sing Glory and Hallelujah!: Historical and Biographical Guide to *Gospel Hymns
Nos. 1 to 6 Complete*
Samuel J. Rogal, compiler

Orchestration Theory: A Bibliography
James E. Perone, compiler

Brass Music of Black Composers: A Bibliography
Aaron Horne, compiler

The Music and Dance of the World's Religions: A Comprehensive, Annotated
Bibliography of Materials in the English Language
E. Gardner Rust

Twentieth-Century American Music for the Dance: A Bibliography
Isabelle Emerson, compiler and editor

ELECTRONIC AND COMPUTER MUSIC

An Annotated Bibliography

ROBERT L. WICK

Music Reference Collection, Number 56
Donald L. Hixon, Series Adviser

GREENWOOD PRESS
Westport, Connecticut • London

Riverside Community College
'00   Library
MAY 4800 Magnolia Avenue
Riverside, CA 92506

ML 128 .E4 W53 1997

Wick, Robert L., 1938-

Electronic and computer
  music

Library of Congress Cataloging-in-Publication Data

Wick, Robert L., 1938–
    Electronic and computer music : an annotated bibliography / Robert
L. Wick.
        p.   cm.—(Music reference collection, ISSN 0736–7740 ; no.
56)
    Includes indexes.
    ISBN 0–313–30076–3 (alk. paper)
    1. Electronic music—History and criticism—Bibliography.
    2. Computer music—History and criticism—Bibliography.   I. Title.
II. Series.
    ML128.E4W53   1997
    016.7867—dc20   96–43573

British Library Cataloguing in Publication Data is available.

Copyright © 1997 by Robert L. Wick

All rights reserved. No portion of this book may be
reproduced, by any process or technique, without the
express written consent of the publisher.

Library of Congress Catalog Card Number: 96–43573
ISBN: 0–313–30076–3
ISSN: 0736–7740

First published in 1997

Greenwood Press, 88 Post Road West, Westport, CT 06881
An imprint of Greenwood Publishing Group, Inc.

Printed in the United States of America

The paper used in this book complies with the
Permanent Paper Standard issued by the National
Information Standards Organization (Z39.48–1984).

10 9 8 7 6 5 4 3 2 1

For my wife Norma,
who always supports my "crazy" projects.

Contents

Preface

This annotated bibliography of electronic and computer music books is intended to be a desk reference for musicians, music teachers, and all who are interested in music created through electronic means. The works included cover only the basic sources concerned with the composition and performance of electronic and computer music. Related subjects, e.g., sound recording and studio engineering, electronic engineering, computer programming, etc., are not covered with the exception of a few important works which, while not directly concerned with electronic music production, have become standard sources for electronic musicians. Also, with a few exceptions, books written in languages other than English have not been included. The reason for not including books written in languages other than English is simply to contain the size and scope of the project, and not because the author feels that these non-English works are not important.

The sections of this bibliography are divided into the basic kinds of works written on electronic music, i.e., histories and general works, electronic music synthesis and synthesizers, electronic music instruments and devices, electronic music composition, MIDI (musical instrument digital interface), teaching electronic and computer music, composers, dictionaries, and electronic music conferences. Making all the books fit into these categories is done in a somewhat arbitrary manner due to the various combinations of subjects authors often use. Generally, the predominant subject of a book is used to classify it into a particular section. Works which cover several subjects are included with "histories and general works."

Each entry follows standard bibliographic form including author, title, place of publication, publisher, date, pages, an indication of the inclusion of illustrations, the ISBN (International Standard Book Number) and the LCCN (Library of Congress Catalog Number) if provided in the source. Also, any indication of the work being part of a series, or the inclusion of a recording is listed. Only books which have been examined have been included.

The annotations have been kept as brief as possible, but the size of an annotation should not be construed as indicating the importance of the book being considered. Also, the annotations should not be considered "reviews" of the work in the sense that they indicate accuracy or value. For the most part the annotations attempt to indicate what information the book contains, and how it may be used to enhance the reader's knowledge or performance of electronic music. Whenever possible, a complete list of the contents of a work has been included. Many of the works are compilations of articles by a number of authors and it was considered important to recognize each author. In addition, the listing of individual articles and authors makes it possible to create more useful indexing.

Both a name index and a subject index have been provided. The name index lists the authors of the works included, and all references to names in the annotations or in the introductions to the chapters. Additional appendices include a list of theses and dissertations on electronic and computer music, a list of systems manuals which are in print, a list of online sources, and a brief list of prominent electronic and computer music periodicals.

I would like to thank the University of Colorado at Denver for providing me with a sabbatical leave to finish the manuscript. And I would especially like to thank the staff at the Auraria Library Interlibrary Loan Department for finding all of the books not held by local libraries. Eveline Yang (ILL Librarian), Joe Neer, Connie Whitson, Geraldine (Dina) Gold, and Jeanne Lyon were all very dedicated to the project, and went the extra distance to locate and obtain the books included.

Introduction

Electronic music is defined by *The New Grove Dictionary of Music* as "music which is produced or modified by electronic devices so that electronic equipment is required for it to be heard." (Page 107, Vol. 6) The term 'electronic music' comes from experiments in Cologne at the Westdeutscher Rundfunk broadcasting network (later called Nordwestdeutscher Rundfunk) which were referred to as *elektronische musik* during the last years of the 1940s. Early electronic and musique concrète experimentations attempted to use natural or 'concrete' sound sources recorded directly to tape rather than through normal performance. Both electronic music and musique concrète eventually evolved into basically the same type of music using electronic instruments recorded directly to tape.

While experiments in making music through the use of electronic instruments were carried out early in the century, little actual music was produced until after World War II when the tape recorder became available at a reasonable cost. It was then possible to record a wide variety of sounds directly to tape, eliminating the usual step provided by musicians playing standard instruments. One of the first organized experiments with concrète music was at the Radiodiffusion Television Francaise in Paris in 1954 where a young electrical engineer, Pierre Schaeffer, produced music recorded directly on a disc-cutting lathe, and later on a primitive tape recorder.

Early experiments with music produced electronically are well documented in the literature. A number of experimenters with electric devices in the last half of the nineteenth century showed how sounds could be generated. The earliest serious attempt was probably the development of the Telharmonium by Thaddeus Cahill in the 1890s. Cahill registered a patent in 1897, but his device was not shown to the public until 1906 in Holyoke, Massachusetts. The patent shows a massive machine weighing almost 200 tons which developed tones by using dynamos to generate alternating currents of varying frequencies. The device required hundreds of individual sound generators which could be controlled by a keyboard similar to that of an organ. Cahill's intention was to sell the music over existing telephone lines, but the whole project collapsed into bankruptcy before World War I. Several devices followed Cahill's attempt including the Theremin in 1924, the Spharophon in 1927, the Dynaphone in 1928, the Ondes Martenot in 1928, and the Trautonium in 1930. All of these devices, with the exception of the Theremin, were keyboard instruments which used various kinds of sound oscillators. Theremin invented a hand-operated electronic instrument using one vertical rod and one horizontal loop both of which were capacitive detectors sensitive to the distance from the player's hand.

By World War II electrically produced sounds were becoming more controllable through the use of vacuum tubes which greatly reduced the size and weight of the equipment. And another important breakthrough for electronic music and music concrète was the development of wire and tape recorders. These devices made it possible to produce music which could later be played back in a performance. It was also soon recognized that these recording devices could in themselves be electronic instruments through manipulating the recording process. During this period a number of important electronic compositions were presented.

The next important development in the history of electronic music was the development of the transistor during the 1960s and later in the 1970s the integrated circuit. These semiconductors made it possible to create electronic sounds through the development of specific devices, e.g., the electronic guitar, electronic organs, and other specific sound-producing instruments. Computers were of interest to electronic musicians from the beginning of their existence, but the high cost of access to large mainframes necessary for the generation of sounds made them unavailable to all but a few prominent experiments in specially constructed studios mainly in France, Germany and the U.S..

By the beginning of the 1980s desk-top computers made it possible for electronic instruments to be controlled by computer programs. These devices created a great leap forward for electronic musicians. It was now possible to create music electronically and record it directly on floppy disks to be played back from the computer or recorded on tape. Electronically composed music became commonplace with popular music composers and, at the same time, serious music composers were becoming more involved. Electronic music was now coming into the mainstream of the music world.

From the first experiments with electronic music and musique concrète a literature was being developed to both chronicle the developments and provide information on how to create and use the new devices. Early experimenters often
wrote about their work and scholars were interested in the history of this new
music.

The literature of electronic and computer music is now entering into a period of
transition. No longer is the distinction between "electronic" and "computer"
music valid. These concepts are merging into one, single music created through
electronic means. Keyboard synthesizers are being given powerful microprocessors which make them stand-alone composing and recording instruments.
Through the use of the MIDI controls, all instruments, including string, percussion, and keyboard are being controlled and manipulated in what might be considered an electronic orchestra. And the development of sound sampling, an
electronic technique where sounds are analyzed by a microprocessor for their
inherent musical qualities and then reproduced in different forms, will no doubt,
add a completely new dimension to electronic music composition in the future.

The electronic music literature of the future will most likely not be divided into
"computer," "electronic," "MIDI," etc., but will concentrate on the art of performance and composition of music through electronic means no matter if the
source of the musical elements is acoustic or electronic.

ELECTRONIC AND COMPUTER MUSIC

Histories and General Works

Some important early works documenting the beginnings of electronic music and musique concrète include three articles in 1906: two from the journal *Electrical World* , and R. S. Baker's article "New Music for an Old World," in *McClure's Magazine*;[1] and later two short publications including *Sketch of a New Aesthetic of Music* (see item 9) by Ferruccio Busoni, and *The Art of Noise [Futurist Manifesto, 1913]* (see item 50) by Luigi Russolo. These early works attempted to declare the legitimacy of using electrically produced sounds, and the necessity for music to break away from its traditional roots and allow for "pure sound" experimentation. The articles in *Electrical World* document the development of the Telharmonium by Thaddeus Cahill,[2] and R. S. Baker's "New Music for an Old World,"[3] also discusses the Telharmonium and leads to Russolo's prophecy in the *Futurist Manifesto* in 1913.

Ferruccio Busoni's *Sketch of a New Aesthetic of Music* (1911) (see item 9) makes a case for the use of electronically produced tones in music. Busoni refers to the device invented by Dr. Thaddeus Cahill that "makes it possible to transform an electric current into a fixed and mathematically exact number of vibrations." This work is one of the first to discuss the idea of electronic music and how such music will lead to a new aesthetic understanding.

---

[1] Ray Stannard Baker. "New Music for an Old World." *McClure's Magazine*. 27 (1906), 291.

[2] "The Generation and Distribution of Music by Means of Alternators." *Electrical World*. 47: 10 (March 10, 1906): 519-521.

[3] "Electric Musical Instruments." *Electrical World*. 47:13 (March 31, 1906): 665-666.

The Art of Noises by Luigi Russolo [*Futurist Manifesto*, 1913], was translated from a portion of *L'arte dei Rumori* by Robert Filliou. The work has become one of the benchmarks in the history of electronic music and musique concrète. Luigi Russolo declares that the future of music must include the realization that what we consider "noise" must become part of our musical raw material in order to keep the musical art relevant to modern life. In his conclusion he points out that "one day we will be able to distinguish among ten, twenty, or thirty thousand different noises. We will not have to imitate these noises but rather to combine them according to our artistic fantasy." (see item 50) The pamphlet is signed by Russolo in the following manner: "Director of the futurist movement, Corso Venezia, 61, Milano." Also, an announcement of the "First Concert of Futurist Noise Instruments" is reprinted at the end of the pamphlet.

With the development of the gramophone in the 1920s came additional experiments. Musicians would play discs backwards at different speeds, and often the grooves were altered to produce special effects during performance. While some reporting of these experiments occurred during the 1920s and 1930s, few major documents chronicling these attempts were published. Most of the work on electronically produced music was stopped during World War II, but the development of the tape recorder shortly after caused a dramatic upsurge in experimentation. Pierre Schaffer began his experiments during the late 1940s into what he called *musique concrète*, and explained the process as the use of natural, or 'concrete' sound sources and a method of composing 'concretely' on tape. This system would avoid the problem of composing through notation for performance. Out of these experiments came the first electronic music studios in the late 40s and early 50s including the Club d'Essai in Paris (1948), the Columbia-Princeton Electronic Music Center in New York (1951), and the Studio fur Elektronische Musik in Cologne (1951).

Between 1955 and 1962 the short-lived German-language annual *Die Reihe'* (see item 22), edited by Karlheinz Stockhausen and Herbert Eimert, attempted to further the cause of electronic music. Its eight numbers, each with a distinctive title, were also published in an English-language edition (1958-68). The English edition carried the subtitle "A Periodical Devoted to Developments in Contemporary Music." Topics of its eight issues are suggested by their titles: *Electronic Music*; *Anton Webern*; *Musical Craftsmanship*; *Young Composers*; *Reports Analysis*; *Speech and Music*; *Form-Space*; *and Retrospective*. The first issue contained articles by the two editors and by an international group of musicians, among them such now well known figures as Pierre Boulez, Gottfried Michael Koenig, Ernst Krenek, Henri Pousseur, and H. H. Stuckenschmidt. Other well known contributors over the years included Stravinsky, Webern, Schoenberg, John Cage, and Gyorgy Ligeti.

During the 1960s and the early 1970s experiments in producing sounds electronically were expanding do mainly to the continued development of reliable tape recorders and the transistor. As mentioned above, Pierre Schaeffer is considered to be the originator of "musique concrète" with his tape compositions in 1948. In *La Musique Concrete* (see item 51) he begins his analysis of electronic music with discussions of Varèse, Cage, Messiaen, Boulez, XENAKIS, and Stockhausen. In the fall of 1966 the Joint Computer Conference was held in San Francisco. A fascinating series of discussions were held on the use of computers to produce musical sounds.

By the 1970s electronic music was well established and the instruments & compositional techniques were being studied in colleges and universities throughout Europe and North America. A number of important histories and general works were published. Later in the 1970s more summing up of developments was underway with publications such as Herbert Deutsch's *Synthesis: An Introduction to the History, Theory, and Practice of Electronic Music* (1976) (see item 19) and David Ernst's *The Evolution of Electronic Music* (1977) (see item 24).

By the 1980's electronic instruments and the computer were merging into one electronic technique. It was now possible to compose electronic music using a home computer and a synthesizer within the means of average musicians. Many additional books were published to meet the demands of the increasing number of electronic composers. Basic textbooks were needed for college courses on electronic music, and a new demand for basic "how to" books was being met. In 1984 the editors of *Keyboard* magazine reproduced a number of the major articles from past years in a work entitled *The Art of Electronic Music* (see item 34).

Recently the use of electronic and computer generated music is becoming so commonplace that much of the research is being combined into regular music studies on composition, orchestration, history, etc.. A few books are still devoted specifically to electronic and computer music. Also, basic reference materials are becoming more common.

The following works are either histories of electronic and computer music, or works that cover a number of subjects of a general nature.

1.   Apollonio, Umbro, ed. Apollonio, Umbro, ed. **Futurist Manifestos.** New York, NY: Viking Press, c1970, 1973. LCCN 72-89124. ISBN 0-670-01966-6.

        This book is a compilation of a number of essays loosely referred to as the "Futurist Manifestos" which began with a front page article called the "Manifesto of Futurism" on February 20, 1909, by the Italian poet F. T. Marinetti which demanded that writers and artists reject the classical art forms he considered "passéist" and embrace the modern technology. Several essays concerning music became part of the manifestos including the famous *Art of Noises* (1913) (see item 50) which declares that the future of music must include the realization that what we consider "noise" must become part of our musical raw material in order to keep the musical art relevant to modern life. While a number of the manifesto writers referred to music, the only other essay directly related to musical composition was Balilla Pratella's *Manifesto of Futurist Musicians* which was published as a pamphlet by *Poesia* (Milan) on April 11, 1910. Pratella reviews a list of 11 "conclusions" in his pamphlet which included a call for free study at the conservatories and musical academies, a call to combat the "venal and ignorant" critics of music, for musicians to abstain from participating in competitions with admission charges, to destroy the prejudice for "well-made" music, and to promote in the public a hostility toward the playing of old works which prevent the appearance of new, revolutionary music.

2.   Austin, William W. **Music in the 20th Century.** New York, NY: Norton, 1966. xx. 708p. illus.

While this work deals with contemporary music in general, it does contain a brief section on electronic and experimental music. Of interest is a chronology of the history of electronic music beginning with Thadius Cahill (1897) and continuing up to 1963 and integrated circuit technology.

3.   Backus, John. **The Acoustical Foundations of Music.** 2nd. ed. New York, NY: W. W. Norton, 1969, 1977. xiv. 381p. illus. ISBN 0-393-09096-5.

This work is one of the more popular basic introductions to acoustics especially designed for musicians who have little or no background in physics. Included are brief but informative sections on electronic music, electronic music equipment, and other related subjects. This work is useful for presenting the basic physics of sound, room acoustics, and the structure of musical instruments. Often used as a textbook, Mr. Backus' work defines the physical properties of musical instruments, what they have in common and how they differ, and basic acoustics. The book contains a brief but definitive bibliography. (pgs. 294-304)

4. Baggi, Denis. **Readings in Computer-Generated Music.** Los Alamitos, CA: IEEE Computer Society Press, 1992. ix, 221p. Illus. (IEEE Computer Society Press Tutorial) LCCN 92-15303. ISBN 0-8186-2747-6.

This is the first of the "Readings in.." series published by the IEEE Computer Society Press. Each volume in the series is coordinated with a special issue of *Computer* magazine, the IEEE Computer Society's flagship periodical. *Readings in Computer-Generated Music* is a tutorial volume designed to acquaint musicians with the systems and methods of composing electronic music. The volume consists of 14 individual articles by separate authors writing on topics including the computer as a musical instrument, composing music & solving musicological problems, and contemporary and future trends in electronic & computer composition. Each article provides a different aspect of computer-generated music. The contents include: "Formula: A Programming Language for Expressive Computer Music," by David P. Anderson and Ron Kuivila, "A Functional Language for Sound Synthesis with Behavior Abstraction and Lazy Evaluation," by Roger B. Dannenberg, Christopher L. Fraley, and Peter Velikonja. "An Expert System for the Articulation of Bach Fugue Melodies," by Margaret L. Johnson, "ScoreSynth: A System for the Synthesis of Music Scores Based on Petri Nets and a Musical Algebra," by Goffredo Haus and Alberto Smetti, "NeurSwing: An Intelligent Workbench for the Investigation of Swing in Jazz," by Denis L. Baggi, "HARP [Hybrid Action Representation and Planning]: A Framework and a System for Intelligent Composer's Assistance," by Antonio Camurri, Corrando Canepa, Marcello Frixione, and Renato Zaccaria, "Tone Context by Pattern Integration over Time," by Marc Leman, "Sound Synthesis by Dynamic Systems Interaction," by Gianpaolo Borin, Giovanni De Poli, and Augusto Sarti, "Sound Works: An Object-Oriented Distributed System for Digital Sound," by Jonathan D. Reichbach and Richard A. Kemmerer," "'Furies and Voices': Composition- Theoretical Observations," by Otto E. Laske, "Algo- Rhythms: Real-Time Algorithmic Composition for a Microcomputer," by Thomas E. Janzen, and "Composition Based on Pentatonic Scales: A Computer-Aided Approach," by Yap Siong Chua. Each article concludes with a bibliography. There is also a brief discography (9 items), but no index.

5. Bateman, Wayne. **Introduction to Computer Music.** New York, NY: John Wiley & Sons, Inc., 1978, 1980. vii. 256p. illus. LCCN 79-026361. ISBN 0-471-86839-6.

This book is "intended for composers and students of contemporary music who are interested in the application of electronic technology in the arts." (Preface) The work discusses computer music in terms of theory but does not provide information concerning specific computers. Sections include "The Computer and the Musician," "Tones and Harmonics," "How the Computer Operates," "Computer Programming in Tone Generation," "Modulation and Dynamics," "Waveform Analysis in the Frequency Domain," "Synthesis of Complex Tones," "Modification and Processing of Recorded Sounds," "Simulation and Reproduction of Natural Sounds," "Scales and Tonality," "Composition with the Computer," and "Machines and Human Creativity." Also included are bibliographies at the end of the chapters, a glossary, appendices on programming in Basic and Fortran, and an index.

6.   Beauchamp, N. W., and Von Foerster, eds. *Music by Computers*. New York, NY: John Wiley and Sons, Inc., 1969. xviii, 139p. illus. LCCN 69-19244. ISBN 0-471-91030-0.

This work is a collection of addresses given at the 1966 Fall Joint Computer Conference in San Francisco. It presents a fascinating series of discussions on the use of computers to produce musical sounds. Included are "Sounds and Music," by Heinz Von Foerster, "On-Line Generation of Sound," by M. David Freedman, "A Computer System for Time-Variant Harmonic Analysis and Synthesis of Musical Tones," by James W. Beauchamp, "Some New Developments in Computer-Generated Music," by Arthur Roberts, "Some Compositional Techniques Involving the Use of Computers," by Lejaren Hiller, "Graphical Language for the Scores of Computer-Generated Sounds," by M. V. Mathews and L. Rosler, "Infrudibles," by Herbert Brün, "Operations on Wave Forms," by J. K. Randall, "Control of Consonance and Dissonance with Nonharmonic Overtones," by J. R. Pierce and M. V. Mathews, and "The Problem of Imperfection in Computer Music," by Gerald Strang.

7.   Berenguer, Jose. **A La Musica Electroacustica. [An Introduction to Electronic Music]** Valencia, CA: Torres Press, 1974. 116p. illus. ISBN 8-47366-020-X.

This is the first study of electronic music published in Spain. The work is directed toward musicians and students and attempts to keep technical concepts to a minimum. The author points out that the use of electronic music does not eliminate the conventional methods, but unites with them. Even though electronic methods can create music to stand alone, it can be associated to vocal and instrumental groups. And that electronic musical instruments would be integrated into traditional orchestras.

8.   Borko, Harold, ed. **Computer Applications in the Behavioral Sciences.**
       Englewood Cliffs, NJ:Prentice Hall, Inc., 1962. 633p. illus.

       Chapter 18 of this work is entitled "Computer Music," and was written
       by Lejaren A. Hiller, Jr. & Robert Baker. They discuss experiments in
       computer composition, the composition of the *Iliac Suite*, and models for
       musical composition, the statistical analysis of style, the analytical
       method as applied to musical structures, and programing for music syn-
       thesis. A short bibliography is provided at the end of the chapter.

9.   Busoni, Ferruccio. **Sketch of a New Aesthetic of Music.** New York,
       NY: G. Schirmer, 1911. 45p.

       This little book, translated from the German by Theodore Baker in 1911,
       makes a case for the use of electronically produced tones in music. Bu-
       soni refers to a device invented by Dr. Thaddeus Cahill that "makes it
       possible to transform an electric current into a fixed and mathematically
       exact number of vibrations." (p. 33) This work is one of the first to dis-
       cuss the idea of electronic music and how such music will lead to a new
       aesthetic understanding. (Ray Stannard reported on Cahill's "Dynamo-
       phone" in *McClure's Magazine*, July, 1906.)

10.   Busoni, Ferruccio. **The Essence of Music, and Other Papers.** New
       York: NY:Dover Publications, 1957. viii. 204p. LCCN 65-26072.

       Busoni has become known as a prophet of twentieth-century musique
       concrète and electronic music. In addition, he predicted the minimalist
       movement and the use of new tonalities in modern music. In this work
       his major essay *The Essence of Music* (written in July of 1922), and
       many of his letters and other comments on the future of music are com-
       bined to provide, in a single source, a complete understanding of Bu-
       soni's view. While Busoni doesn't speak directly about electronic and
       computer music, much of what is predicted relates to these develop-
       ments.

11.   Ceely, Robert. **Electronic Music Resource Book.** Newton, MA: NEV
       Multimedia Publications, 1980, 1981. 370p. illus. LCCN 81-82292. IS-
       BN 0-9606426-0-9.

       First published in 1980, this impressive volume provides a wealth of in-
       formation on electronic music. It begins with an introduction that pro-
       vides a brief history of electronic music, the function of electronic music
       studio, sound sources, sound modification, and the organization of sound

material. Additional chapters include "Waveforms," "Modifiers," "Controllers," "Connections," "The Tape Recorder as a Compositional Tool," "Putting it all Together," "Notation," "Suggested Class Assignments," "Studio Configurations," "Compositional Limitations of Current Electronic Music Synthesis," "ARP™ 2600 Synthesizer," "Buchla™ Music Easel," "EML-101™ Synthesizer," "EML-301™ Controller," "EML-Sequencer™," "Mini-Moog™ Synthesizer," "Modular Moog™ Synthesizer," "Polyfusion™ Modular Synthesizer," and "Synare 2™ Synthesizer." Appendices include a glossary of electronic music terms, a bibliography of books and periodicals (205 items), a discography (25 items), and a list of useful addresses. Often used as a textbook, this work is one of the most complete sources of information on electronic synthesizers available. It is especially important to electronic and computer music historians for information on the subject written before 1981. Some of the effectiveness of the book is damaged by the lack of an index.

12.   Chavez, Carlos. **Toward a New Music: Music and Electricity.** New York, NY :Da Capo, c1937, 1975. 180p. illus. LCCN 74-28308. ISBN 0-306-70719-5.

This is a reprint of the 1937 edition published by W. W. Norton. Carlos Chavez became fascinated with "electric" music after a 1923-24 trip to New York where he was introduced to new developments in the area of radio, electric communication, and sound reproduction. This book provides a composer's view of the early applications of electronics to music. Sections include "Music and Physics," "Musical Production and Reproduction," "Electric Instruments of Musical Reproduction," "The Sound Film," and "Electric Apparatus or Sound Reproduction."

13.   Chion, Michel. **La Musique Electroacoustique.** [**Electronic Music**] 2d ed. Paris, France: Presses Universities de France, 1976, 1982. 127p. (Que sais-Je? [series]) ISBN 2-13-037362-7.

The first edition (1976) of this work was co-authored by Guy Reibel. The book provides an introduction to the study of electronic music with emphasis on French contributions. A brief history of music concrète and electronic music is provided along with chapters on equipment & electronic music composition. A detailed time line for important concerts, studios, and other significant events is provided. Appendices include a list of individuals, groups, and studios important to the history of electronic music (101 items), and a brief bibliography (10 items).

14.   Clough, Rosa Trillo. **Futurism: the Story of a Modern Movement, A**

New Appraisal. New York, NY: Greenwood Press, 1961, 1969. 297p. illus. ISBN 0-8371-2166-3.

Mr. Clough's work, while dealing mainly with futurist writings in the area of architecture, painting, and sculpture, contains a chapter on the future of music. His study is "not a treatise on art...[but rather] an historical and critical account of the Futurists' writings with emphasis on their manifestos..." (Foreword) In his chapter concerning music, he traces the developments to the 1960s in the area of "noises" and suggests the involvement of music and electronics through the development of the Theremin.

15.   Commission on Electronic Music. [Sweden] **Electronic Music in Sweden.** Stockholm, Sweden: Swedish Music Information Center, 1985. 87p. ISBN 9-18547-021-X.

Electronic Music in Sweden is representative of a series of monographs using this general title published by the Swedish Music Information Center. The series covers various aspects of music. This work begins with a brief history of electronic music in Sweden and then continues with a list of 12 Swedish electronic music composers. A short biography is provided for each composer. Included are Karl-Birger Blomdahl, Lars-Gunnar Bodin, Gunnar Bucht, Sven-Erik Bäck, Bengt Hambraeus, Sten Hanson, Ake Hodell, Bengt Emil Johansson, Ralph Lundsten, Arne Mellnas, Jan W. Morthenson, and Leo Nilson. A final portion of the book provides a description of the Electronic Music Studio in Stockholm. A complete description of the PDP 15/40 is provided, along with a discography.

16.   Computer Music Coalition. **Computer Music Sourcebook.** Peoria, IL: CMC, 1991. 207p. looseleaf. ISBN 0-945505-00-0.

This looseleaf is a publication of the Computer Musician Coalition. It provides information on all aspects of computers as they are applied to music. The looseleaf format is used so separate sections can be updated individually. Sections include "General Articles," "Product Catalogs" (321 items), "Test Reports & Reviews" (57 items), "News & New Products," "Potpourri," "Consultant Directory," "Dealer Directory," "User Groups" (13 item), and a "Manufacturer's Directory." General articles published in the original 1991 looseleaf include "Computers in Music Education," by Cindy Bridges, "MIDI for Music Educators," by John Larson, "The 30 Minute MIDI Workshop," by Ron Wallace, "Apple Serenade," by Cynthia E. Field, "Musical Liberation: Evolution of the Species," "How to Enhance the Whole Church Ministry with Electronic

Keyboards & MIDI," (no author) "Thoughts to Create By," by Korey Ireland, "Collaborating with Computers," by Korey Ireland & "The Big Stretch," by Korey Ireland. This work will provide much needed information on all aspects of computer music if it is updated as planned.

17.   Cope, David H. **New Directions in Music.** 4th ed. Dubuque, IA: Wm. C. Brown, 1971, 1984, 1989. xv. 439p. illus. ISBN 0-697-03342-2.

Mr. Cope's book, first published in 1971, has now gone through several editions in order to keep current. While all aspects of modern music are discussed, it does have chapters on electronic and computer music which provide good introductions to these areas. Electronic music is discussed from the standpoint of fundamentals, esthetics, synthesizers, studios, etc.. In addition, a section on "Notable Composers and Works" is provided. The chapter on computer music provides information on composition, computer-generated sound, hybrid composition, etc.. The work is well documented and detailed bibliographies are provided.

18.   Cowell, Henry. **New Musical Resources.** New York, NY: Something Else Press, Inc., 1930, 1969. xxiii. 158p. illus. LCCN 67-16291.

Originally published in 1930 by Alfred A. Knopf, Inc., *New Musical Resources* has become known as an important early publication predicting the future of electronic and experimental music. In his introduction Mr. Cowell points out that his work was "first written during 1919, with the literary assistance of Professor Samuel S. Seward, of Stanford University...[and] in this early form it embraced most of the applications given here of the theory of musical relativity." (Introduction, xxii) He discusses the present and future possibilities of polyharmony, tone quality, the use of overtones, time, metre, dynamics, form, tempo, tone clusters, and the building of chords from different intervals.

19.   Deutsch, Herbert. **Synthesis: An Introduction to the History, Theory, and Practice of Electronic Music.** Port Washington, NY: Alfred Publishing Co., 1976, 1985. 250p. (includes recording) LCCN 85-88284. ISBN 0-88284-348-6.

Although this book is designed for the beginner, it assumes that the reader has a working knowledge of music and musical terminology as it attempts to provide a general background to the world of electronic music. A short, but very inclusive, history of electronic music is provided along with additional sections on "Tape Recorder as a Musical Instrument," "The Electronic Synthesis of Sound," "...Synthesizers," and "The

Studio." In addition a glossary of terms and an index is included. The synthesizers and other electronic equipment talked about in this work were generally outdated by the early 1980s but the work remains an important source in the history of electronic music. There is a record included with the book that demonstrates synthesis and basic recording techniques.

20.   Deutsch, Herbert A. **Electroacoustic Music: the First Century.** Miami, FL: Belwin Mills, 1993. 130p. illus. (1 sound disk-CD)

Mr. Deutsch begins his history of electroacoustic music with several brief chapters beginning with Thaddeus Cahill's Teleharmonium; then he continues with descriptions of Leon Theremin's "Etherovox" (now referred to as the Theremin), Maurice Martenot's Ondes Martenot, Harald Bode's "polyphonic synthesizer," and Les Paul's electronic guitar. Also information is provided on Otto Luening's and Vladimir Ussachevsky's historic October, 1952, concert at the Museum of Modern Art where compositions were performed with tape recorders. Additional chapters include "The Columbia University Electronic Studio," "Raymond Scott and the 'Electronium'," "The Minimoog," "Max Mathews, the Father of American Computer Music," and "Dave Smith, The 'Prophet,' MIDI and the Japanese Connection." The second part of the work surveys the more recent developments in electroacoustic music including an introduction to the technology, basic concepts of sound and electroacoustics, tape recording, including DAT (digital audio technology) & multitracking, synthesis, MIDI, and personal computers' use of MIDI. Appendices include a setup chart for a typical MIDI studio, a setup chart for a computer based MIDI studio, a setup chart for a computer-based multimedia studio, and a list of software. No bibliography is provided. The book has an accompanying CD recording that provides examples of music which illustrates some of the material discussed in the history portion of the book, and short sound bites selected to demonstrate electroacoustic techniques.

21.   Douglas, Alan. **The Electrical Production of Music.** London, England: Macdonald & Company, 1957. 223p. illus.

Mr. Douglas begins this work by describing the physics of acoustical musical instruments, musical scales & intervals, noise & stating transients, and harmonic analysis. He then continues with electrical tone or waveform generation, electrical tone formation, and loudspeakers. In a final chapter entitled "Existing Limitations and Possible Future Trend of Research" he investigates a number of devices which he feels will contribute greatly to the music of the future.

22.   Eimert, Herbert & Hans Ulrich Humpert. **"Electronic Music," Die
       Reihe 1.** Bryn Mawr, PA: Theodore Presser Co., 1965. [*Die Reihe* Ser.;
       No. 1]

       This is number one of a periodical originally published in Germany in
       1955 which was reprinted as a monograph by Theodore Presser in 1965.
       Additional numbers of *Die Reihe* were published in Germany but not all
       were translated. This volume consists of 11 articles by various authors:
       "What is Electronic Music?" by Herbert Eimert. "The Third Stance," by
       H. H. Stuckenschmidt, "A Glance Over the Shoulders of the Young," by
       Ernst Krenek, "First Practical Work," by Giselher Klebe, " 'At the ends
       of fruitful land...'," by Pierre Boulez, "Formal Elements in a New Com-
       positional Material...," by Henri Pousseur, "The Sound Material of Elec-
       tronic Music," by Karel Goeyvaerts, "Serial Technique," by Paul Gen-
       dinger, "Actualia," by Karleheinz Stockhausen, "Studio Technique," by
       Gottfried Michael Koenig, and "Statistic and Psychologic Problems of
       Sound," by Werner Meyer-Eppler. Additional numbers of *Die Reihe* in-
       clude "Anton Webern, No. 2," "Musical Craftsmanship, No. 3," "Young
       Composers, No. 4," "Report Analysis, No. 5," "Sprache Und Musik, No.
       6," "Form-Raum, No. 7," and "Musikalishe Rotationstechnik, No. 8."

23.   Emmerson, Simon, ed. **The Language of Electroacoustic Music.**
       London, England: Macmillan Press Ltd., 1986. viii, 224p. illus. ISBN 0-
       333-39759-2.

       The Language of Electroacoustic Music reprints 10 important articles by
       as many electronic music experts. The book opens with the classic 1977
       article "Technology and the Composer," by Pierre Boulez, which fore-
       shadowed many of the developments discussed by many of the other arti-
       cles in the collection. The additional articles are grouped under three
       broad headings: "Materials and Language," which discuss and categorize
       the musical material used by composers since the inception of electroa-
       coustic music; "Problems of Language," which discuss the rapid devel-
       opment of the technical resources of electronic music, and finally "The
       Influence of Computer Technology," which broadly discuss the applica-
       tion of computers to the production of music. Articles included are "The
       Relation of Language to Materials," by Simon Emmerson, "Sound Sym-
       bols and Landscapes," by Trevor Wishart, "Spectro-morphology and
       Structuring Processes," by Denis Smalley, "At the Threshold of an Aes-
       thetic," by David Keane, "Language and Resources; A New Paradox," by
       Bruce Pennycook, "Computer Music: Some Aesthetic Considerations,"

by Mike McNabb, "Computer Music Language Design and the Composing Process," by Barry Truax, "The Mirror of Ambiguity," by Jonathan
Harvey and "A Stubborn Search for Artistic Unity," by Tod Machover.
The editor suggests that this work "seeks to lay the foundations for discussion about aesthetic matters by clarifying the central issues...[and] it
is hoped that the book will contribute to a genuine critique of the medium as it approaches the start of its fifth decade." (Preface, p. 4) The
work has a selected bibliography (31 items), and a list of recordings of
electronic music cited in the text. There is no index.

24. Ernst, David. **The Evolution of Electronic Music.** New York, NY:
Schirmer Books, 1977. xi. 174p. illus. LCCN 76-041624. ISBN 0-02-
870880-6.

Mr. Ernst has concentrated on three general classifications: "Solo Tape,
Performer with Tape, and Line Electronics in this overview of the history
and development of electronic music." (Preface) In addition, there are
sections concerning electronic and concrète sounds, compositional techniques, and a chronological list of pre-1948 events related to electronic
music. The work is clearly written and well illustrated, and has a brief
bibliography (9 items) and an index.

25. Ernst, David. **Musique Concrète.** Boston, MA: Crescendo Publishing
Co., 1972. ii. 37p. illus.

"The purpose of this book is to provide both teachers and students with
enough information to begin study in the field of musique concrète."
(Preface) Chapters include: "I. Introduction," "II. Basic Concepts," "III.
Developments Leading to First Electronic Music Composition," "IV.
Survey of Musique Concrète," and "V. Exercises in Composition." In addition the work contains a discography (50 items), and a bibliography
(19 items).

26. Fowler, Charles B., ed. **Electronic Music: Music Educators Journal.**
Washington, DC: Music Educators National Conference, 1968. 97p.
illus.

This study was originally published as the November, 1968 issue of the
Music Educators Journal. Contents include "An Unfinished History of
Electronic Music," by Otto Luening, "Electronic Music & Music Tradi-
tion," by J. K. Randall, "New Sounds in the Classroom," by Eunice
Boardman, "Challenge to Music Education," by Wayne Barlow, "Ex-
tending the Stuff Music is Made Of," by Morton Subotnick, "What Goes

Into an Electronic Music Studio," by James Scawright, "The Making of Four Miniatures," by Vladimir Ussachevsky, "Electronic Composition in the Junior High School," by Virginia Hagemann, "Electronic Composition in the Senior High School," by Ann Modugno, "Project Pep," by Lloyd Schmidt, "Electronic Music Workshop for Teachers," by Jean E. Ivey, "Musique Concrète at Home..." by Merrill Ellis, "The Sound-Generation Gap: A Student View," by David Friend, "It's Electric: the Faculty View," by Lindsey Merrill, "The Humanization of Electronic Music," by John Eaton and, "Electronic Sounds and the Sensitive Performer," by Barry L. Vercoe. Also included is a bibliography, a list of equipment for electronic music laboratories, a discography, and readers' comments.

27.   Gerhard, Roberto. "Concrète and Electronic Sound Composition," in **Music Libraries and Instruments.** London, England: Henrichsen, 1961. 300p. illus.

Music Libraries and Instruments is a collection of the papers read at the Joint Congress of the International Association of Music Libraries and the Galpin Society held at Cambridge, England, during 1959. Roberto Gerhard presented a paper discussing electronic music and musique concrète. Analysis of several electronic music and musique concrète compositions are presented including *Metazioni* by Berio, *Song of the Young Men* by Stockhausen, and *Symphonie pour un Homme seul* by Schaeffer -Henri. No bibliography is provided.

28.   Griffiths, Paul. **A Guide to Electronic Music.** New York, NY: Thames and Hudson, Inc., 1979, 1981. 128p. illus. ISBN 0-500-272-034.

This little book provides a concise introduction to electronic music. Mr. Griffiths begins with sections on the development of electronic music historically and continues with what he calls the electronic repertory which includes sections on electronic music instruments, line electronic ensembles, and rock applications of electronic music. In addition, a list of recordings and a glossary of terms are contained in appendices. The work also contains a brief bibliography and an index.

29.   Griffiths, Paul. **Modern Music: A Concise History.** Rev. Ed. New York, NY: Thames and Hudson, 1994. 216p. illus. LCCN 94-60288. ISBN 0-500-20278-8.

Although this book is concerned with modern music in general, it contains information on a number of electronic musicians including Luciano

Berio, Pierre Boulez, Ferruccio Busoni, John Cage, Lejaren Hiller, Karlheinz Stockhausen, Edgard Varèse, and Iannis Xenakis. Also Chapter 11 is devoted to electronic music and provides a very good introductory discussion of the early developments, musique concrète, electronic music studios, and composers. The book is well-illustrated with interesting art work and photographs of composers, and contains a bibliography and an index.

30.   Haus, Goffredo, ed. **Music Processing.** Madison, WI: A-R Editions, Inc., 1993. x. 395p. illus. (Computer Music & Digital Audio Series) LC-CN 93-13288. ISBN 0-89579-268-0.

Music Processing is one of a series entitled The Computer Music and Digital Audio Series, John Strawn, Series Editor. It has been a favorite series of books with electronic musicians and includes *Digital Audio Signal Processing*, edited by John Strawn, (see item 96) *Composers and the Computer*, edited by Curtis Roads, (see item 143) *Computer Applications in Music: A Bibliography & Supplement 1*, by Deta S. Davis, (see item 217) *The Compact Disc Handbook;* by Ken C. Pohlmann, (not included) *Computers and Musical Style*, by David Cope, (see item 124) *MIDI: A Comprehensive Introduction*, by Joseph Rothstein, (see item 185) and *Synthesizer Performance and Real-Time Techniques*, by Jeff Pressing (see item 93). The editor points out "that previous books on computer music have been mainly devoted to discussion of sound processing and related analysis/synthesis techniques and systems... [and] given this..*Music Processing* has been conceived as an answer to the need for an organized treatment of its topic. It takes as its starting point advanced research into the subsymbolic, symbolic, and structural description and processing of music." (Preface, viii) The work contains 12 articles by various authors divided into three parts. Part one entitled "Tutorials" includes "Music Analysis by Computer," by Eleanor Selfridge-Field, and "Music composition and Editing by Computer," by Giovanni De Poli. Part two entitled Music Description and Processing includes "An Epistemic Approach to Musicology," by Otto Laske, "Symbolic and Subsymbolic Description of Music," by Mark Leman, "Formal Music Representation; a Case Study: the Model of Ravel's *Bolero*" by Petri Nets, Goffredo Hause and Antonio Rodriguez, "Applications of Artificial Intelligence Methodologies and Tools for Music Description and Processing," by Antonio Camurri, and "Tools for Music Processing: The CARL System at Ten Years," by Gareth Loy. And part three entitled "Reports from Laboratories" includes "Computer Music at Carnegie Mellon University," by Roger Dannenberg, "Computer Music at CCRMA, by Douglas Keislar, "Computer Music at IRCAM," by Marc

Battier, and "Computer Music at LIM," by Goffredo Haus. There are important lists of references at the end of each of the chapters.

31.   Holmes, Thomas B. **Electronic and Experimental Music.** New York, NY: Charles Scribner's Sons, 1985. viii. 278p. illus. LCCN 84-26715. ISBN 0-684-18135-5.

This book is intended to "serve as an enjoyable guide to the world of electronic music for the listener, the fan, the composer, the performer, and anyone else who is instructed in the future of music." (Preface) Mr. Holmes' work provides a basic introduction and history of electronic music. Sections include "Part I: Electronic Music: What It Is, How It Is Made," "Part 2: A History of Electronic Music Technology," "Part 3: Experimental Music," "Part 4: Rock Music and Electronics," "Part 5: An Electronic Music Record Guide," "Part 6: Glossary of Technical and Musical Terms," & "Part 7: Information Sources." Information sources include a list of mail order record retailers, periodicals (18 items), a selected bibliography (46 items), a list of equipment suppliers, and an index.

32.   Howe, Hubert S., Jr. **Electronic Music Synthesis: Concepts, Facilities, Techniques.** New York, NY: Norton, 1975. xv. 272p., illus. ISBN 0-393-09257-7.

Herbert Howe points out in his introduction that "this is a technical book about electronic music. It is intended for readers who are interested in gaining first-hand knowledge of how electronic music is created. All...major methods of producing electronic music are discussed in detail: tape-splicing and editing techniques, electronic music synthesizing equipment, and computers." (Preface) The work is divided into three parts: Part I covers acoustics and psychoacoustics; Part II covers the electronic music studio; and, Part III covers computer music. Chapter titles include "Physical Attributes of Sound," "Psychological Attributes of Sound," "Recording and Playback Equipment," "Signal Generating and Processing Equipment," "Control Equipment," "How to Design an Electronic Music Studio," "Basic Concepts of Computer Music," "Detailed Description of a Computer Sound-Generated Program: MUSIC 4BF," and "System of the Future."

33.   Judd, Frederick Charles. **Electronic Music and Music Concrète.** London, England: Neville Spearman, Ltd., 1961. 92p. illus.

This little book deals with music concrète, electronic music, radiophonics, and abstract sound reproduction using magnetic tape. Sections include "The Elements of Electronic Music," "Electronic Sound Sources and Tone Shaping," and "The Composition of Electronic Music and Musique Concrète." The work is illustrated with photographs of equipment and schematics of sound-generating components. Several appendices provide information concerning techniques, technical data, and additional reading.

34. Keyboard Magazine. **The Art of Electronic Music.** New York, NY: William Morrow & Co., 1984. x. 320p. illus. LCCN 85-60142. ISBN 0-688-03106-4.

The articles reproduced in this volume were originally published in *Keyboard* magazine between 1975 and 1983. Included is a foreword by Dr. Robert Moog entitled "Technology and Art" which discusses the concept of "natural" instruments as compared to modern electronic devices. Articles on the history of electronic music and artists are included. The following individuals are discussed in some detail: Robert Moog, Don Buchla, Tom Oberman, Dave Smith, Max Mathews and John Chowning, Wendy Carlos, Keith Emerson, Isao Tomita, Jan Hammer, Klaus Schulz, Larry Fast, Roger Powell, Brian Eno, Barton & Pricella McLean, and Ben Burt (*StarWars* sound). This book also contains a brief bibliography and a glossary of terminology.

35. Kirby, Michael. **Futurist Performances.** New York, NY: E. P. Dutton & Co., Inc., 1971. xvi, 335p. illus.

While this work deals with futurist performance in a variety of areas, Michael Kirby does include a brief overview of Russolo and *The Art of Noises* (see item 50) Additional chapters cover "The Origins of Futurist Performance," "The Variety Theatre Manifesto," "Dynamic and Synoptic Declamation," "The Synthetic Theatre," "The Theatre of Surprise," "Futurist Scenography," "Acting and Costumes," "Futurist Cinema," "Radio," and "Extension of Categories." Appendices contain various manifestos and play scripts translated from Italian.

36. Kondracki, Miroslaw. **International Electronic Music Discography.** New York, NY: Schott Publishing, 1979. 174p. ISBN 3-7957-0150-3.

This is the first attempt to list most of the electronic and computer music recordings on an international basis. The list grew out of a survey done in Paris by the *Groupe de Recherches Musicales* of electronic music recordings in 1962 which was updated in 1967. According to the Preface the listing is of recordings of musique concrète, electronic music, music

for magnetic tape, music for instruments and tape, text-sound compositions, synthesizer music, computer-synthesizer music, and computer-
composed music. Gottfried Koenig, who has written an Introduction to
the list, points out that "this discography contains around 2000 titles; a
respectable number, justifying publication of this catalogue at this time.
Its purpose is to guide not only music-lovers but music salesmen too, not
only to supply musicologists with a documentation but to orient composers, music students and music teachers." (Introduction, ii.) Each entry is coded with composer, title, disc number, place of production, i.e.,
studio, university, broadcasting station, etc., and title of the complete al-
bum if appropriate. Appendices include a list of abbreviations of record
companies with addresses, a list of electronic studios, and an index to
composers.

37.   Kostelanetz, Richard. **The Theatre of Mixed Means: an Introduction
       to Happenings, Kinetic Environments, and other Mixed-Means Per-
       formances.** New York, NY: The Dial Press, Inc., 1968. xix. 311p. illus.
       LCCN 68-10828.

       While Mr. Kostelanetz's book is devoted mainly to the "new theatre" and
       what he calls "happenings," it contains an interesting interview with John
       Cage (pages 50-63) at Cage's home in Stony Point, New York. Cage dis-
       cusses his theories concerning the relation between electronic music and
       modern theatre and provides some insight into the genus of several of his
       compositions including *4' 33"* (1952), *Rozart Mix* (1965), *Variations V*
       (1965), and *Variations VII* (1966).

38.   Mackay, Andy. **Electronic Music: The Instruments, the Music, the
       Musicians.** Cambridge, MA: MIT Press, 1981, 1985. 128p. illus. (Re-
       printed by Phaidon 1985.) ISBN 0-714-82176-4.

       This book is an illustrated introduction to electronic music. The first part
       is devoted to the history and development of electronic music instru-
       ments, part two is a survey of the music that has been written for elec-
       tronic sources, and part three contains biographies of 50 important fig-
       ures in the field of electronic music. The illustrations are very well done.
       Appendices include a glossary of terms and an index.

39.   Manning, Peter. **Electronic and Computer Music.** Oxford, England:
       Clarendon Press, 1987, 1994. 408p., illus. (2d ed. Clarendon Press 1994)
       ISBN 0-1931-1923-4.

       This work covers the whole spectrum of electronic and computer music including "The Background to 1945," "Developments from 1945 to 1969," "New Horizons in Electronic Design," "The Electronic Repertory from 1960," and "The Digital Revolution." The history of electronic music emphasizes developments in Cologne, Milan and the United States. Also, new developments in computer music are included. A limited discography and bibliography are included.

40.   Mathews, Max V. and J. R. Pierce, eds. **Current Directions in Computer Music Research.** Cambridge, MA: MIT Press, 1989. vi. illus. 432p. (includes CD recording) LCCN 88-21777. ISBN 0-262-13241-9.

Current Directions in Computer Music Research is a collection of essays describing the state of computer-generated music at the end of the 1980s. The editors point out that "much...has been learned, and this book illustrates some of this new knowledge of sounds and hearing, through descriptions of how sounds are generated and through digital recording ('sound examples' on an accompanying compact disk) illustrating sounds and their musical utility." (Introduction, p.3) The essays are written by leading electronic musicians and cover subjects ranging from the synthesis of speech to timbral manipulations and automatic counterpoint. Chapters include "Compositional Applications of Linear Predictive Coding," by Paul Lanksy, "On *Speech Songs*," by Charles Dodge, "Synthesis of the Singing Voice," by Gerald Bonnet and Xavier Rodet, "Synthesis of Singing by Rule," by Johan Sunderberg, "Frequency Modulation Synthesis of the Singing Voice," by John M. Chowning, "Spatial Reverberation: Discussion and Demonstration," by Gary S. Kendall, William L. Martins, and Shawn L. Decker, "Spatialization of Sounds over Loudspeakers," by F. Richard Moore, "Fourier-Transform-Based Timbral Manipulations," by Mark Dolson, "VLSI Models for Sound Synthesis," by John Wawrzynek, "Paradoxical Sounds," by Jean-Claude Russet, "Additive Synthesis of Inharmonic Tones," by Jean-Claude Russet, "The Bohlen-Pierce Scale," by Max V. Mathews and John R. Pierce, "Residues and Summation Tones--What Do We Hear?" by John R. Pierce, "Simulating Performance on a Bowed Instrument," by Chris Chafe, "Automatic Counterpoint," by William Schottstaedt, "Real-Time Scheduling and Computer Accompaniment," by Roger Dannenberg, "The Conductor Program and Mechanical Baton," by Max V. Mathews, "Zivatar: A Performance System," by Janos Negyesy and Lee Ray, and "Composing with Computers--a Survey of Some Compositional Formalisms and Music Programming Languages," by Gareth Loy. The articles vary in complexity: some are extremely technical and require a basic understanding of the subject being discussed and others are relatively easy for the electronic music novice to follow. Each article contains a brief bibliography at the end. The illustrations are generally clear and help to explain the text in most cases. Gareth Loy's article entitled "Composing with Computers --a Survey of Some Compositional Formalisms and Music Programming Languages," provides an important overview of the history of computer-generated music, and is followed by an impressive bibliography. Appendices include an analysis of the sound examples on the accompanying compact disk, a list of contributors, and an index.

41.   Moles, Abraham A. **Les musiques experimentales: Revue 'une tendance important de la musique contemporaine. [Experimental Music: A Review of the Important Trends in Contemporary Music.]** Paris, France: Editions Du Cercle D'Art Contemporain, 1960.166p. illus.

This work reviews the progress of electronic music from the beginnings to current developments in 1960. Chapters include a history of electronic music, electronic music instruments, theories, compositional techniques, and problems. Appendices include a list of electronic music compositions, a discography and a bibliography. (126 items)

42.   Morgan, Christopher P. **The Byte Book of Computer Music.** Petersborough, NH: Byte Books, 1979. 144p. illus. LCCN 78-027681. ISBN 0-07-043097-7.

This book was designed to help computer enthusiasts get the most out of their computer music experiments. The work is made up of the best articles (as selected by the editors) from past issues of *Byte* (magazine) along with some new materials. Articles include "Scartos: Implementation of a Music Language," by Hal Taylor, "A Two Computer Music System," by Jeffrey H. Lederer," "The Micro Computer and the Pipe Organ," by Jef Raskin, "Tune in With Some Chips," by Ted Sierad, "A $19 Music Interface," by Bill Struve, "A Sampling of Techniques for Computer Performance of Music," by Hal Chamberlain, "Walsh Functions," by Benjamin Jacoby, "Simple Approaches to Computer Music Synthesis," by Thomas G. Schneider, "Notes on Anatomy: the Piano's Reproductive System," by Chris Morgan, "Interfacing Pneumatic Player Pianos," by Carl Helmers, "Electronic Organ Chips for Use in Computer Music Synthesis," by Robert Grappel, "Last Fourier Transforms On Your Home Computer," by William D. Stanley, "Fast Forier Transforms for the 6800," by Richard Lord, "Polyphony Made Easy," by Steven K. Roberts, "Music from the Altair 8800 Computer," by Loring White, "Teach KIM to Sing," by Peter H. Myers, and "A Terrain Reader," by Richard Gold. References are listed at the end of each article.

43.   Nielzen, Soren & Olle Olsson. **Structure and Perception of Electro-acoustic Sound and Music: Proceedings of the Marcus Wallenberg Symposium Held in Lund, Sweden, on 21-28 August, 1988.** New York, NY: Excerpta Medica, 1989. 214p. illus. (International Congress Ser. No. 846) ISBN 0-444-81105-2.

This volume is a collection of essays written for the Marcus Wallenberg Symposium held in Lund, Sweden, August 21-28, 1988. The title of the symposium was Structure and Perception of Electroacoustic Sound and Music and contained three parts: a Master Class for composers, a series of concerts, and a scientific conference. The purpose of the symposium was to bring eminent composers and established scientists together to provide a basis of communication and inspiration concerning the development of techniques and equipment in electroacoustic composition. In addition, it was the aim of the symposium to explore the complex processes of the human brain as it relates to music. The essays include "Music Psychology and the Composer," by John A. Sloboda, "Sound Structure and Musical Structure: The Role of Sound Color," by Wayne Slawson, "Concerning the Use of the Term 'Sound Material' in Tape Music: A New Definition of Musique Concrète," by Michel Chion," "Aspects of Structure," by Johan Sundberg, "Why is Musical Timbre so hard to Understand?" by Carol L. Krumhansl, "Music as a Skill," by John A. Slobada, "Some New Musical Paradoxes," by Diana Deutsch, "Perception and Physiology in the Hearing of Computed Sound," by Edward C. Carterette, "Physiology of Hearing," by W. Dixon Ward, "Hearing and Perception in Different Mental States," by Reinhard Steinberg, Lydia Raith, Wilfried Gunther, "Representation of Complex Sounds in the Peripheral Auditory System with Particular Reference to Pitch Perception," by Edward F. Evans, "Electric, Magnetic and Acoustic Activity from the Human Auditory System," by Claus Elberling, "Description of Complex Sounds," by Armin Kohlrausch, Adrianus JM Houtsma, "MASCAM: Using Psychoacoustic Masking Effects for Low Bit-Rate Coding of High Quality Complex Sounds," by Gerhard Stoll, Gunther Theile, Martin Link, "On Music and its Cerebral Correlates," by David H. Ingvar, "Evoked Response and Multiple Channel Recording," by Svetlana Frkovic-Marrow, "Music, Composers and Scientists: A Relationship of Equals," by John A. Sloboda, and "Practical Comments on Composers and Scientists," by Denis Smalley. The work also contains a name and subject index.

44.   Nyman, Michael. **Experimental Music: Cage and Beyond.** New York, NY: Schirmer Books, 1974, 1981. 154p. Illus. LCCN 81-1166. ISBN 0-02-871660-4.

Mr. Hyman's book begins with a definition of experimental music and continues with a discussion of the Cage's synthetic structures and methodology, Satie's experiments, Charles Ives, Earle Brown Russolo, and other electronic composers. Additional sections include "Inauguration 1950-60: Feldman, Brown, Wolff, Cage," "Seeing, Hearing, Fluxus," "Electronic Systems," "Indeterminacy 1960-70: Ichiyanagi, Ashley, Wolff, Cardew, Scratch Orchestra," and "Minimal Music, determinancy and the new tonality." The work also contains a bibliography (66 items), but no index.

45.   Pellman, Samuel. **An Introduction to the Creation of Electroacoustic Music.** Belmont, CA: Wadsworth Pub. Co., 1994. xv. 441p. LCCN 93-11562. ISBN 0-534-21450-9.

Designed mainly as a textbook, Samuel Pellman's work covers most aspects of the production of electronic music. The author defines electroacoustic music as "the field of scientific study that deals with the transformation of energy between electrical forms and acoustical forms..." (Introduction) Basically the work deals with music produced through a combination of electronic and acoustical means. The primary purpose of the text "is to provide a broad and secure base of practical knowledge regarding the creation of music with electroacoustic instruments." (Preface) Sections include "From Sound to Electricity, and Back," "Music from Tape Recorders," "Digital Recording," "Multiple-Track Recording and Mixing," "The Musical Instrument Digital Interface [MIDI]," "Advanced MIDI Networks," "Tone Colors," "Analog Sound Synthesis," "Digital Sound Sampling and Synthesis," "Composing Electroacoustic Music," "The Audience for Electroacoustic Music," and "Technology and Music: From the Past to the Future." Appendices include a list of hints for microphone placement, further data on MIDI, a case study of the interaction of music and technology, and a discography of electronic music (257 items). Each chapter provides an introduction to the specific subject, examples and well-drawn illustrations, a list of "important terms" and a short bibliography for further reading. The work is clearly written and well illustrated.

46.   Penfold, R. A. **Computers and Music; An Introduction.** West Sussex, England: L. R. Printing Services, Ltd., 1989, 1992. vi. 174p. ISBN 7-80-7075-07-4.

In his Preface Mr. Penfold explains that many musicians shy away from producing electronic music because of a fear that they will have to devote a large amount of time learning the technology. This book is designed to produce "some basic knowledge about such things as disk drives, the various computers and types of software that are available, interfaces, and a lot of general information on computers." (Preface) Chapters include "Computer Basics," "Storage Media," "Poets and Peripherals," "Real Computers," "About MIDI," "Music Software," and "MIDI Instruments." Appendices include a glossary of electronic terms, a hexadecimal numbers table, and a checklist of points to remember before purchasing or combining electronic music equipment. This work is designed for the layman with some knowledge of both electronics and music.

47.   Roads, Curtis, and John Strawn, eds. **Foundations of Computer Music.** Cambridge, MA: M. I. T. Press, 1985. xiii, 736p. illus. ISBN 0-262-68051-3.

This work is a compilation of 36 articles published in the first three volumes of the *Computer Music Journal.* Mr. Roads points out in his Foreword that "in the past two decades a new kind of musical instrument has been invented. It is so different from its predecessors that musicians may need another two decades to learn to play it. In the future, it will be considered the outstanding musical innovation of the twentieth century." The book attempts to sum up the past and present uses of the computer as a musical instrument. The volume is divided into four parts based on an informal classification of the articles. The parts include Digital Sound-Synthesis Techniques, Synthesizer Hardware and Engineering, Software Systems for Music, and Perception and Digital Signal Processing. Most of the articles tend to be technical in nature, but attempts are made to bring the novice up to speed with detailed explanations of terms and techniques. Articles include "The Synthesis of Complex Audio Spectra by Means of Frequency Modulation," by J. Chowning, "Trumpet Algorithms for Computer Composition," by D. Morrill, "Improved FM Audio Synthesis Methods for Real-Time Digital Music Generation," by S. Saunders, "The Simulation of Natural Instrument Tones Using Frequency Modulation with a Complex Modulating Wave," by B. Schottstaedt, "A Derivation of the Spectrum of FM with a Complex Modulating Wave," by M. LeBrun, "Organizational Techniques for c:m Ratios in Frequency Modulation," by B. Truax, "A Tutorial on Nonlinear Distortion or Waveshaping Synthesis," by C. Roads, "Brass-Tone Synthesis by Spectrum Evolution Matching with Nonlinear Functions," by J. Beauchamp, "An Analysis/Synthesis Tutorial," by R. Cann, "Granular Synthesis of Sound," by C. Roads, "PILE--A Language for Sound Synthesis," by P. Berg, "An Introduction to the SSSP Digital Synthesizer," by W. Buxton, E. A. Fogels, G. Fedorkow, L. Sasaki, and K. C. Smith,

"The DMX-1000 Signal-Processing Computer," by D. Wallraff, "A Portable Digital Sound-Synthesis System," by H. Alles, "The 4C Machine," by J. A. Moorer, "Use of High-Speed Microprocessors for Digital Synthesis," by J. F. Allouis, "Design of a Digital Oscillator That Will Generate up to 256 Low-Distortion Sine Waves in Real Time," by J. Snell, "Table Lookup Noise for Sinusoidal Digital Oscillators," by F. R. Moore, "A Recipe for Homebrew ECL," by C. Hastings, "The Evolution of the SSSP Score-Editing Tools," by W. Buxton, "Grammars as Representations for Music," by C. Roads, "The Use of Hierarchy and Instance in a Data Structure for Computer Music," by W. Buxton, "A Composer's Notes on the Development and Implementation of Software for a Digital Synthesizer," by N. Rolnick, "Automated Microprogramming for Digital Synthesizers," by C. Abbott, "A Software Approach to Interactive Processing of Musical Sound," by C. Abbott, "An Introduction to the PLAY Program," by J. Chadabe, "A Microcomputer-Controlled Synthesis System for Live Performance," by M. Bartlett, "Considering Human Memory in Designing User Interfaces for Computer Music," by O. Laske, "An Interview with Gottfried Michael Koenig," by C. Roads, "Controlled Indeterminacy: A First Step Toward a Semistochastic Music Language," by J. Myhill, etc.

48. Roads, Curtis, ed. **The Music Machine: Selected Readings from [the]** *Computer Music Journal.* Cambridge, MA: MIT Press, 1989.

This work is a follow-up to *Foundation of Computer Music* (MIT Press, 1985) edited by Curtis Roads & John Strawn (see item 46) which contains articles from the *Computer Music Journal* between 1977 and 1979. *The Music Machine* adds four parts to the earlier work: interviews, composition techniques, music applications of artificial intelligence, and MIDI. Additional sections include "Music Software," "Synthesis and Signal Processing," "Signal Processing Hardware," and "Musical Performance: A Synthesis-By-Rule Approach." The work contains a total of 54 articles by almost as many authors. Each section is proceeded by an overview article containing a brief bibliography, and the bibliographies of the original articles are included. Both a name and subject index is included.

49. Russcol, Herbert. **The Liberation of Sound: An Introduction to Electronic Music.** Englewood Cliffs, NJ: Prentice-Hall, Inc., 1972, 1987. xxv. 337p. illus. LCCN 84-17649. ISBN 0-13-535393-9.

Mr. Russcol begins this impressive history with an introduction entitled "Why Electronic Music?" where he provides a brief history of the concept and controversy surrounding electronic music. Additional sections include "The Breakup of the Harmonic Era," "The Search for a New Music," "The First 'Schools' of Electronic Music in the 1950s," "The Experimental Sixties," "Music and Computers," and "Electronic Music on Records." Chapter XII contains a chronology of electronic music from the beginning of "Musique Concrète" (1948), to the death of Varèse in 1965. Detailed reviews of over 60 recordings are provided. Appendices include a discography (over 350 items), three articles the author feels are "of the highest interest" to scholars including "A Documented History of the Cologne School," by Otto Luening, "Some Thoughts on Computers and Music," by Dr. J. R. Pierce, Bell Laboratories, and "The Composer and Computer Music," by Hubert S. Howe, Jr.. Also included is a glossary of electronic terms, a bibliography (96 items), and an index. (This work was reprinted by Da Capo in 1987 and 1994.)

50.   Russolo, Luigi. **The Art of Noises (Futurist Manifesto, 1913).** New York, NY: Pendragon Press, 1967, 1986. 87p. (Monographs in Musicology, no. 6)

This pamphlet was translated from a portion of *L'arte dei Rumori* by Robert Filliou. The work has become one of the benchmarks in the history of electronic music and music concrète. Luigi Russolo declares that the future of music must include the realization that what we consider "noise" must become part of our musical raw material in order to keep the musical art relevant to modern life. In his conclusion he points out that "one day we will be able to distinguish among ten, twenty or thirty thousand different noises. We will not have to imitate these noises but rather to combine them according to our artistic fantasy." (p. 13) The pamphlet is signed by Russolo in the following manner: "Director of the futurist movement, Corso Venezia, 61, Milano." Also, an announcement of the "First Concert of Futurist Noise Instruments" is reprinted at the end of the pamphlet.

51.   Schaeffer, Pierre. **La Musique Concrète. [Music Concrète]** Paris, France: Presses Universitaires de France, 1967. 127p. illus.

Pierre Schaeffer is considered the originator of "musique concrète" with his tape compositions in 1948. In this work he begins his analysis of electronic music with discussions of Varèse, Cage, Messiaen, Boulez, XENAKIS, and Stockhausen. Also chapters are included on the "Paris school" from 1951 to 1967. The book includes a bibliography (19 items), a discography (17 items), but no index.

52.   Schrader, Barry. **Introduction to Electro-Acoustic Music.** Englewood
       Cliffs, NJ: Prentice-Hall, Inc., 1982. xvi. 223p. illus. ISBN 0-13-481515-
       7.

       Mr. Schrader defines "electro-acoustic" music as "any music that is pro-
       duced, changed, or reproduced by electronic means."(Introduction) This
       work generally covers the whole of what would be considered electronic
       music or all music which is not acoustic.   Early musique concrète and
       tape manipulation techniques of Pierre Schaeffer, Steve Rich, John Cage,
       Hugh Le Caine, Kenneth Gaburo, Vladimir Ussachevsky, Otto Luening,
       Tod Dockstader, Toru Takemitsu, Luciano Berio, and Krzysztof Pen-
       derecki are discussed.   Additional chapters include "Electro-Acoustic
       Musical Instruments," "Electronic Music and Optical Sound Effects,"
       "Classical Studio Electronic Music: The Cologne Studios and Its Precur-
       sors," "Classical Studio Electronic Music: The Development of the
       Classical Studio," "Electronic Music Synthesizers," "Computer Music,"
       and "Live/Electronic Music." The final section of the book consists of
       interviews with electroacoustic composers and selected works: Luciano
       Berio, *Thema: Omaggio a Joyce* : Pauline Oliveros, *I of IV* ; Morton
       Subotnic, *Until Spring* ; Jean-Claude Risset, *Mutations I* ; and, Gordon
       Mumma, *Cybersonic Cantilevers.* Also included are a bibliography (128
       items) and an index.

53.   Schwartz, Elliott. **Electronic Music: A Listener's Guide.** New York,
       NY: Praeger, 1975, 1989. xii. 306p. illus. (Reprint Da Capo Pr., 1989.)
       LCCN 84-021508. ISBN 0-306762-60-9.

       Mr. Schwartz points out in his Preface that his "primary aim has been to
       make the basic facts of electronic music as clear as possible for the typi-
       cal 'listener' - the person who cares about music...but has little or no
       background in either music or the science of electronics." The work is
       divided into five parts: "Part I: The Musical Past, 1906-60," "Part II:
       The Musical Present, 1960-70," "Part III: Some Consideration for the
       Future." "Part IV: Observations by Composers," and "Part V: Do-It-
       Yourself: Tape Composition at Home." Part IV includes short, anecdotal
       essays by the following composers: Jon H. Appleton, Larry Austin,
       Robert Ceely, Joel Chadabe, David Cope, Lucas Foss, Kenneth Goober,
       William Hellermann, Lejaren A. Hiller, Jr., Hubert S. Howe, Jr., Jean
       Eicheberger Ivey, Gottfried Michael Koenig, Daniel Lent, Alvin Luckier,
       Otto Luening, Robert Moran, Giordon Mumma, Pauline Oliverous, Steve
       Reich, Gerald Shapiro, Barry Vercoe, Raymond Wilding-White, and
       Charles Wuorinen. The work includes a short bibliography, discography
       and index.

54.   Varèse, Edgard.   "The Liberation of Sound." In **Perspectives on American Composers.** ed. Benjamin Boretz & Edward T. Cone. New York, NY: W. W. Norton, 1971. x. 268p. illus. (pgs. 25-33) LCCN 79-128039.

This chapter contains excerpts from lectures by Edgard Varèse including "New Instruments and New Music," given at Mary Austin House, Santa Fe, 1936, "Music As An Art-Science," given at the University of Southern California, 1939, "Rhythm, Form and Content," given at Princeton University, 1959, and "The Electronic Medium," given at Yale University, 1962. The lectures were edited by Chou-Wen-Chung.

55.   Wallace, Ronald A. **Computer Musicians Source Book.** Peoria, IL: Computer Musicians Coalition, 1987. 221p. looseleaf. illus. ISBN 0-945505-00-0.

The *Computer Musicians Source Book* is published by the Computer Musician Coalition which is a division of Ron Wallace Enterprises, Inc.. The work is published as a looseleaf allowing for updating by the Computer Musician Coalition, 1024 W. Willcox Ave., Peoria, IL 61604. Sections include "CMC Messages & Contents," "General Articles," "Product Catalog," "Test Reports & Reviews," "Potpourri," "News & New Products," "Consultant Directory," "Dealer Directory," "User Groups," and "Manufacturer Directory." This work contains a lot of useful information concerning electronic music. The section entitled "Potpourri," includes a computer music glossary, a member forum which includes notes on various electronic musicians, and happenings which is a list of electronic and computer music events throughout the U. S.. Articles reproduced in the manual (at least in the original version) include "Computers in Music Education--Computers Don't Byte!," by Cindy Bridges, "An Introductory Guide: MIDI for Music Educators," by John Larson, "The 30 Minute MIDI Workshop," by Ron Wallace, "Apple Serenade," by Cynthia E. Field, and "Musical Liberation: Evolution of the Species," by Ron M. Goldberg.

56.   Wells, Thomas H. & Eric S. Vogel. **The Technique of Electronic Music.** New York, NY: Schirmer Books, 1974, 1981. xvi. 303p. illus. (2nd ed. 1981 by New York: Macmillan, Inc.) LCCN 78-8819. ISBN 0-02-872830-0.

"This book is concerned with the presentation and explanation of the techniques of electronic music production and is intended as a textbook for college courses in electronic music." (Preface)   Probably the best book to this date on the theory of voltage-controlled synthesis, the work is well illustrated with block diagrams and patchings, and contains sections at the end of chapters to help the reader understand the concepts presented. Sections include "Psychoacoustics and Electronic Music," "Oscillators," "Mixing," "Modulations," "Filters," "Control Signals," "Tape Recording," "Studio Layout and Design," "Text Equipment and Measurements," and "Electronic Music Scores." Examples of scores by Ligeti (*Artikulation*), Stockhausen (*Kontakte, Telemusik, Mixtur, Kurzwellen*), Wells (*12.2.72, Electronic Music & Systems of Electronic and Instrumental Music*), Korte (*Remembrances*), and Faulconer (*Electronic Music: 1973*). Each section contains a selected bibliography. Appendices include trigonometric tables, voltage and power ratios to decibels, frequencies of notes in the tempered scale, sound power output from a simple source in terms of the maximum volume displacement, logarithms, journals, and manufacturers. The work also includes a glossary, selected discography and index.

57.   Wittlich, Gary E. et al **Microcomputers and Music.** Englewood Cliffs, NJ: Prentice-Hall, 1986. xiii. 321p. illus. ISBN 0-13-580515-5.

"The primary aim of this book is to demonstrate how microcomputers can be used effectively in the solution of problems of interest to musicians." (Preface) Chapters include: "Introduction to Top-Down Design and Structured Programming." "Data Processing and Manipulation," "Data Structures for Music Applications," "Structured Programming for Computer-Assisted Instruction Lessons," "Microcomputer Graphics," "Computer-Generated Sound," and "Top-Down Design: Examples." Most programming examples are done in BASIC, and programs are written for easily obtainable desktop computers, e.g., Apple II™, Commodore 64™, & IBM PC™. Appendices include a guide to BASIC, instructions for using the Apple "Shape Maker," machine codes for screen scrollers for melody making programs, and solutions to exercises.

58.   Yelton, Gary, ed. **The Musical PC.** Decatur, GA: MIDI America, Inc., 1992. 362p. illus. ISBN 0-9623397-8-4.

This work presents over 30 articles. Contributors include Gary Yelton on using the PC at home, stage & studio & rudiments of music and acoustics, Bob Moog on music education software & electronic software systems, Dr. Marc Apfelstadt on music printing software, Mark Lang on multimedia applications, and Doug Kraul on PC hardware & system software. Appendices include tips for using music software by Dr. Marc Apfelstadt, and a DOS primer by Connor Freff Cochran.

Electronic Music Synthesis
and Synthesizers

A synthesizer is an electronic machine that produces and processes sounds in real time. Most synthesizers are voltage-controlled and produce sound through amplitude variation, and can produce a wide variety of sounds controlling pitch, envelope, amplitude, timbre, reverberation, modulation, etc.. Until the late 1970s, the synthesizer was relegated to the professional electronic studio. They were expensive and extremely hard to operate because they required extensive patching (wiring). With the application of the transistor (and later the integrated circuit chip) to the electronic circuitry of the synthesizer, both the cost and difficulty of operation were reduced. Many musicians found that they could construct their own synthesizers at less cost and, at the same time, make them better suit their needs. A number of construction and synthesizer theory books were published during this period, but only a few stand out and are included here.

As the integrated circuit (IC) became more common in the construction of synthesizers, new techniques of operation were developing. By the middle of the 1980s, a number of commercial synthesizers were available both for the novice musician and the professional. The combination of the synthesizer and the digital computer required additional technical knowledge.

The complete marriage of synthesizers and computers occurred by the end of the 1980s. Even live performances began to depend on a combination of the two machines. By the beginning of the 1990s digital synthesizers dominated. These modern synthesizers were becoming cheaper, more powerful, and extremely common.

The following books provide an historical overview of the development of the music synthesizer including the early electronic music studios, the analog machines, and the more modern digital versions.

59.   Casabona, Helen & David Frederick. **Beginning Synthesizer.** Cupertino, CA: GPI Publications, 1986. v. 105p. illus. ISBN 0-88284-353-2.

As one of a series of books on electronic music produced by *Keyboard* Magazine (Tom Darter, editor), this book provides 13 basic lessons for the beginning synthesizer player. The lessons are divided into 6 sections: "Introduction" "Using Presets," "Performance Controls," "Editing Presets," "Editing in Performance," and "Solos to Play." A glossary of terms is provided at the end of the volume.

60.   Chamberlain, Hall. **Musical Applications of Microprocessors.** Rochelle Park, NJ: Hayden Book Co., 1985, 1987. 672p. illus. ISBN 0-31700-632-3.

Mr. Chamberlain's impressive work covers "the application of all important electronic and computer music performance techniques to micro processors..." (Preface) In addition, he covers some new techniques for microprocessors and extremely large computers. The work is divided into four major sections: background material, computer-controlled analog synthesis, digital synthesis and sound modification, and product application and the future. Chapter titles include "Music Synthesis Principles," "Sound Modification Methods," "Voltage Control Methods," "Direct Computer Synthesis Methods," "Microprocessors," "Basic Analog Modules," "Digital-to-Analog and Analog-to-Digital Converters," "Signal Routing," "Organ Keyboard Interface," "Control Sequence Display and Editing," "Digital-to-Analog to Digital Conversion of Audio," "Digital Tone Generation Techniques," "Digital Filtering," "Percussive Sound Generation," "Source-Signal Analysis," "Digital Hardware," and "Music Synthesis Software." The work is concluded with an interesting section entitled "The Predictions." A short bibliography (19 items) and an index are provided.

61.   Chowning, John M. *"Computer Synthesis of the Singing Voice."* in **Sound Generation in Winds, Strings, Computers.** Stockholm, Sweden: Musikaliska Akademien, 1980. 248p. illus. (includes one sound disc: 45 rpm) ISBN 91-85428-18-3.

Mr. Chowning delivered this paper at a seminar at the Royal Institute of Technology (KTH) arranged by the Committee for Music Acoustics of the Royal Swedish Academy of Music in November 1979. The work contains 14 papers in addition to Mr. Chowning's which deals with acoustics of wind and bowed instruments. In his Introduction he explains that the "work represented here demonstrates above all that acceptable synthesis of a sung tone demands careful attention to rather simple characteristic details of the real target tone which are largely independent of the synthesis technique... [and that] the purpose of this paper is to show a strategy for the use of FM in the synthesis of two cases of the singing voice 1) a soprano, and 2) an un-naturally low male voice we might call basso profundissimo."

62.   Chowning, John M. and David Bristow. **FM Theory and Applications: by Musicians for Musicians.** Tokyo, Japan: Yamaha Music Foundation (Hal Leonard Books), 1987. v. 195p. illus. ISBN 4-636-17482-8.

FM Theory and Applications: by Musicians for Musicians grew out of a conversation with Pierre Boulez at an IRCAM Conference in Paris where he encouraged the authors to prepare a short tutorial on the fundamental of FM (frequency modulation) synthesis. The emphasis of this volume is to make it possible for musicians to obtain more expressively potent control over their FM instruments. Emphasis is placed on producing music in this book, and not on setup, patching, and programming. Examples are provided by David Bristow for the Yamaha DX™ series synthesizers. The work begins with an Introduction that provides an overview of the use of FM synthesizers and continues with sections on the theory of synthesizers, how sounds are produced, and a number of applications including "Noise, Inharmonic Spectra," "Envelopes and Bandwidth," "Resonances or Formats," "Feedback," and "Building Finished Sounds." Appendices include "Logarithmic Representation and 'Pitch Frequency'," "'X' Synth Comparisons by Index vs. Op. Output Level," "Bessel Functions Graphs," "A Short Bibliography," (18 items), "A Glossary of Terms," and "The Sampling Rate of the [Yamaha ™] DX7." There is no index.

63.   Creely, Robert. **Electronic Music Resource Book.** Newton, MA: NEV Multimedia Publications, 1980. 370p. illus. ISBN 0-9606426-1-7.

Mr. Creeley's book contains both general information on the history and composition of electronic music, and information concerning specific synthesizers. The work is written for musicians with little or no electronic background. General information chapters include "Waveforms," "Modifiers," "Controllers," "Connections," "The Tape Recorder as a Compositional Tool," "Putting It All Together," "Notation," "Suggested Class Assignments," "Studio Configurations," and "Compositional

Limitations of Current Music Synthesizers." Chapters on specific synthesizers include the ARP 2600™, the Buchla Music Easel™, the EML-
101™ & EML-200™, the EML-3-1 Controller™, the EML-401 Sequen-
cer™, the Mini-Moog™, the Modular Moog™, the Polyfusion Modu-
lar™, and the Synare 2 Percussion Synthesizer™. The work is well
illustrated and appendices include a glossary of synthesizer terminology,
a bibliography & discography, and a list of useful addresses of publishers
and studios.

64.   Crombie, David. **New Complete Synthesizer: a Comprehensive Guide
        to the World of Electronic Music.** London, England: Omnibus Press,
        1983, 1985. 112p. illus. ISBN 0-7119-0701-3.

"The aim of this book is to provide the reader with a reference work that
will help him or her to understand the increasingly complex world of
electronic music synthesis. This book caters for both the person with
little or no knowledge of synthesizers, and for those with a working understanding of these electronic instruments." (Introduction, [p.2]) Mr.
Crombie's book begins with a preface that provides background on electronic music in general and synthesizers specifically, and then continues
with chapters on sound, types of synthesizers, subtractive synthesis, additive and FM synthesis, phase distortion synthesis, controls and controller techniques, interfacing and accessories, computers and music, and
using the synthesizer. A final chapter provides a very good introduction
to MIDI. This book is very well written with clear illustrations and provides a good introduction for students and beginning electronic musicians.

65.   Crombie, David. **The Synthesizer & Electronic Keyboard Handbook.**
        New York, NY: Alfred K. Knopf, 1984, 1986. 160p. illus. LCCN 84-
        47863. ISBN 0-394-54084-0.

This book is designed to be an introduction to the new generation of
electronic keyboards. In the Forward, Thomas Dolby points out that "before you spend your cash, read this book, study what it has to say, and
think hard." The work is divided into four main sections; "Sound and
Electricity," which provides basic information about how sounds are
formed; "The Instruments," which begins with a brief history of the early keyboards, Hammond™ organs through to modern synthesizers including most major brands (also in this section the use of microprocessors and home computers as interface devices is discussed); "Playing
Techniques" which explains notation, patching, and other performance
techniques; and a final section covers all aspects of amplification and

recording including information on MIDI. The work is well illustrated and contains a complete glossary of electronic music terms and an index. The book was reprinted by Music Sales Corp. 1986.

66.   Darter, Tom, comp. **The Art of Electronic Music.** New York, NY: William Morrow & Co., 1982. iv. 312p. LCCN 85-60142. ISBN 0-688-03105-6.

Dr. Robert Moog points out, in the Forward to this work, that these "musicians have produced a dazzling variety of high-quality music. Their experiences and thoughts remind us that music is made by people, and that the electronic part of electronic music simply tells us how the musicians went about their work." (Forward: "Technology and Art. IV") The book is divided into three major sections: "1. The History of Electronic Musical Instruments"; "2. Pioneers of Synthesizer Design"; and, "3. Artists of Electronic Music." Section 1. contains ten articles written by Tom Darter including "Introduction: The Acceleration of History," "Electro-Mechanical Instruments," "Photo-Electronic Instruments," "Electric Piano," "Early Tube Oscillators," "Monophonic Keyboards," "The First Synthesizers," "Beginning of the Modern Age," "Music and the Computer," and "Then and Now: Into the Land of the Synthesizer." Section 2. contains eight articles including "Introduction: From Garage Workshop to Industrial Complex," by Tom Darter, "Robert Moog," by Dominic Milano, "Don Buchla," by Jim Aikin, "The Rise and Fall of Arp Instruments," by Craig Walters, "Tom Oberheim," by Dominic Milano, "Dave Smith," by Tom Darter, "Max Mathews/John Chowning," by Jim Aiken, and "The New Pioneers: From Designer to Design Team," by Tom Darter. Chapter 3. contains twenty-two articles including "Introduction: A Short History of Electronic Music," by Tom Darter, "Wendy Carlos," by Dominic Milano, "Keith Emerson," by Dominic Milano, "Columbia/Princeton," by Bob Moog, "Isao Tomita," by Michey Yoshino, "Tangerine Dream," by Dominic Milano, "Jan Hammer," by Dominic Milano, "Klaus Schultz," by John Diliberto, "Larry Feast," by Dominic Milano, "Kraftwerk," by Jim Aikin, "Robert Powell," by Dominic Milano, "Brian Eno," by Jim Aikin, "Barton & Priscilla McLean," by Jim Aikin, "*StarWars* Sound/Ben Burtt," by Dominic Milano, "Michael Boddicker," by Dominic Milano, "Susan Ciani," by Dominic Milano, "Soundtrack to *Apocalypse Now*," by Bob Moog, "Vangelis Papathanassiou," by Bob Doerschuk, "Thomas Dolby," by Michael Davis & Dominic Milano, "Soundtrack to *Tron*," by Bob Moog, "Wendy Carlos," by Bob Moog, and "Progress and Art: The Future of Electronic Music," by Tom Darter. Articles are generally brief and often contain short discographies. Appendices include a glossary of electronic music terms, a list of recommended readings (22 items), short biographies of the authors, and an index.

67.   Darter, Tom, ed. **The Whole Synthesizer Catalogue.** Cupertino, CA: GPI Publications, 1985. 160p. illus. ISBN 0-88188-396-4.

The stated goal of this work is "to give our readers an objective look at the new synthesizers, drum machines, sequencers, and sampling units as they arrive in the marketplace." (Forward) Over 120 synthesizers and related units are discussed in the work. Articles are brief and only include basic information, first release date, and list price. Larger, more expensive machines, e.g., Fairlight CMI™ and Synclavier II™, are not included because of cost. In many respects this work is a synthesizer buying guide.

68.   Devarahi; Rappaport, Steven. **The Complete Guide to Synthesizers.** Englewood Cliffs, NJ: Prentiss-Hall, Inc., 1982. vii. 214p. illus. ISBN 0-13-160630-1.

"This book has been written for the musician or student who knows nothing of either synthesis or electronics and who wants to understand how analog synthesizers work. It is a combination of theoretical explanation and hands-on experience: 99 experiments are offered and discussed in detail." (Preface, p. vii) The work is presented in seven chapters which progress from basic concepts necessary to understanding synthesizers, through synthesizer modules and approaches to synthesis, and ending with an overview of synthesizers. Each chapter is designed for a student to read and understand in about an hour, and is then followed by a series of experiments which help the reader understand the concepts presented. Since the work attempts to present specific synthesizers, the equipment needed for each chapter is listed at the beginning. Most of the experiments can be performed on the ARP 2600™ patchable synthesizer which is widely available in schools and colleges. Chapter seven lists a number of additional synthesizers and provides descriptions and comparisons of capabilities including: the ARP Solus™, the Crumar Stratus™, the Electro-Harmonix Mini-Synthesizer™, the Korg Sigma™, the Minimoog™, the Moog Opus 3™, the Moog Source™, the Oberheim OB-1™, the Roland SH-09™, and the Sequential Circuits Pro One™ among others. Appendices include sections on the ARP 2600™, a list of synthesizer manufacturers (36 companies), a glossary of synthesizer terminology, a discography (15 items), an index of experiments & a general index, and an annotated bibliography of books and periodical articles on synthesis (19 items).

69.   Dodge, Charles & Thomas A. Jerse. **Computer Music: Synthesis, Composition, and Performance.** New York, NY: Schirmer Books, 1985. 400p. illus. ISBN 0-02-837100-X.

"The purpose of this book is to provide the musician with an entry into the three main fields of computer music - synthesis, composition, and performance." (Preface) The authors have presented the material for the person with little background in programming or mathematics. All programming examples are written in Fortran. Chapters include "Fundamentals of Computer Music," "The Acoustics and Psychoacoustics of Music," "Synthesis Fundamentals," "Synthesis Using Distortion Techniques," "Subtractive Synthesis," "Speech Synthesis," "Reverberation," "Composition with Computers," and "Real-Time Performance of Computer Music." Notes are provided at chapter ends and the work contains a glossary of electronic music terms and an index.

70.   Douglas, Alan. **Electronic Music Production.** 2d ed. Blue Ridge Summit, PA: TAB Books, Inc., 1982. 140p. illus. ISBN 0-2733-1523-4.

"This is not a construction book in the sense that complete designs for pianos, organs, or synthesizers are shown...It is hoped that this book will help the newcomer gain an understanding of the many facets of this new medium." (Preface) Chapters include "Properties of Conventional Musical Instruments," "Musical Scales, Temperament and Tuning, Concord and Discord," "Electronic Music Generators," and "Electronic Music and the Composer." The work is well illustrated and contains appendices on multi vibrator circuits, tuning oscillators, pitch in terms of organ stops, and carillon or chime synthesis. Also included is a 53 item bibliography.

71.   Eaton, Manford L. **Electronic Music: A Handbook of Sound Synthesis & Control.** 2nd. ed. Kansas City, MO: Orcus Research, 1971. 95p. illus.

"The book contains information which will enable the reader to design and evaluate electronic music systems. It is the first authoritative presentation of the basic theories of sound generation and control." (Introduction) The work is written for people interested in electronic music but who have no previous technical training. Sections include "Sound, Electronics & Transducers," "Sound Waves & Music," "Parameters of Sound," "Some Properties of Hearing," "Electronics," "Black Box Synthesis...," "Microphones, Loudspeakers and Tape Recorders," "Techniques of Generation Complex Waves," "Control Techniques," "Compositional Procedures," "Electronic Music in the Future," and "Charts." Also included are a glossary of electronic music terms, a short bibliography, and an index.

72.   Eiche, Jon F. **What's a Synthesizer? Simple Answers to Common Questions about the New Musical Technology.** Milwaukee, WI: Hal Leonard Books, 1987. 61p. illus. LCCN 87-12149. ISBN 0-88188-671-8.

This little book is intended as a simple introduction to synthesis and synthesizers. The work begins with an explanation of sound waves, pitch, & other music basics, and then proceeds to explain keyboards, how digital synthesis works, and MIDI. The chapter on MIDI is one of the best introductions to the topic in print.

73.   Freff. **What's a Sampler? A Basic Guide to the World of Digital Sampling.** Milwaukee, WI: Hal Leonard Pub. Co., 1989. 42p. illus. ISBN 0-88188-883-4.

This short book is a basic introduction to the electronic music synthesizer. It begins with a definition of sampling and then continues to explain the basics of sound, digital recording, and the types of sampling instruments. Other chapters include "Truncating and Looping," "Taking Samples Farther," "Juggling Memory," "Knowing What to Play," and "Sample-Editing (and Creating!) Software." There is also a glossary of electronic music terminology. While this is a very elementary introduction, it does provide excellent explanations and examples of synthesis with an emphasis on sampling.

74.   Friedman, Dean. **Synthesizer Basics.** New York, NY: Amsco Publications, 1986. xii. 135p. illus. ISBN 0-8256-2409-6.

Mr. Friedman has attempted to present synthesizers "in such a way that whether you own a synthesizer, or regardless of its make, you will still be able to get something out of this book." (Introduction, p. 2). In order to do this he recommends a procedure he calls "getting neutral," designed to allow any synthesizer to work with the projects outlined. The exercises are designed for analog synthesizers only, the Yamaha DX7™ and the Casio CZ101™ can not be used with this book. The work begins with a brief history of synthesizers beginning with Thaddeus Cahill's Telharmonium (1897), and continues with explanations of sound waves, waveforms, and different kinds of synthesis. Additional chapters include "The Voltage-Controlled Synthesizer," "Synthesizer Components," "Performance Controls," "Neat Extra Features," "Additional Features and Capabilities," "FM Synthesis and the [Yamaha] DX7™," "Other Synthesizers, Samplers, Systems," "MIDI," and "A Final Word About

Synthesis." The chapters are clearly written and well illustrated. Electronic musicians with little or no technical knowledge should be able to follow the explanations provided.

75.   Fryer, Terry. **A Practical Approach to Digital Sampling.** Milwaukee, WI: Hal Leonard Publishing Co., 1989. 45p. illus. ISBN 0-88188-925-3.

This brief volume provides a complete introduction to sound sampling beginning with a short history and continuing through the techniques and equipment used. Some of the concepts covered include "Nyquist limit," "Aliasing," and "Quantization error." Chapters include "Sampling Resolution Bit By Bit," "A Good Reason to Dust Off that Calculator-- Sampling Rate," "How to Control Aliasing by Filtering and Half-Speed-Mastering Your Samples," "More Distortion Solutions," "Stop, Look & Listen Before You Sample," "Share the Wealth and the Memory Through Multisampling," "Transposing Samples: Not for the Squeamish," "Better Samples Through Equalization," "Realistically Sampling Multi-Register Acoustic Instruments," "The Legality of Sampling from Unauthorized Sources," "It's a Sampler and a Drum Machine," "Just Don't Get Soap Suds in the Microphone!-- How to properly Prepare for A Sampling Recording Session," "Logging, Miking, SMPTE, & the Marauding Iguana," "Techniques for Sampling Drums," "Attack of the Armchair Sampler," "Sampling Basics: Setting Levels & Truncating," "What To Do When Your Samples Exceed the Dynamic Range of your Sampler," and "Make Your Samples Work Together." A short biography of the author is also included. There is no bibliography or index.

76.   Graham, Bruce. **Music and the Synthesizer.** Herts, England: Argus Books, Ltd., 1985. 144p. ISBN 0-85242-695-X.

"This book is suitable for anyone who wishes (i) to know about synthesizers: (ii) to buy one (for Pianists and Organists this is a very easy way to add a further dimension to a group): (iii) to expand his knowledge of Electronic Music Systems (without having to learn all the technicalities of Electronics)": (iv) to learn more about how music, and sound in general, is built up from its elements." (Preface) While the work is technical in nature, terms are well defined and explanations are written so they can be understood by someone with a minimal electronic background. Appendices include a glossary (51 terms), a bibliography (33 items), and an index.

77.   Henry, Thomas. **Build a Better Music Synthesizer.** Blue Ridge Summit, PA: TAB Books, Inc., 1987. vii. 176p. illus. LCCN 86-5742. ISBN 0-

8306-0255-0.

Mr. Henry points out in his introduction that "you can always build a better synthesizer than you can buy." The purpose of this volume is to explain exactly how to build one. The book is written for the musician who has had some background in electronics. The work begins with basic electronic theory and then covers the components of sound, typical synthesizer modules, control levels, impedance, power supply requirements, and mechanical considerations. Clear instructions are given for construction along with circuit diagrams. Ten projects are included in the book: a deluxe VCO (voltage-controlled oscillator), a four-pole lowpass VCF (voltage-controlled filter), a retriggerable ADSR, a super controller, a two-chip VCA (voltage-controlled amplifier), a digital keyboard, a quadrature function generator, a ring modulator, and a power supply. Appendices include a list of electronic parts supplies and a bibliography. A limited index is also included.

78.   Horn, Delta T. **Troubleshooting and Repairing Electronic Music Synthesizers.** Blue Ridge Summit, PA: TAB Books, 1992. x. 206p. illus. LCCN 91-33305. ISBN 0-8306-3921-7.

Mr. Horn points out that "all too often, it is inconvenient or even impossible to send [electronic instruments] to an authorized repair center [and] with older equipment, the manufacturer might have gone out of business..." (Preface) further complicating troubleshooting. This book is intended to make it possible to troubleshoot and repair the type of circuits commonly found in both analog and digital electronic music synthesizers. The main emphasis of the work is to provide "tips" on how to troubleshoot common problems in synthesizers and related equipment. No specific design details of specific synthesizers are provided primarily to avoid violating patents and trade secrets of the manufacturers. The work is divided into two sections: "Analog Synthesizers," and "Digital Synthesizers." Also, an extensive "patching troubleshooting" section is included. The work is very general in its approach but should provide valuable routines not found in the synthesizers' manuals. An index is provided for quick reference. There is no bibliography.

79.   Horn, Delton T. **The Beginner's Book of Electronic Music.** Blue Ridge Summit, PA:TAB Books, Inc., 1982. viii. 376p. LCCN 82-5912. ISBN 0-8306-2438-4.

This book is aimed primarily toward the hobbyist and the semi-professional musician. The first section discusses basic synthesis and the types of circuits used in electronic music. Schematics and parts lists are provided for experimenters. The second section describes the procedure for setting up an electronic music studio for line and recorded performances. And finally, a number of useful appendices are provided including: a glossary of terms related to electronic music, a bibliography for recommended additional reading (14 items), a list of manufacturers and their addresses, a discography with short annotations (77 items), and a section of sample patches for common synthesizers. The book is well illustrated and progresses from simple electronic devices to the operation of complete synthesizers. This book was reprinted by Silver Burdett Press in 1984.

80.   Horn, Delton T. **Digital Electronic Music Synthesizers.** 2d. ed. Blue Ridge Summit, PA: TAB Books, Inc., 1988. xi. 258p. illus. LCCN 87-18108. ISBN 0-8306-9695-4.

In his preface to this second edition, Mr. Horn points out that "the synthesizers of today are fundamentally different from those of a few years ago,...the majority use...digital circuitry [and] many have no dedicated modules at all." This book is intended to familiarize readers with synthesizers and how they work. Chapters include "Components of an Analog Synthesizer," "Digital Sound Synthesis," "MIDI," "The SMPL Tape Automation System," "PAIA Kits," "Casio™ Electronic Musical Instruments," "Siel™ Synthesizers," "The Emulator," "Oberheim Electronics™, Inc.," "Korg/Unicord™ Synthesizers," "Yamaha™ Synthesizers," "Sequential Circuits," "The Synclavier™," "Kawai™," "Wersi™ Organs," "Accessories," "Electronic Drums," and "Software." Also included are specifications and electronic diagrams to build a number of small projects including an Op Amp organ, a digital poly-syngan, and modulators and drones. Appendices include a section on universal patch diagrams, TTL IC pinouts, and CMOS IC pinouts. The work also contains index and bibliography.

81.   Horn, Delton T. **Electronic Music Synthesizers.** Blue Ridge Summit, PA: TAB Books, 1980. 168p. illus. ISBN 0-8306-9722-5.

"This book is intended to familiarize the reader with just what a synthesizer is and what it can do." (Introduction) Included in the work are a number of construction projects, an overview of some of the commercial synthesizer available, and sample patch diagrams that can be duplicated on various kinds of equipment. Chapter titles include "Components of a Synthesizer," "Moog™ Modular Systems," "Mini-Moog™ and Poly-moog™," "ARP 2600™ and ARP Odyssey™," "PAIA Modules,

Gnome™ and Oz™," "Oberheim™ Polyphonic Synthesizers," "EML Synkey™," and "RMI Keyboard Computer™." Project instructions provide clear schematics and parts lists. The book contains an index, but no bibliography.

82.   Howe, Hubert S., Jr. **Buchla Electronic Music Systems Users Manual for CBS Musical Instruments.** Fullerton, CA: Columbia Broadcasting Systems, Inc., 1970. 28p.

The Buchla™ synthesizer was developed during the late 1960s by CBS Musical Instruments, and was the first to provide a modular system approach. An introduction by Dr. Will Gay Boltje of Southern Illinois University provides an overview of electronic music. The manual also provides a complete list and description of each module available, a sequence of tutorial examples, and complete patching instructions. The work is now considered a seminal writing in the history of electronic music. No index or bibliography is included.

83.   Hurtig, Brent, ed. **Synthesizers and Computers.** 2d ed. Milwaukee, WI: Hal Leonard Pub. Corp., 1985, 1987. v. 128p. illus. (Keyboard Synthesizer Library, Vol. 3) ISBN 0-88188-716-1.

Synthesizers and Computers is a collection of reprints from *Keyboard* Magazine. The articles are written by leading programmers, designers, educators, and musicians who are active in the field of electronic music. The work is valuable for advanced electronic music enthusiasts, and the beginner who wishes to gain an understanding of the MIDI protocol. The 1987 edition brings the volume up to date by including several articles that appeared in the magazine between 1985 and early 1987 including articles on digital sounds sampling, MIDI, art programs, mass storage, and backing up electronic music data.

84.   Keyboard Magazine. **Synthesizer Basics.** Cupertino, CA: GPI Publications, 1984. vii. 109p. illus. ISBN 0-88188-289-5.

Compiled from several years of articles appearing in *Keyboard* Magazine, this book presents step-by-step explanations and hands-on advice concerning many aspects of synthesizers from the foremost authorities. The work is divided into four sections: "Perspectives on Synthesizers," "Basic Concepts and Components," "Sound Systems and Accessories," and "Recording and Specsmanship." Authors include Tom Rhea, Robert Moog, Jim Aiken, Roger Powell, Steve Porcaro, and Dominic Milano. The preponderance of the work is authored by Robert

Moog. Appendices include "Questions and Answers," "Recommended Reading," (20 items), short biographies of authors, and a glossary of synthesizer terminology. There is no index.

85.   *Keyboard* Magazine. **Synthesizer Technique.** Rev. Ed. Cupertino, CA: GPI Publications, 1984, 1987. v. 129p. illus. ISBN 0-88188-715-3.

This is the second volume in *Keyboard Magazine's* Keyboard Synthesizer Library series. Chapters are excerpted from past issues of *Keyboard* Magazine with additional material added to introduce each section. Authors include Jim Aikin, Craig Anderton, Tom Coster, Tom Darter, George Duke, Patrick Gleeson, Bob Moog and Roger Powell. The work is divided into three sections: "Recreating Timbres," "Pitch-Bedding, Modulation, and Expression," and "Soloing and Orchestration." The articles included are well illustrated and written for musicians with little or no experience with synthesizers. Appendices include biographies of the authors, a bibliography of recommended readings (20 items), and a glossary of synthesizer terminology. This work was first published under the same title in 1984. The 1987 edition was revised with about 15 added pages.

86.   Massey, Howard, Alex Noyes, & Daniel Shklair. **A Synthesist's Guide to Acoustic Instruments.** New York, NY: Amsco Publications, 1987. 224p. illus. ISBN 0-7119-1124-X.

A Synthesist's Guide to Acoustic Instruments is designed to be a handbook for synthesizer users of all ability levels. The book begins with some basic information on audio principles, and then continues with a description of the four most common synthesis systems currently in use: subtractive, digital phase distortion, digital FM, and digital sampling. The main part of the book contains twenty-five chapters covering the most commonly simulated acoustic instruments including woodwind instruments, keyboard instruments, stringed instruments, and percussion instruments. Each acoustic instrument is covered in detail with explanations of how to link the instrument to MIDI and how to work with the digital signals. Sampling techniques are also discussed for each instrument. The work is written for electronic musicians who understand the basics, but it is not overly technical in its explanations. There is an appendix on reading the wave shape and FFT illustrations. There is no index or bibliography.

87.   Mayer, Alfred. (The Boys from Putney) **Electronic Music for the Seventies.** Morrison, NJ: Ionic Industries, Inc., 1970. ii. 45p. illus.

This little volume is interesting for two reasons: 1) it is an operations manual for the Putney VCS3™ (Voltage Controlled Studio Mk3™) synthesizer, and 2) it clearly represents the electronic music state-of-the-art of the late 1960s.   Mr. Mayer explains in the Introduction that "electronic music is now coming of age. Heretofore, there may have been questions of its importance, its validity, its direction. Currently, it would be difficult to pinpoint exactly the avenues it will pursue; my thought, at the moment, is that it no longer can be shrugged off, lightly." Sections include: "General Introduction," "Connecting the Putney VCS3™ and Using the Matrix Board," "Detailed Operation of Devices," "External Equipment and Special Patches," and "Specimen Patches." Also, a bibliography (68 items) and a glossary are included.

88.   Milano, Dominic, ed. **Synthesizer Programming.** Milwaukee, WI: Hal Leonard Books, 1987. vii. 109p. illus. ISBN 0-88188-550-9.

"This book will give you the capability to understand and control...your [electronic] musical equipment." (Forward, iv.) The work is divided into three main sections: 1. "Synthesizer Programming," including "First Steps in Programming," "Data Storage," "Parameters," "Trouble-Shooting," "Fine Points of Basic Patches," "Factory Programmers," "Studio Programmers," "Additive Synthesis," and "Modular Synthe-sizers"; 2. "Clinics in Programming," including "The [Yamaha™] DX7," "The Oberheim Xpanders™," "The [Casio™] CZ-101," and "The Roland™ JX8P +JX10"; 3. "Basic Synthesis," including "Learning the Lingo," "Modulation and Voltage Control," "Ins, Outs, and Modulation Attenuation," "Attenuators, More or Less," "Oscillators and Other Vibrating Objects," "Oscillator Pitch Control," "Waveforms," "Oscillator Waveforms and Harmonic Spectra," "Filters," "Filter Cutoff Fre-quencies," "Filter Feed-Back," "Bandpass Filters," "Envelopes," and "Test Yourself." The work is clearly written and well illustrated. Appen-dices include a bibliography (16 books, 8 *Keyboard* columns, & 18 *Keyboard* articles), a glossary of synthesizer & programming terms, and an index.

89.   Newquist, H. P. **Music and Technology.** New York, NY: Watson-Guptill Publications, Inc., 1989. 208p. illus. LCCN 89-9818. ISBN 0-8230-7578-8.

This is a well-written guide for beginners who wish to familiarize them-selves with MIDI specifically, and the application of computers to music composition in general. Chapters are included covering keyboard syn-thesizers, samplers, MIDI and home recording. The explanations are clear and are generally accompanied by appropriate illustrations. *Music and Technology* will answer a great many of the beginning electronic musicians' commonly asked questions, and at the same time, clarify much of the confusion encountered when first using MIDI and electronics in music composition.

90.   Olson, Harry F. **Music, Physics and Engineering.** 2d. ed. New York, NY: Dover, 1967. xi. 460p. illus.

The first edition (1952) of Mr. Olson's book was titled *Musical Engineering*. This book covers most aspects of the physics of sound including a chapter on electronic music which discusses music synthesis by animation, electronic music synthesis by the generation and modification of original sound, synthesis by digital computer, and the RCA™ electronic music synthesizer. Much of the development of synthesized sound in the early years is discussed here.

91.   Pellegrino, Ronald. **The Electronic Arts of Sound and Light.** New York, NY: Van Nostrand Reinhold Co., 1983. xiii. 256p. illus. ISBN 0-4422-6499-2.

Mr. Pellegrino's work begins with a short history of the application of technology to art and continues with an explanation of the nature of waves and the theory behind the synthesizer. In addition, there are chapters on the computer, oscillographics and film, video graphics & the electronic arts studio, laser light forms, and electronic composition. The book is clearly written and informative. Each section attempts to provide both theory and practical information. Complete bibliographies are provided at the end of each chapter, and there is an index.

92.   Polyphony Magazine. **The Source Book of Patching and Programming from Polyphony: a Compilation of the Best from the Readers of Polyphony Magazine.** Oklahoma City, OK: Polyphony Publishing Co., 1978. 124p. illus. LCCN 78-111946. ISBN 0-933338-00-7.

The Source Book of Patching and Programming... is designed as a handy patch manual to be used as a reference for standard synthesizers. This patch book is strongly oriented toward PAIA modules, so these patches can be used as starting points on any synthesizer. Some computer programs for interfacing synthesizers and computers are found at the back of the book.

93.   Pressing, Jeff. **Synthesizer Performance and Real-Time Techniques.**

Madison, WI: A-R Editions, Inc., 1992. 462p. illus. (The Computer Music & Digital Audio Series 8) LCCN 91-39700. ISBN 0-89579-257-5.

Mr. Pressing provides an elaborate volume that makes the case for the synthesizer as a genuine musical instrument. He points out that since MIDI (Musical Instrument Digital Interface) has become standard, it in connection to the synthesizer, make a complete instrument. The book contains a history of electronic music, group studies for practice on an electronic keyboard, and a very complete bibliography.

94.   Sear, Walter. **A Guide to Electronic Music and Synthesizers.** London, England: Alfred Publishing, Co., 1978. 96p. ISBN 0-8600-1210-7.

It is the intent of this work to "describe the basic ideas [of electronic music], and to explain the basic vocabulary needed for an elementary understanding of sound, acoustics, basic electricity, and magnetism necessary to the understanding of electronic music." (Preface) Chapters include "Sound," "The Electronic Generation of Sound," "The Recording of Songs," "Some Classical Tape Recorder Electronic Music Techniques," "The Electronic Music Synthesizer," "Using Electronic Music Synthesizers to Create Music," "Voltage Control Sources," "Additional Synthesizer Accessories," "Interconnecting Various Synthesizer Components," and "Salient Features of Various Synthesizers." There is no index or bibliography.

95.   Sear, Walter. **The New World of Electronic Music.** New York, NY: Alfred Publishing Co., 1972. 131p. illus. LCCN 72-091956. ISBN 0-88284-001-0.

This work is a primer on the basic concepts of electronic music. Chapters are short and to the point. The concepts presented include: "The Electronic Generators of Sound," "The Electronic Music Synthesizer," "Voltage Control Sources," "Interconnecting Various Synthesizer Components," and "Salient Features of Various Synthesizers." A useful index is provided but no bibliography.

96.   Strawn, John. ed. **Digital Audio Signal Processing.** Los Altos, CA: William Kaufmann, 1985. x. 283p. illus. (The Computer Music and Digital Audio Series) LCCN 84-17133. ISBN 0-86576-028-9.

As another in the extremely popular Computer Music and Digital Audio Series, this book contains reprints of articles published in journals and original material. John Strawn points out that "signal processing is a subfield of engineering, drawing heavily on signal transmission theory, communications theory, and feedback theory, with contributions from theoretical and computational mathematics. The theory relies on mathematical advances that are often a century old or older. Digital signal processing is much more recent, coming into prominence since the Second World War." (Preface, xi, xii.) Now that many recording studios are all digital, this book will be valuable both for the novice recording technician and the professional as a reference work, and as a history of the art. Selections include "An Introduction to the Mathematics of Digital Signal Processing," by F. R. Moore, "An Introduction to Digital Filter Theory," by J. O. Smith, "Spiral Synthesis," by T. L. Petersen, "Signal Processing Aspects of Computer Music: A Survey," by J. A. Moorer, and "An Introduction to the Phase Vocoder," by J. W. Gordon and J. Strawn. There is a subject and a name index.

97.   Thomas, Terence. **Sound Synthesis: Analog and Digital Techniques.** Blue Ridge Summit, PA: TAB Books, 1990. x. 166p. illus. LCCN 89-20464. ISBN 0-8306-3276-2.

Mr. Thomas points out that "the purpose of [his] book is to clear up some of the confusion and provide the reader with an anatomy of analog and digital synthesizer systems." (Introduction, vii.) The work begins with power requirements and test equipment, and continues through synthesizer sources, filters, amplifiers, envelopes, sequencers, keyboards, attenuators & processors, system planning, MIDI, digital synthesizers, and parts identification. Most of the book is devoted to musicians who wish to construct their own synthesizer, but the final three chapters do provide information on using and programming a pre-made instrument. Some of the circuit diagrams provide information for building instruments which can operate along side a commercial synthesizer. The book also contains foil patterns for etching circuit boards. The simple circuits provided can be wired on pre-etched boards that are available commercially, and the more complex circuits can be built with custom-etched boards. The book is clearly written and the circuit diagrams are easily followed. The chapter on parts identification provides needed information for organizing and building an instrument. An index is provided.

98.   Vail, Mark. **Vintage Synthesizers: Groundbreaking Instruments and Pioneering Designers of Electronic Music Synthesizers.** San Francisco, CA: GPI Books, 1993. x. 300p. illus. LCCN 93-24714. ISBN 0-87930-275-5.

It may be difficult to think of electronic music synthesizers as being "vintage," but as Mr. Vail points out in his Introduction, "in the fast-paced world of electronic music, synths less than a decade old can be labeled 'vintage'." This well-illustrated book (over 200 photos) provides a brief history, pricing (both new and used), basic patching information, range & sampling abilities, and other important information for over 25 ground breaking synthesizers manufactured between 1962 and 1992. The work includes comprehensive articles by well known electronic musicians such as Dominic Milano, Connor Freff Cochran, Craig Waters, Jim Aikin, Ted Greenwald, Mark Vail, and Robert Moog. In addition there are in-depth interviews with numerous synthesizer manufacturers and engineers. Even though this is a book specifically about synthe-sizers, it provides important information concerning the history of electronic music in general. A lot of information can be gleaned from these articles concerning the early days of electronic music performance. While *Vintage Synthesizers...* is basically concerning individual instru-ments, the authors of the separate articles provide insights and historical information about the early days of electronic music that makes the work extremely valuable as a general history. It is suspected that much of what is being offered here (often in an anecdotal manner) is information not written before. The book is divided into 6 sections: "Hearts of the Modern Synth Industry," "Modular Synthesizers," "Famous Analog Synths," "Digital Synths & Samplers," "Miscellaneous [instruments]," and "The Patchbay" which includes pricing information, the purchasing of synthesizers, support & service companies, "MIDI Retrofits & MIDI-To-CV Converters," and a section on European manufacturers. The work also includes a useful glossary of electronic music terms and short biographies of the authors.

99.   Wilkinson, Scott R. **Tuning In: Microtonality in Electronic Music.** Milwaukee, WI: Hal Leonard Pub. Corp., 1988. 120p. illus. LCCN 87-37831. ISBN 0-88188-633-5.

This work is a basic guide to alternate scales, temperaments and micro tuning using synthesizers. Mr. Wilkinson points out that "there has been a resurgence of interest in widening [the] musical palette. The relation-ships between the tones are being reconsidered and many new tones are finding a voice as a result. The 'notes in the cracks' of the familiar equal tempered scale are appearing, adding new scales, tunings, and harmonies to the musician's vocabulary." (Introduction, p. 6) Chapters include "Music, Mathematics and Microtuning," "Acoustics and Psychoa-coustics," "The History of Tuning and Temperament," "Using Tunings," "Alternate Tunings and Scales," and "Tuning Electronic Instruments." "The history of Tuning and Temperament" presents a brief history of music temperament beginning with Lun & Pythagoras and continuing through micro tuning in electronic music. "Microtonal synthesizers" covered include the Motorola Scalatron™, The Prophet 5™ (which was one of the earliest instruments to include digital patch memory), the Grey Mater E for the Yamaha™ DX7, the Yamaha™ (FB01, TX81Z, DX711D/FD, DX75, DX11, & TX802), the Synergy™ and MuLogix Slave 32™, the Rayna Systems Digital Synthesizer™, the Kurzweils™, the Ensoniq Mirage™ & EPS™, the Kawai Digital Pianos™, the Roland Digital Harpsichord™, the Synclavier™, and various computers. Appendices include a glossary of electronic music and micro tuning terms, a bibliography of books and articles (115 items), a discography (61 items), and a list of manufacturers of synthesizers, and an index.

100.   Yelton, Geary & Larry Fast. **The Rock Synthesizer Manual.** Rev. Ed. Woodstock, GA: Rock Technical Publications, 1986. 128p. illus. LCCN 86-4918. ISBN 0-914283-25-1.

This is the second edition of Geary Yelton's *Rock Synthesizer Manual.* As with the original edition, the book is intended for the beginning electronic musician who wishes to learn the basics of synthesis and gain an understanding of synthesizers. The work is intended to "give...a detailed introduction to the art and technology of electronic music...[and] a lot of the information [found] here can be applied to various forms of digital synthesis." (Introduction, p. 6) The work begins with a brief history of the synthesizer beginning with Thadeus Cahill (Telharmonium), Don Buchla, and Robert Moog, and then reviews the basics of electronic sound, sound sources, amplifiers and envelopes, filters, modulation, and FM (frequency modulation) synthesis. Additional sections review the basics of circuit control, keyboards, continuous controllers, MIDI, and sequencers. Lists of instruments and software are provided along with information on pricing, and availability of used instruments. The book is well written and the illustrations are effective. Appendices include a glossary of electronic music terminology, a list of electronic music manufacturers and publishers the author calls "contacts," and a bibliography (24 items). There is also a detailed index.

Electronic Music Instruments and Devices

By 1948 there was enough experimentation going on with electronic music instruments that S. K. Lewer published his book entitled *Electronic Musical Instruments* (see item 114) where he describes the use of various systems including tape recorders, the Theremin, and others. Few additional books were published until Richard Dorf wrote his history entitled *Electronic Musical Instruments* in 1968 (see item 108). By this time it was possible to describe the early synthesizers in addition to tape techniques. By the 1970s additional volumes were being published. The development of the integrated circuit (IC) made it possible for electronic instruments to be made from kits, or even to be designed from scratch. This possibility created a market for do-it-yourself electronic music project books.

The following books are concerned with electronic musical instruments and devices that are generally not synthesizers alone, but peripheral devices and computer interfaces.

101. Anderton, Craig. **Electronics Projects for Musicians.** Saratoga, CA: Guitar Player Productions, 1975. 140p. illus. ISBN 0-825695-02-3.

Electronics Projects for Musicians is a basic manual which presents both the rudiments of electronics, and projects for building electronic music devices. Information includes where to buy electronic parts, how to use the necessary tools for construction, how to understand electronic circuits and codes, and trouble shooting completed projects. Projects tend to be limited to small devices of a hobby nature. No information is given to construct larger projects.

102.   Anderton, Craig. **The Digital Delay Handbook.** New York, NY: Amsco
       Publications, 1985. ix. 133p. illus. ISBN 0-8256-2414-2.

       Mr. Anderton's book is the most complete analysis of digital delay equip-
       ment written to date. The first part of the work explains how the digital
       delay line controls work and subsequent chapters cover short-delay line
       applications, echo applications, special effects, using the delay line feed-
       back loop jacks, drum delay line applications, Echotron™ applications,
       using the control voltage input, and multiple delay line applications. The
       chapter on Echotron™ describes the operation of the popular delay line
       (device) made by DeltaLab Research including synchronizing synthe-
       sizer arpeggiator to quarter notes, synchronizing synthesizer arpeggiator
       to various note values, flanged drums, flanged drums with psycho-
       acoustic panning, two-measure Echotron™ echo, altering the Echotron™
       sync output signal, using the control voltage input, and a number of other
       operations. The work ends with a chapter on multiple delay line appli-
       cations.

103.   Appleton, Jon. **21 St. Century Musical Instruments: Hardware and
       Software.** New York, NY: Brooklyn College Inst. Studies in American
       Music, 1989. 30p. illus. LCCN 89-82244. ISBN 0-914678-32-9.

       This little volume is no. 29 of the Brooklyn College Institute for Studies
       in American Music. Jon Appleton has worked with electronic music
       since the late 1960s when he became professor of music at Dartmouth
       College. This work is based on two public lectures he delivered during
       his tenure as I.S.A.M. Senior Research Fellow in 1988-89 entitled "Com-
       posing for New Musical Instruments," and "Creating New Musical
       Instruments." Both sections provide a brief historical overview, a
       description of current trends, and some interesting predictions of the
       future of electronic music. There is no bibliography or index.

104.   Briggs, G. A. **Musical Instruments and Audio.** Boston, MA: Herman
       Publishing, 1966. 238p. illus. ISBN 0-89046-025-6.

       This book, one of sixteen in a series on electronic music, is primarily
       concerned with acoustics and the physics of musical instruments.
       Musical Instruments and Audio "is intended to appeal to both the
       concert-goer and the audiophile..." (Introduction) Mr. Briggs begins by
       explaining the fundamentals of acoustics in a very simple manner and
       then proceeds to apply these fundamentals individually to various instru-
       ments, both electronic and acoustic. Chapter headings include "Various
       Sounds - Cause and effect," "Various Instruments," "Characteristics of

Instruments," "Formats," "Electronic Organs," and "Tuning."

105.   Brown, Bob and Mark Olsen. **Experimenting with Electronic Music.**
       Blue Ridge Summit, PA: TAB Books, 1974. viii. 180p. illus. LCCN 73-
       88743. ISBN 0-07-430129-1.

       This work begins by providing basic information on musical electronics,
       continues through an explanation of electronic instruments and their
       components, and then provides a number of electronic projects that can
       be constructed by the reader. The projects range from small devices for
       enhancing electronic devices to actually building relatively simple
       musical instruments, e.g., a Theremin. Parts lists are provided in the
       back of the book. An index is provided.

106.   Crowhurst, Norman H. **Electronic Musical Instrument Handbook.**
       Indianapolis, IN: Sams, Howard W., & Company, 1962. 128p. illus. LC-
       CN 62-15008.

       Norman Crowhurst's *Electronic Musical Instrument Handbook* is one of
       the early works to provide basic information on electronics as applied to
       musical instruments including sound reinforcement with microphones,
       sound reinforcement by electronic pickups, purely electronic musical
       instruments, transducers for musical instruments, and electronic circuit
       elements. In addition there is a chapter on installation and servicing
       equipment. Mr. Crowhurst's chapter on synthesizers provides interesting
       analyses of some of the early machines including the RCA™ Musical
       Synthesizer that worked from a punched roll of paper tape. The work
       includes a glossary of electronic music terminology and an index.

107.   Crowhurst, Norman H. **Electronic Musical Instruments.** Blue Ridge
       Summit, PA: TAB Books, 1971. 188p. illus. LCCN 70-133801. ISBN 0-
       8306-1546-6.

       Mr. Crowhurst provides an overview of the development of electronic
       music instruments and the state of the art in 1971. Chapters include
       "Amplification of Traditional Instruments," "Electronic Modifiers,"
       "Fully Electronic Instruments," "Amplifiers & Speaker Systems," and
       "Synthesizers." The work is illustrated with numerous schematic circuit
       drawings and pictures of early electronic music devices.

108.   Dorf, Richard H. **Electronic Musical Instruments.** 3d ed. New York,
       NY: Radiofile, 1958, 1963. vi. 326p. illus. ISBN 0-686-02581-4.

"The purpose of this new third edition is...to show...from the electronic technical viewpoint what organs are made of and how they work." (Preface) In addition to explaining tone generators, keying and coupling, tone coloring, special effects and equipment, sound production and reverberation, and tuning and servicing. Mr. Dorf provides sections on specific organs including Baldwin™, Schobe™, Thomas™, Lourey™, Gulbransen™, Wurlitzer™, Seeburg™, Hammond™, Rogers™, Allen™, and Conn™.

109. Douglas, Alan. **The Electronic Musical Instrument Manual: A Guide to Theory and Design.** 6th ed. London, England: Putman, 1976. 491p. ISBN 0-8306-6832-2.

"This is not a construction book: its object is to start the reader right at the fundamentals of sound, and progressively work up to examples of current organs." (Preface) In addition, sections are included on commercial electronic instruments & experimental methods. A number of useful tables are provided in a series of 9 appendices including: a frequency table, a color code for resistors, a resonant frequency chart for tone-forming chokes (Hz), a table comparing British and American wire gauges, and an organ bibliography. An index is provided.

110. Friedman, Dean. **The Complete Guide to Synthesizers, Sequencers, & Drum Machines.** New York, NY: Amsco Publications, 1985. xvi. 111p. illus. ISBN 0-8256-2410-X.

This book is designed to be an overview of the equipment available for developing a home or professional electronic music studio, or for live performance of electronic music. Information on more than 28 synthesizers, 5 keyboard controllers, 4 sequencers, and 9 drum machines is included. Each piece of equipment is listed with complete technical detail, a picture, and a detailed explanation of how the machine is set up, connected to other devices through MIDI, and played. Some of the brands of electronic music equipment represented in this book include Casio™, Digital Keyboards (M.T.I.)™, E-MU Systems™, Ensoniq™, Europa Technology™, Fairlight™, Korg™, Kurzweil Music Systems™, Linn Electronics™, Music Technology, Inc.™, New England Digital™, Oberheim™, Octave-Plateau Electronics™, Roland™, Sequential Circuits™, Siel™, Simmons™, and Yamaha International™. Appendices include a software summary, a glossary of electronic music terminology, and a list of manufacturers with addresses and telephone numbers. Now a somewhat older list, this book provides very useful information on electronic instruments.

111.   Heywood, Brian & Roger Evan. **The PC Music Handbook.** Tonbridge,
       England: PC Publishing, 1991. [xii.] 158p. illus. ISBN 1-870775-17-1.

"This book sets out what you need to know to [use your computer to
make music], whether you want to produce parts for your music society,
control your studio, train your ears or experiment with new sound
synthesis methods. You will find this book useful whether you are a professional musician looking for a studio system or a PC owner who wants
to dabble in music." (Preface [vii.])   The authors   assume a basic
knowledge of computers and music on the part of the reader. *The PC
Music Handbook* provides information on the PC and how to use it in
music composition, scoring, MIDI sequencing on the PC, using
MIDI for remote control, and a number system setups. All examples are
provided using the IBM PC™. Each chapter is provided with either a
list of questions that must be asked to fulling understand the use of PC's
in music composition, or useful lists and checklists. Appendices include
MIDI specification 1.0, a list of on-line communications sites, a list of
useful publishers and equipment manufacturers, a bibliography of books
and magazine articles (27 items), a list of MIDI organizations, and a
glossary of terminology used in the book. There is also an index.

112.   Jenkins, John & Jon Smith. **Electric Music: A Practical Manual.**
       Bloomington, IN: Indiana University Press, 1976. 176p., illus. (Midland
       Books; No. 195.) LCCN 75-18233. ISBN 0-253-31944-7.

This work explores the history, development and use of electronic instruments and amplifiers. In addition, the working principles of audio equipment are explained in detail. Chapters include "Sources," [a brief history
of electronic instruments], "Amplifiers and Loudspeakers," "Treat-
ments," "The Stage Set-Up," "Performance," "Recoding," and "Electronic Music." Appendices include "The Physics of Sound," and "Useful
Addresses." (9 items) There is a brief index.

113.   Klein, Barry. **Electronic Music Circuits.** Indianapolis, IN: Sams Pub.
       Co., 1982. 302p. illus. LCCN 81-084278. ISBN 0-672-21833-X.

Mr. Klein's work provides detailed information on a number of specific
electronic music synthesizers and other devices including voltage controlled oscillators, amplifiers, filters, envelope generators, and multipliers. Each project includes a detailed circuit diagram and parts lists. Chapters include "Synthesizer System Design," "Power Supply Circuits,"
"Control Voltage Generators, Processors, and Controllers," "Voltage
Controlled Oscillators (VCOs),"   "Filters," "Analog Multipliers,"

"Miscellaneous Circuits," and "The Modular System." Appendices include synthesizer construction aids, IC data sheets, IC Pin diagrams and an index. *Electronic Music Circuits* is designed for the advanced electronic musician who has a complete knowledge of electronics. The novice will find the work very difficult to follow.

114.   Lewer, Stanley K. **Electronic Musical Instruments.** London, England: Electronic Engineering, 1948. 101p. illus.

This relatively early work on electronic instruments provides a general overview of the developments to 1948. Chapters include "The Acoustics of Music," "Classifications of Instruments," "Electronic Circuit Generation," "Electrostatic Tone Generation," "Photo-electric Tone Generators," and "Amplifiers and Control Circuits." The writing is technical and numerous schematics and equipment layout drawings are provided. The work includes a bibliography and a brief index.

115.   Penfold, R. A. **More Advanced Electronic Music Projects.** London, England: Bernard Babani, Ltd., 1986. [viii] 78p. ISBN 0-85934-148-8.

This books is the third in a series of works Mr. Penfold has written on designing and building electronic music projects. (see items 116, 142) The format is very similar to the earlier works where each project is introduced with a brief essay and then followed by circuit diagrams, descriptions of use, and any necessary construction & wiring instructions. Even though the book contains advanced designs, the author declares that "anyone who has built up a few single electronic projects should have little difficulty in building most of the designs featured." (Preface) The projects included are divided into two types: 1) effects units, and 2) percussion synthesizers; including a phaser, a circuit operation, phase shifters, shaped fuzz, envelope modifier, split phase tremolo, VCO, VCF, chime synthesizer, etc.. As with the earlier works, this book provides clear instructions and easy-to-follow circuit designs.

116.   Penfold, R. A. **Practical Electronic Music Projects.** London, England: Bernard Babani, Ltd., 1980, 1994. 122p. illus. ISBN 0-85934-363-4.

The purpose of this book is to provide the constructor with a number of practical circuits for the less complicated items of electronic music equipment, including such things as a fuzz box, a simple organ, various types of sound generators, tremolo generators, a reverberation amplifier, a metronome, etc. Each project is fully explained and includes a schematic drawing and a parts list. Directions are clear and easy to follow. There is no index or bibliography.

117.　Starr, Greg R. **What's a Sequencer ?: a Basic Guide to Their Features and Use.** Milwaukee, WI: Hal Leonard Pub. Corp., 1990. 62p. illus. LCCN 90-53369. ISBN 0-7935-0083-4.

What's a Sequencer is part of a series of introductory books on electronic music by the Hal Leonard Publishing Co.. Other titles in the series include *What's MIDI: Making Musical Instruments Work Together* by Jon F. Eiche (see item 165), *What's a Sampler?: A Basic Guide To The World of Digital Sampling* by Freff (see item 81), and What's *A Synthesizer?: Simple Answers To Common Questions About The New Musical Technology* by Jon F. Eiche (see item 72). *What's a Sequencer* is written on a very simple level and directed toward the novice electronic musician. It begins by explaining what a sequencer is and continues with explanations of MIDI, how to hook up equipment setups, and operation procedures.

118.　Strange, Allen. **Electronic Music Systems, Techniques, and Controls.** 2d. ed. Madison, IA: Brown & Benchmark, 1972, 1983. xii. 274p. illus. LCCN 80-66305. ISBN 0-697-03602-2.

The first edition of this book published in 1972 was considered the "first comprehensive and useful guide to the subject." (Preface) The 1983 edition is in many respects a new book and is a clearly written guide to working with electronic music instruments and technical procedures of electronic music. The various aspects of electronic music covered include: "Electronic Sound Sources and their Characteristics," "Basic Signal Processing: Amplifiers and Filter," "Concepts of Voltage Control," "Control Voltage Sources," "Sub-Audio Modulation," "Audio Rate Modulation," "Equalization and Filtering," "Magnetic Tape Recording," "Audio Mixing," "Reverberation, Echo and Feedback," and "Panning and Sound Location Control." In addition there are chapters on equipment, and lists of scores for analysis and performance. This work has an extensive, annotated bibliography.

119.　Vilardi, Frank & Steve Tarshis. **Electronic Drums.** New York, NY: Amsco Publications, 1985. 84p. illus. (includes 33 1/3 record) ISBN 0-8256-2440-1.

The authors point out that "the term 'electronic drums' refers to drum synthesizers that are set up and played like conventional drums. The player, however, has control over the sound being generated, and it does not always have to be a drum sound." (p. 1) *Electronic Drums* provides a complete introduction to the synthesis of drum sounds in the application of electronic music ensembles and as solo instruments. The book is divided into four sections: "Electronic Drums," "Digital Drum Computers," "Programming a Song," "and Triggering and Sampling." The electronic drums discussed include the Simmons SDS5™, the Pearl Fightman™, the Simmons SDS8™, the Tama Techstar™, the Simmons SDS7™, the E-Drum™ by E-MU, and the Simmons SDS1™. The digital drum computers discussed include the Linn Drum™, the Oberheim DMX and DX™, the E-MU Drumulator™, the Roland TR909™, the Roland TR707™, the Yamaha RX11 & RX15™, and the Linn 9000™. The section on programming includes techniques for programming drum patterns and writing an electronic song sheet. A 33 1/3 record is included which provides sound examples of electronic drums.

120.   Winston, Lawrence E. **33 Electronic Music Projects You Can Build.** Blue Ridge Summit, PA: TAB Books, 1981. 181p. illus. ISBN 0-8306-1370-0.

This work begins by explaining the importance of electronics in current music production and then proceeds to explain how these devices are constructed. Also, thirty-three projects are provided with complete schematics and instructions. A few of the projects included are a guitar headphone amplifier, an electronic metronome, an integrated circuit metronome, a one-transistor mixer, a four-channel IC mixer, a special effects filter, an electronic microphone booster, a general purpose amplifier, a simple electronic organ, etc.. Instructions are clear and easy to follow.

Electronic Music Composition

Electronic composition books describe the process of composition with computers and electronic instruments from the earliest times to the present. Lajaren Hiller & L. M. Isaacson describe some of the earliest attempts in their *Experimental Music: Composition with an Electronic Computer* (1959) (see item 131). This work chronicles one of the earliest electronic compositions, *Illiac Suite*, and introduces the reader to the aesthetic limits of the computer and defines what can be done with current (1950s) technology. Toward the end of the 1960s more electronic composers were gaining access to main-frame computers, making it possible to do more experimenting with electronic composition. Electronic and computer music was also finding its way into the movie and television studios by the 1970s. Daphine Oram, who wrote *An Individual Note of Music: Sound and Electronics* (see item 139), was reported to be the first to compose an electronic sound track for a BBC television play (*Amphitryon 39*). The personal computer exploded onto the scene early in the 1980s and electronic music composers quickly took advantage of the new machines. It was now possible to compose music without the problems of begging time on a main frame computer, and the marriage of the micro and electronic musical instruments was completed. The early 1990s saw the development of easy-to-use, off the shelf computer composition programs for relatively inexpensive desktop computers.

The following books are representative of works written to explain the art of electronic music composition from the earliest attempts to the sophisticated computer systems of the present day. For the most part, books written for composing electronic music on specific computers have not been included.

121. Adams, Robert T. **Electronic Music Composition for Beginners.**
      Dubuque, IA: William C. Brown, 1986, 1992. xiii. 304p. illus. ISBN 0-
      697-00457-0.

      "This text explores beginning electronic music composition concepts
      through the use of small, widely available set of synthesizer modules
      and/or readily microcomputer options." (Preface) The book is divided
      into four sections: Part I provides background materials along with
      instrument design, score construction, and rehearsal/performance infor-
      mation; Part II presents a module set and its use in designing synthesizer
      instruments; Part III provides general information on microcomputers
      and their use; and, Part IV presents composition strategies and proce-
      dures, including the use of tape recorders. The work is clearly written
      and well illustrated.   Appendices include waveform and harmonic
      spectra information, frequencies of equal-tempered scales, a list of equip-
      ment and software manufacturers, flowchart notation symbols, a glossary
      of terms, and a bibliography & index.

122. Bigelow, Steven. **Making Music with Personal Computers.** La Jolla,
      CA: Park Row Press, 1987. vi. 118p. LCCN 87-32748. ISBN 0-935749-
      21-7.

      "This book provides an introduction to the use of personal computers to
      create and perform music.   It is intended for amateur or professional
      musicians who want to know what personal computers can do, what kind
      of hardware and software is available, and are looking for some guidance
      in setting up their own personal electronic music system."   (Preface)
      Sections include an introduction to sound waves and synthesizer funda-
      mentals, MIDI, personal computer systems, software, system configura-
      tions, synthesizer technique, and pitfalls and possibilities. Appendices
      include a list of hardware and software vendors, a bibliography (25
      items), and lists of online networks and bulletin boards, teaching and
      research centers, electronic music associations, and dealers. The work
      also includes a glossary and products index.

123. Brün, Herbert. **Uber Musik und zum Computer. [Music and It's
      Relation to the Computer]** Karlsruhe, Germany: G. Brown, 1971. 130p.
      illus. (contains 1 - 33 1/3 phonodisc).

      Herbert Brün's work is one of the first to delve into the theoretical use of
      computer composition. His research was supported by the Research
      Board of the University of Illinois, and the United States National
      Science Foundation. The work discusses the elements of computer

compositions, the language of composition, programming, and the concept of "musical" criteria. No specific programs or computer techniques are provided. Appendices include "Music of the New Frontiers," "Reflections of an Interested Party," "The Existence of a Composer," and "Notes to the Accompanying Record." The work contains an 18 item bibliography.

124.   Cope, David. **Computers and Musical Style.** Madison, WI: A-R Editions, 1991. xvii. 246p. (The Computer Music and Digital Audio Series, 6.) LCCN 91-11494. ISBN 0-89579-256-7.

This book presents a computer program the author wrote for the replication of musical styles. It is described as "a nonlinear (not composed beginning-to-end) and top-down compositional approach and an intricate rules-based expert system defined according to experience gained in my twenty-three years of teaching music theory. While all of the aspects considered in this book are critical to the success of the overall program, the crux of style imitation lies in the development of a musical pattern matcher and the inclusion of an ATN (augmented transition network) compositional approach." (Preface, xiii) The work begins with a brief history of automated music with an emphasis on musical style. It then continues by defining the basic concepts and parameters of musical style and examines functional harmonic tonality (expectation-fulfillment-deception) as they relate to the programs presented later in the work. In addition, texture and timbre are discussed, along with harmonic grammars and the forms of linguistic representation in music. Later Mr. Cope presents LISP (LISt Processing) Programming language which the author uses to define an idea and then work toward actual manipulation of data. The specifics of "invention-composing programs" are then described and the complexities of programming the keyboard style of J. S. Bach and Mozart are described. Finally, computer-assisted compositions are demonstrated which range from computer composition of entire pieces to composer-controlled compositions with computer assistance. The work is well illustrated and bibliographies are presented at the end of each chapter. There is a good index.

125.   De Furia, Steve. **The Secrets of Analog and Digital Synthesis.** Rutherford, NJ: Third Earth Productions, 1986. 122p. illus. ISBN 0-88188-516-9.

This book was first published as part of a video/book set. The present volume was designed to stand alone or to be used with the video tape. Five lessons are provided: 1) "The Physics of Sound," 2) "Making

Waves," 3) "The Sound Designers Took Kit," 4) "Synthesizers and Editing Techniques," and 5) "F M Synthesizers," is applicable to any FM synthesizer, such as Yamaha's™ DX and TX series. A glossary of synthesizer terminology is provided at the end of the book. There is no index or bibliography.

126.   De Voe, Robert A. **Electronmusic: A Comprehensive Handbook.** Vernon, CT: Electronic Music Laboratories, Inc., 1977. vi. 175p. illus. LCCN 76-54111.

"Electronmusic...as I define it, is any music produced in which sounds are either electronically modified or electronically generated." (p. 5) Robert De Voe goes on to point out that this work is a manual for composers who want to learn how to produce music on tape. The book is handwritten and contains numerous sketches provided as examples and illustrations. Chapters include "Electronmusic, what is it?" "Vibes - Sound and Acoustics," "Tape Recorder Husbandry," "Creative Tape Work," "Synthesizer Husbandry," "How to Score," and "Putting it all Together." The chapters require that the reader have a good understanding of synthesizers and synthesis. Most of the examples of synthesis are related to EML™ (Electronic Music Laboratories, Inc.) equipment. Appendices include a glossary of synthesizer and compositional terms, a list of patches for the ElectroComp Synthesizer™, and sample score sheets. No bibliography is included.

127.   Drake, Russell, and Ronald Herder. **How to Make Electronic Music.** New York, NY: Educational Audio Visual, Inc., 1975. 108p. illus. ISBN 0-517-52904-1.

How to Make Electronic Music deals with synthesis and recording techniques. The work approaches electronic music from the standpoint of composing with tape recorders. The Introduction points out that "all you need is a tape recorder, some relatively simple skills [and] some curiosity and imagination." Each chapter builds on the previous one and includes experiments to be completed. The final chapter provides technical information on various kinds of recorders and a good primer on recording electronic music. A glossary, bibliography, and an index are provided.

128.   Dwyer, Terence. **Composing with Tape Recorders: Musique Concrète for Beginners.** London, England: Oxford University Press, 1971. v. 74p. illus. ISBN 0-1931-1912-9.

Mr. Dwyer provides a step-by-step procedure for composing music through the use of tape recorders in this little volume. Instructions are simple and clear, and exercises are provided at the end of each chapter. Appendices include a list of useful recordings for source materials, a brief bibliography, tone-producing suggestions, and a glossary of terms.

129.   Hammond, Ray. **The Musician and the Micro.** Dorset, England: Blandsford Press, 1983. 192p. illus. ISBN 0-713712-98-8.

"This book is about the future of music. It assumes that the reader knows something about music but little about computers." (Introduction, p.5) The work provides an introduction to the use of the micro computer in music composition. Sections include "The Micro Concept," "The Personal Micro and Music," "The Micro in the Studio," "The Micro as Teacher," "The Micro and the Percussionist," "The Micro in Performance," "...Instrument Hybrids," "The Micro in Sequence," "...Dedicated Music Computers," and "The Micro and the Musician." The final chapter, "The Micro and the Musician," discusses the work of Warren Cann, John Lewis, Hans Zimmer, and Peter Gabriel. A glossary of "jargon" is also provided. There is no bibliography.

130.   Heifetz, Robin Julia, ed. **On the Wires of Our Nerves: The Art of Electroacoustic Music.** Lewisburg, PA: Bucknell University Press, 1989.

Heifetz points out in the introduction that she has selected the essays contained in this book as "an appreciation of higher aesthetic ideals that have thus far not been demonstrated very often in a musical world rife with technology." (p. 12) To this end she has presented 17 articles divided into three general subject areas: 1) "Overview: Considerations and Problems in the Creative Decision-making Process," 2) "Digital Electroacoustic Music: Problems and Questions," and 3) "Individual Systems: The Development of Personal Style." Many of the articles presented appeared in other publications, both serial and monographic, and are important analyses in electroacoustic composition. The articles include "Tradition and Change: The Case of Music," by Leonard Kasdan & Jon H. Appleton, "Electronic Music," by Otto Luening, "Electronic Music; Art beyond Technology," by Darian Semegen, "Murmur," by Kenneth Gaburo, "Some Practical Aesthetic Problems of Electronic Music Composition," by David Keane, "Aesthetic Dilemmas in Electronic Music," by Jan W. Morthenson, "Aesthetic Direction in Electronic Music," by Jon H. Appleton, "The Development of Personal Compositional Style," by Barry Schrader, "Computer Music Warmware: The Human Perspective," by Robin Julia Heifetz, "*Computer* Music or

Computer *Music*," by John Melby, "The Quest for 'Musically Interesting' Structures in Computer Music," by David Keane, "Aesthetic Appeal in Computer Music," by Thomas E. Janzen, "Electronic Sonata," by Lajaren Hiller, "Composer's Input Outputs Music," by Herbert Brün, "Fire and Ice: A Query," by Priscilla McLean, "Otahiti: The Evolution of a Personal Style," by Jon H. Appleton, and "Loudspeakers and Performers: Some Problems and Proposals," by Dexter Morrill. The book also includes a large bibliography (102 items), a discography of electroacoustic recordings (458 selections by 182 composers), and a short biography of each contributor.

131.   Hiller, Lejaren A. & Leonard M. Isaacson. **Experimental Music: Composition with an Electronic Computer.** New York, NY: McGraw-Hill, Inc., 1959, 1979. vi. 197p. illus. LCCN 79-21368. ISBN 0-313-22158-8.

First published in 1959 and reprinted in 1979, this work describes in detail the techniques used in the late 1950s to create computer music. Chapter titles include: "The Aesthetic Problem," "Experimental Music," "The Technical Problem," "Experimental Details," "Experimental Results: The *Iliac Suite*," and "Some Future Musical Applications." The book introduces the reader to the aesthetic limits of the computer and then defines what can be done with the current (1950s) technology. Also included is an interesting discussion of information theory. As an example of the creation of a piece of computer music, the *Iliac Suite* is described in detail. Also, a full score of the *Iliac Suite* is provided in an appendix. The work suffers from the lack of an index.

132.   Jaxitron. **Cybernetic Music.** Blue Ridge Summit, PA: TAB Books, Inc., 1985. vii. 344p. LCCN 85-17305. ISBN 0-8306-0856-7.

Jaxitron points out in his Introduction that "a composition is a scheme in which musical sounds are ordered; Composition is the act of designing such schemes. Whether the notes emerge from the composer's pencil or his computer is incidental to the total result that is the product of his mind." In the book, Jaxitron works with K. E. Iverson's Programming Language (APL) in which he injects the needed code for musical composition. (APL is written in BASIC.) Sections include "The Theme of APL," "Scoring in APL," "Rhythm," "Raw Material," "Melody," "Form," "Harmony," "Combining Harmony and Melody," "Harmonic Continuity," "A Systematic Approach," and "Advanced Techniques and Examples." The work shows the musical possibilities of combining the computer and artistic abilities of the musician. Appendices include "The

Cybernetic Song Book" which contains examples of computer-composed music, a "Harmonization/Melodization Workspace," and an index.

133.   Keane, David. **Tape Music Composition.** London, England: Oxford University Press, 1980. x. 148p. illus. ISBN 0-1931-1919-6.

David Keane explains in his Preface that "this book is as much about how sounds may be used in music as it is about how sounds may be made." The book is written for readers with little or no experience in technology, and attempts to explain how to compose music using tape recorders. Chapter titles include "Principles of Tape Recorders," "Principles of Tape Recording," "Composition Using Basic Recording Techniques," "Compositions Using Basic Tape Editing Techniques," "Composition Using Two Tape Recorders," "Mixers," "Treatment Devices: Filtering, Reverberation and Variable Speed Control," "Composition with Synthesizers," "Basic Aesthetic Considerations," and "Setting Up An Electronic Music Studio." Appendices include equipment specifications, patch cord and panel directory, passive mixer and pan control designs, tape-loop guide systems, and noise reduction systems. The book also contains an annotated bibliography and an index.

134.   Lang, Paul Henry, ed. **Problems of Modern Music: The Princeton Seminar in Advanced Musical Studies.** New York, NY: G. Schirmer, 1960. pgs. 145-259. (Reprinted from *The Musical Quarterly*, April 1960, vol. XLVI, no.2. Special Issue.)

This is a collection of papers presented at the Seminar in Advanced Musical Studies at Tanglewood during the summer of 1960, directed by Roger Sessions with Milton Babbitt, Edward T. Cone, Robert Craft, and Ernst Krenek assisting. Titles of papers include: "Problems and Issues Facing the Composer," by Roger Sessions, "Analysis Today," by Edward T. Cone, "Shop Talk by an American Composer," by Elliott Carter, "Notes on *A Piece for Tape Recorder*," by Vladimir Ussachevsky, "Extents and Limits of Special Techniques," by Ernst Krenek, "Bartok's 'Serial' Composition," by Allen Forte, and "Twelve-Tone Invariants as Compositional Determinants," by Milton Babbitt.

135.   Lincoln, Harry B., ed. **The Computer and Music.** Ithaca, NY: Cornell University Press, 1970. 372p. illus. LCCN 74-8065. ISBN 0-8014-0550-5.

"This book documents the efforts of a number of composers and music researchers who use the computer in their work, and it illustrates the wide range of possibilities by the computer in music composition and research." (Preface) Sections include: "Musichke's Handmaiden: Or Technology in the Service of the Arts," by Edmund A. Bowles, "From Musical Ideas to Computers and Back," by Herbert Brün, "Ethics and Esthetics of Computer Composition," by Gerald Strang, "Music Composed with Computers - A Historical Survey," by Lejaren Hiller, "MUS-PEC," by Jack P. Citron, "Webern's use of Motive in the 'Piano Variations'," by Mary E. Fiore, "Towards a Theory of Webernian Harmony, Via Analysis with a Digital Computer," by Ramon Fuller, "Harmony Before and After 1910: A Computer Comparison," by Roland Jackson, "Automated Discovery of Similar Segments in the Forty-Eight Permutations of a Twelve-Tone Row," by Gerald Lefkoff, "Fortran Music Programs Involving Numerically Related Tone," by Ian Morton and John Lofstedt, "Theoretical Possibilities for Equally Tempered Musical Systems," by William Stoney, "Root Progression and Composer Identification," by Joseph Youngblood.

136.   Mathews, Max V. **Technology of Computer Music.** Cambridge, MA: M.I.T. Press, 1969. 200p. illus. ISBN 0-262-13054-5.

"This book is intended for people who plan to use computers for sound processing." (Preface) The work, while not specifically written for engineers and physicists, does require an advanced knowledge of acoustics, physics, mathematics, and the computer language Fortran to be understood. Sections cover fundamentals, tutorial examples of sound generation, and a detailed description of the operation of the Music V program. (A Program designed to be run on the IBM™ 7094 or the GE™ 645 computer.) Two appendices on psychoacoustics and music, and mathematics are provided.

137.   Moore, F. Richard. **Elements of Computer Music.** New York, NY: Prentice-Hall, 1990. xiv. 560p. illus. LCCN 89-8679. ISBN 0-13-252552-6.

Often used as a college textbook for electronic music composition, this book provides information on how computers can analyze, process, and synthesize musical sounds and structures. This work is written at a rather high level and assumes that readers have more than a cursory knowledge of music, mathematics, computer programming, and electronics. The author points out that he assumes "that the reader is computer literate at the level of being able to read and write computer programs in some 'high-level' computer language." (Preface, xi) Subjects covered by the book include sound representations and sound digitization, additive and subtractive synthesis, concert hall acoustics, and computer-mediated composition. Appendices include sections of the mathematics of music, a table of units of measure, tuning, and 'cmusic' which is an acoustic compiler program based on the C computer language written by the author.

138.   Moore, Janet L. S. **Understanding Music Through Sound Exploration and Experimentation.** New York, NY: University Press of America, 1986. xxi. 121p. LCCN 85-29462. ISBN 0-8191-5231-5.

The purpose of this book is to "guide the inexperienced student toward discovering musical elements and ways they can be used to create music." (Preface) The work includes 26 experiments covering all elements of musical sound. Each experiment includes an explanation of the purpose, the material needed, and the procedure. Common musical materials and a piano, organ, and synthesizer are required. Appendices include "Tables of Musical Notes and Terms," a "General Survey of Contemporary Uses of the Musical Elements," a "Sampler of Electronic Music Recordings," and "A Glossary of Electronic Terms." Also a list of references (18 items) is included.

139.   Oram, Daphine. **An Individual Note of Music, Sound and Electronics.** New York, NY: Galaxy Music Corp., 1972. v. 145p. illus. ISBN 0-85249-109-3.

Daphine Oram, who was reported to be the first to compose an electronic sound track for a BBC television play (*Amphitryon 39*), is internationally known for her work in films, television, theatre, and radio. This work approaches the production of electronic music from a practical, compositional standpoint of a more personal nature. The first 13 chapters trace electronic sound production beginning with the energized, tuned circuit and continues through filters and formats, tape recording, feedback, and echo. In addition, she discusses the "human elements" which go into electronic music. Appendices include a discography, a list of Ms. Oram's compositions, and a guide to contents by subject.

140.   Paturzo, Bonaventura Anthony. **Making Music with Microprocessors.** Blue Ridge Summit, PA: TAB Books, Inc., 1984. viii. 286p. ISBN 0-8306-0729-3.

"This book shows how microprocessors and microprocessor-based computers can be used to create and produce electronic music. It is not, however, a generalized account of computer music techniques that never quite gets beyond the introductory stage." (Introduction) Mr. Paturzo begins his study with simple explanations of how a microprocessor makes music, and then proceeds with chapters on basic music theory, characteristics of musical sounds, microprocessors and microcomputers, synthesizer design, and finally provides actual designs for software and hardware use. Circuit diagrams are clear and easily understood. All projects are based on a SYM-1™ using 6502 microprocessor. Lists for additional reading are included at the end of each chapter.

141. Pellegrino, Ronald. **An Electronic Studio Manual: for Use With R. A. Moog's Voltage Controlled, Modular Synthesizing Equipment.** Columbus, OH: Ohio State University College of the Arts, 1968. viii. 234p. illus.

This manual (published in manuscript) was designed to be a companion book to Ronald Pellegrino's *The Tale of the Silver Saucer and the Transparent Apple* music drama. The manual concentrates on the compositional problems which are related to the electronic phase of the work. "It retraces the steps of the authors lengthy and systematic inquiry into the electronic sound synthesizing equipment by examining the theoretical and practical bases of the functional characteristics of the individual modules and modules in combination." (Preface) The first part of the manual is devoted to solutions to compositional problems, and the second is made up of circuit diagrams and their variations. No index or bibliography is included.

142. Penfold, R. A. **Computer Music Projects.** London, England: Bernard Babani, Ltd., 1985. 112p. ISBN 0-859341-47-X.

The purpose of this book is to show some of the ways in which a home computer can be used to produce electronic music. The topics covered include sequencing and control through analog and MIDI interfaces, computers as digital delay lines, and sound generators for computer control. The book is written for the novice who has some understanding of both electronics, computers, and music. All examples are clearly written and accompanied by well-illustrated examples. Projects covered include circuits for CV interface, drum synthesizers, cymbal and metallic sound generators, audio digitizer, compounder and MIDI interface systems, and multi-channel CV generator and keyboard CV reader etc..

143. Roads, Curtis, ed. **Composers and the Computer.** Los Altos, CA: William Kaufmann, Inc., 1985. xxi. 201p. illus. LCCN 84-23323. ISBN 0-86576-085-3.

This book is one of *The Computer Music, and Digital Audio Series,* edited by John Strawn and published by William Kaufmann, Inc.. Mr. Roads has brought together a series of articles & interviews concerning a number of aspects of computer music. Sections include: "Interview with Herbert Brün," by Peter Hamlin with Curtis Roads, "John Chowning on Composition," & "Interview with Janus Dashow," by Curtis Roads, "In Celebration: The Composition and Its Realization in Synthetic Speech," by Charles Dodge, "Improvisation with George Lewis," by Curtis Roads, "Thoughts on Computer Music Composition," by Tod Machover, "Digital Techniques and Sound Structure in Music," by Jean-Claude Risset, "The Realization of NSCOR," by Curtis Roads, and "Music Composition Treks," by Iannis Xenakis. An index and detailed bibliographies are provided.

144.   Robson, Ernest and Larry Wendt. **Phonetic Music with Electronic Music.** Parker Ford, PA: Primary Press, 1981. 127p. illus. (includes cassette tapes) LCCN 81-90189. ISBN 0-934982-02-3.

This work presents twelve compositions of phonetic music with electronic realization. The phonetic sounds are created by Ernest and Marion Robson with the help of Larry Wendt who produced the works on tape. Mr. Wendt points out that "these works do not deal with the complete dissolution of word-based systems like some other sound poetry might; despite their acoustical construction they retain a great deal of integrity with notable written words... What we have done here is to retain the clarity of the text while relying on electronic techniques to provide an acoustical underpinning and to accent particular aural-lingual events as an aid towards their differentiation." (Preface) Mr. Robson defines phonetic music "as a somewhat special region of sound poetry [which] is any acoustic pattern of 'speech' independent of grammar or meaning. It may or may not be reinforced, acoustically, by meaningful text, or instrumental music, or by environmental noise." (Discussion I) Additional discussions include "Notation for Phonetic Music," "Format Music in Vowel and Diphthong Tones," and "Tonal Matrix." Each section contains a brief bibliography.

145.   Schwanauer, Stephen M. and David A. Levitt. **Machine Models of Music.** Cambridge, MA: MIT Press, 1993. ix. 544p. illus. LCCN 92-17179. ISBN 0-262-19319-1.

Schwanauer and Levitt's compilation of many of the important materials concerning computer composition of music provide, in one source, a fascinating history of the quest to both model traditional music in order to understand its composition through the use of computers, and to create new music based on the use of this technology. The editor's point out that *"Machine Models of Music* has its origins in systematic efforts to model the mind's musical creative process. If it is possible to model thought, it should be possible as well to model creative thought and, in particular, musically creative thought. If there is a process, musically creative or generally creative or otherwise, duplicating the process should be possible with the precision and consistency of symbolic manipulation afforded to us by machine models of mind." (Preface) Each selection is provided with a brief introduction. Many of the selections provide historical accounts of the past attempts to generate and test composition, to explain the foundations of computer composition, and to explain and demonstrate heuristic composition. Selections include "Musical Composition with a High-Speed Digital Computer," by Lejaren Hiller and Leonard Isaacson, "An Experiment in Musical Composition," by F. P. Brooks, Jr., A. L. Hopkins, Jr., P. G. Neumann, and W. V. Wright, "A Technique for the Composition of Music in a Computer," by Stanley Gill, "A Program for the Analytic Reading of Scores," by Allen Forte, "Patterns in Music," by Herbert A. Simon and Richard K. Sumner, "Linguistics and the Computer Analysis of Tonal Harmony," by Terry Winograd, "Simulating Musical Skills by Digital Computer," by John Rothgeb, "Musical and Computer Composition," by James Anderson Moorer, "Process Structuring and Music Theory," by Stephen W. Smoliar, "In Search of a Generative Grammar for Music," by Otto E. Laske, "A Method for Composing Simple Traditional Music by Computer," by Gary M. Rader, "Generative Theories in Language and Music Descriptions," by Johan Sundberg & Bjorn Lindblom, "An Overview of Hierarchical Structure in Music," by Fred Lerdahl & Ray Jackendoff, "An Artificial Intelligence Approach to Tonal Music Theory," by James Meehan, "Music, Mind, and Meaning," by Marvin Minsky, *"Protocol:* Motivation, Design, and Production of a Composition for Solo Piano," by Charles Ames, "An Expert System for Harmonizing Four-Part Chorales," by Kemal Ebcioglu, "A Computer Model of Music Composition," by David Cope, "Flavors Band: A Language for Specifying Musical Style," by Christopher Fry, "A Representation for Musical Dialects," by David A. Levitt, "The Perception of Melodies," by H. Christopher Longuet-Higgins, "MUSCAT: A Connectionist Model of Musical Harmony," by Jamshed J. Bharucha, and "A Learning Machine for Tonal Composition," by Stephen M. Schwanauer. All documentation and bibliographies originally published with the selections are reproduced here. The work provides a valuable single source for the theory of computer composition of music. Appendices include an analysis and explanation of Mozart's *Musical Dice Game* along with the score.

146.   Whitney, John. **Digital Harmony: On the Complementarity of Music
        & Visual Art.** Peterborough, NH: Byte Books/McGraw-Hill, 1980.
        235p. illus. LCCN 80-22150. ISBN 0-07-070015-X.

"This book documents how the application of graphic harmony, in that
'real' sense of ratio, interference and resonance, produces the same effect
that these physical facts of harmonic force have upon musical structures.
The book points to these forces of visual *harmony* at work in a number
of my recent films." (Foreword, p. 5) Mr. Whitney continues to document what he calls a "personal revolution" concerning computer composition for all media. Several chapters deal with particular compositional
problems including "How Shall Motion Pattern Time," "The Instrument-
-Not Pure Hypothesis--Not a Piano," and "The idea of Differential
Dynamics -- Pythagoras Revisited." A final chapter entitled "Do It Yourself" contains the implementation of some Pascal programs that were
used to generate the digital harmony patterns that illustrate some of the
figures featured in the work. A step-by-step procedure for these figures
and their transformations is included.   A number of appendices are
provided including "Audio-Visual Music: Color Music -- Abstract film,
1944," "Audio-Visual Music and Program Notes, 1946," "Moving
Pictures and Electronic Music, 1959," "Interview with John Whitney,
1970," "Democratizing the Audio-Visual Arts, 1974," and "Film Music,
1977." This work is a fascinating account of John Whitney's personal
system for producing computer-generated sounds for and through the use
of graphic images.

147.   Winsor, Phil. **Computer Composer's Toolbox.** Blue Ridge Summit, PA:
        TAB Books (Windcrest), 1990. xxi. 246p. illus. LCCN 89-20384. ISBN
        0-8306-3384-7.

This book provides a collection of procedures and functions that serve
either synthetic or analytic compositional goals. There are 117 computer
subroutines organized into six groups including utilities, series and
motive operations, probability distribution functions, sorting and search-
ing, sound/text composition, and general composition. Mr. Winsor
explains that it is the "author's objective...to present a wide selection of
useful algorithms, leaving a detailed discussion of specific musical con-
texts to another volume." (Preface, xix) Each subroutine is written out in
the book using the Microsoft Basic programming language on a Texas
Instruments™ Professional Computer with 256K of RAM, and is
preceded by a brief explanation of purpose, the notes that will be
generated, and ideas for programming it into other compositions. This
work is especially useful to computer enthusiasts who wish to try some

music subroutines on their machines without purchasing a MIDI interface, or as a source of inspiration for beginning composers who wish to
introduce some computer music into their compositions. Most of the
routines are no longer than 30 or 40 lines of code. There is a subroutine
index which provides access to each of the computer subroutines in addition to a general index. The author has provided both a 5 1/4" and a 3
1/2" computer floppy disk with the 117 subroutines requiring 360K on an
IBM PC™ or compatible with DOS version 2.0 or more recent.

148.   Winsor, Phil. **Computer-Assisted Music Composition: A Primer in
        Basic.** Princeton, NJ: Petrocelli Books, Inc., 1987. ix. 330p. ISBN 0-
        89433-262-7.

        "This book is addressed to people who wish to develop programming
        skills necessary for the composition of computer music, but who have
        neither the time or inclination to acquire expertise via traditional
        business applications approaches." (Preface)   All programs used as
        examples are written in BASIC. The book begins with an introduction to
        how a small, digital computer can create music and then proceeds to
        develop a step-by-step plan for writing programs in BASIC. In a chapter
        entitled "Stochastic Music," Mr. Winsor reviews the various methods
        used for making a computer perform music including the "Monte-Carlo
        Method: Compositional Algorithms," and the bundling of options. Two
        computer music pioneers (Lejaren Hiller and Jannis Xenakis) are
        discussed. Appendices include "Areas for Experimentation," "Refer-
        ences," (19 items), a "Glossary," "ASCII Character Codes," "Computer
        Music Scores and Recordings for Study," (61 items) "File Management,"
        "Program Directory," and an index.

149.   Xenakis, Iannis. **Formalized Music: Thought and Mathematics in
        Composition.** Bloomington, IN: Indiana University Press, 1971. x. 273p.
        LCCN 76-135017. ISBN 0-253-32378-9.

        Mr. Xanakis explains in this work what he sees as "free stochastic music-
        theory," "Mackovian Stochastic Music-Applications," "Musical
        Strategy," "Free Stochastic Music by Computer," "Symbolic Music,"
        "Towards a Metamusic," "Towards a Philosophy of Music," and "New
        Proposals in Microsound Structure." In his chapter on "Free Stochastic
        Music by Computer," Xenakis outlines a stochastic work executed by the
        IBM-7090™. A program is presented in Fortran IV. Much of this book
        is concerned with a mathematical basis for art. An Appendix provides
        "Two Laws of Continuous Probability." The work also includes a bibli-
        ography (42 items).

MIDI
(Musical Instrument Digital Interface)

The Musical Instrument Digital Interface (MIDI) was established in 1983. MIDI is a microprocessor-based system that allows communication between electronic music devices that enables hardware of different manufacture and design to exchange messages. The MIDI protocol carries the messages that allow a computer to interface with musical instruments, and for that matter, each other. The original MIDI specification was oriented towards live performance, but over the years it has been widened to include non-real-time composition. Continual updates on MIDI specifications are controlled by the International MIDI Association in Los Angeles, California. MIDI has provided the needed link for combining electronic musical instruments and other devices with computers and synthesizers.

The following works are related to the general use of MIDI for establishing the relationships between electronic music devices to create music. In addition, books concerned with specific MIDI devices are included.

150. **Yamaha MIDI System Guide: Digital X Book.** New York, NY: Amsco Publications, 1986. 135p. illus. ISBN 0-8256-1061-3.

The *Yamaha MIDI System Guide: Digital X Book* is a comprehensive manual designed to explain basic operating information for the Yamaha 'X' series of synthesizers. It is a vital guide for both the beginner and the experienced synthesist. The work is divided into six sections: "1) Hardware Guidance for Yamaha™ DX7, DX1, DX5, DX21, DX27, DX100, DX9, KX88, KX1, KX5, TX7, TX816, QX1, QX7, RX11, RX15, RX21, CX5M"; "2) MIDI Seminar that explains the MIDI protocol, implementation charts, and a section on FM synthesis; 3) Connecting Up the 'X' Series"; "4) Dave Bristow Workshop entitled 'What is Computer Music?'"; "4) A Practical Manual which includes live techniques for solo performance, ensemble playing, recording techniques, system recording set-up, and mixdown techniques"; and "5) Data Bank which includes a digital system glossary, DX7 voice charts, and RX rhythm patterns." Complete information is provided for each 'X' series synthesizer including connections, playing modes, performance modes, edit modes, and MIDI specifications. The work is rather technical but written in clear language making it valuable to beginners. There is no index or bibliography.

151.   Anderton, Craig. **MIDI for Musicians.** New York, NY: Amsco Publications, 1986. xiii. 105p. illus. ISBN 0-8256-2214-X.

Written as an introduction to MIDI (Musical Instrument Digital Interface), this short work provides the novice with information on the history of MIDI, how MIDI works, the MIDI language, applications both live and in the studio, equipment required, software, and the future of MIDI. The book is written in simple and clear language and provides ample illustrations of both concepts and process. Appendices include MIDI specification charts, a section on equipment & program trouble shooting, interpreting a MIDI implementation sheet, and a list of MIDI organizations and publications (5 items).

152.   Boom, Michael. **Music Through MIDI: Using MIDI to Create Your Own Electronic Music System.** Redman, WA: Microsoft Press (Penguin Books), 1987. xvi. 302p. LCCN 87-7831. ISBN 1-55615-026-1.

Mr. Boom's book begins with an explanation of MIDI basics and proceeds to more advanced techniques making it of value to both the novice and the more advanced electronic musician. Chapter 1 "MIDI: An Overture" provides a brief explanation of MIDI, including its history and development. Chapter 2 "Sound and Music" explains the basic attributes of sound and an overview of the system of musical notation. Chapter 3 "Synthesizing Sound" gives a detailed explanation of the fundamentals of sound synthesis and how synthesizers work. Chapter 4 "MIDI Connections" shows how MIDI connections are made and the basic methods of wiring synthesizers to computers. Chapter 5 "MIDI Messages" provides information on how MIDI carries information from one component to another to make the MIDI system work. Chapter 6 "Computers and MIDI" shows how a computer in a MIDI system can control all of the components and explains various types of software and how they are used. Chapters 7 and 8 "Real MIDI Equipment & Computerized MIDI Systems" show the actual equipment available today and how these components relate. Chapters 9 through 12 "MIDI in Live Performance, MIDI in the Recording Studio, MIDI in Education, and MIDI at Home" provide a discussion of actual MIDI applications including Tim Gouman's system, Tom Scott's MIDI recording studio, the Mills College Electronic Music Laboratory, and David Ocker's home MIDI system. Appendices include an explanation of MIDI specifications, a list of manufacturers and publishers mentioned in the book, and a list of books and magazines for further study, and finally, a list of MIDI users' groups. In addition there is a glossary of electronic music and MIDI terms and an index.

153. Casabona, Helen & David Frederick. **Using MIDI. A volume in the Keyboard Magazine Library for Electronic Musicians.** Cupertino, CA: Alfred Pub. Co. Inc., 1987. iv.122p. illus. LCCN 87-1354. ISBN 0-88284-354-0.

This work provides a step-by-step tour of using MIDI. It is designed for the beginner who has a little knowledge of synthesizers but no prior knowledge of computers or computer languages, and is written in clear, non-technical language. A brief history of MIDI introduces the work and then it continues through MIDI basics, MIDI applications, and advanced applications and accessories. The section on MIDI basics provides three lessons which can be used to review the reader's understanding of MIDI. The work then goes on to explain the use of MIDI keyboards, sequencers, drum machines, digital delays & reverbs, computers & computer software, synchronization interfaces, guitars, electronic drums, audio mixers, lighting systems, and much more. The advanced applications discussed include computer-to-MIDI interfaces, voicing & librarian software, MIDI data delays, synchronization, junctions and routings, alternate controllers, and slave systems. Appendices include MIDI implementation charts, the MIDI 1.0 specification, and a list of MIDI manufacturers. Also provided are short biographies of the authors and an index. There is no bibliography.

154. Conger, Jim. **C Programming for MIDI.** Redwood City, CA: M & T Publishing, 1988. 219p. illus. ISBN 0-934375-86-0.

Mr. Conger's book also has an MS-Dos computer disk which may be ordered directly from the company. In his Forward he points out that "...in its simplest sense, MIDI allows notes to be turned on and off by a computer. It can also monitor an instrument and remember every note that is played. The logical conclusion is that entire compositions can be stored and edited in computer memory." This work contains the following chapters: "An Overview of MIDI and Programming," "Experimenting with MIDI," "Displaying Screens," "Curson Movement and Error Message Functions," "Building a Patch Library," "Sending and Receiving Patch Data," "File and Directory Utilities," "Editing Patch Parameters," "Utilities and Printing," "Sequencing Experiments," "A MIDI One Track Recorder," "Communications with the Synthesizer," "ROM BIOS Assembly Language Routines," and "Conclusion." In addition appendices include a glossary, a bibliography (10 items), a function location cross reference, library functions used table, screen files for PATCHLIB and RECORD, and an index. This book if for anyone who wishes to write programs for music applications using MIDI and attempts to guide the reader toward good programming practice while also creating useful programs and libraries of software tools. All examples of programming are for the IBM PC or similar systems.

155.   Conger, Jim. **MIDI Sequencing in C.** Redwood City, CA: M & T Books, 1989. 471p. (includes 1 computer disk - 5 1/4 in.) LCCN 89-32620. ISBN 1-55851-046-X.

This book continues where *C Programming for MIDI* (see item 154) left off. It approaches recording, editing, and playback of MIDI data from the perspective of the user and the programmer. A computer disk is provided in a back pocket of the book which provides examples of programs covered in the text. The author points out that "sequencing is a term describing the process of recording, editing, and playing back sequences of musical notes. All major manufacturers of musical instruments and equipment now support the MIDI (Musical Instrument Digital Interface) standard for sending and receiving musical data. This allows one program to act as a sequencer for any group of MIDI instruments." (Introduction, p. 17)   The work approaches MIDI sequencing on the IBM PC™ and allows for an understanding of MIDI on several levels: 1) for the non-programmer, the MT sequencer provided on the program disk has a ready-to-use, 8-track sequencer with editing features; 2) for the developing programmer, the source code for the MT sequencer is provided that follows the programming examples in *C Programming for MIDI*, and; 3) for the experienced programmer, the source code provides functions that can be applied to a wide range of MIDI projects. The first three chapters provide a tutorial that describes MT from the user's point of view, and the remaining chapters describe how the MT program works. Some information is repeated from *C Programming for MIDI* and readers will find it familiar in that some of the discussions are repeated. This book assumes, for the most part, that the reader is familiar with MIDI and the C language. Certainly a complete knowledge of both is necessary before it will be possible to tackle the final three chapters. Appendices include "MIDI note numbers and percussion sound assignments for the MT-32," "MT Screen Messages," "Function finder lists," "Microsoft and Turbo C Compiler differences," and "MIDI 1.0 detail specification table." Both a bibliography and an index are provided. There is also a brief sketch of the author.

156. Crigger, David. **The MIDI Drummer: By a Drummer For a Drummer...** Newbury Park, CA: Alexander Publishing, 1987. 54p. illus.

The *The MIDI Drummer* begins with a definition of the MIDI protocol and how it applies to drumming, and then goes on to explain how MIDI is used by drummers. Chapters include "Basic Tools," "MIDI: A Keyboardist's Tool Adapted to Drummers," "Making MIDI Work," "Triggering," "Playing the Melody," "Synchronization," "Monitoring; Hearing What You're Doing," and "System Setups From an Audio Standpoint." Mr. Crigger's work is simply written and can easily be understood by the beginning electronic drummer. Illustrations are clear and provide all patching information necessary to apply the MIDI protocol to drumming. There is no index or bibliography.

157. De Furia, Steve & Joe Scacciaferro. **MIDI Programming for the Macintosh.** Redwood City, CA: M & T Publications, 1988. 371p. illus. LCCN 88-13801. ISBN 1-55851-022-2.

This book shows how to write music software for the Macintosh™ using MIDI conventions. The book is designed for experimenters with little experience with computers or music and, at the same time, it offers projects for the more advanced electronic musician. Sections include an overview of MIDI specifications (1.0), how the MIDI systems are put together, a MIDI quick reference, an overview of program creation, a list of MIDI library commands, and an explanation of how to build a Pascal MIDI application, and a Basic MIDI application. There is a disk available (an order form is provided) which includes the programs discussed in the book. Appendices include a "Procedure and Function Listing for Real-Time MIDI Lab," a "Source Code Listing for Real-Time MIDI Labs," a "Subroutine Listing for SysEx MIDI Lab," and a "Source Code Listing for SysEx MIDI Lab." Also, short biographies of the authors and an index are included.

158. De Furia, Steve & Joe Scacciaferro. **The MIDI Programmer's**

Handbook. Redwood City, CA: M & T Books, 1989. 275p. illus. LCCN 89-043676. ISBN 1-55851-068-0.

The *MIDI Programmer's Handbook* has become a popular reference for both beginning and advanced electronic musicians. Often used as a textbook in college music classes, it is not specific to any particular computer language or computer system. It is written to be useful for MIDI programming on IBM™, Apple™, Commodore™, or Atari™ computers. The book begins by explaining the basics of MIDI and then provides sections on synchronization of MIDI systems. A second part of the work includes a section called "MIDI in the Real World" which provides information on MIDI implementation, and MIDI hardware profiles. Part three is entitled "MIDI Programmers Reference" and explains channel voice messages, channel mode messages, system common messages, system real-time messages, system exclusive messages, universal non-real-time system exclusive, and universal real-time system exclusive. A final part covers writing MIDI software which allows the reader to learn to design real-time MIDI software applications through the use of a generic system. An appendix provides MIDI programming examples. An index is provided.

159.   De Furia, Steve & Joe Scacciaferro. **The MIDI Resource Book.** Pompton Lakes, NJ: Third Earth Pub. Co., 1987. 148p. illus. ISBN 0-88188-587-8.

The *MIDI Resource Book* is designed to be a guide through the MIDI maze. In conjunction with the other two books in the series, *The MIDI Implementation Book* (see item 162) and *The MIDI System Exclusive Book* (see item 160), it can act as both a dictionary and an encyclopedia on the subject of MIDI. (Introduction) The work introduces the musician to the history of the establishment of the MIDI convention, technical information, and additional references and resources. While the book begins with relatively elementary explanations of MIDI, it quickly becomes technical. System exclusive formats are provided for Akai™, Casio™, Kawai™, Korg™, Roland™, & Yamaha™. Appendices include lists of MIDI organizations, manufacturers, on-line bulletin boards, educational sources, and a bibliography (30 items).

160.   De Furia, Steve & Joe Scacciaferro. **The MIDI System Exclusive Book.** Pompton Lakes, NJ: Third Earth Publishing, Inc., 1987. 360p. illus. ISBN 0-88188-586-X.

This work is the third in a trilogy on MIDI. The first two are on MIDI resources (see item 161) and MIDI implementation charts. (see item 162) This book is concerned with "system exclusive," i.e., those MIDI commands that are exclusive to specific equipment or programs which are allowed by the universal system. System exclusive charts are provided for Akai™, ARP™, Casio™, E-mu Systems™, Ensonig™, Fender™, Hohner™, J. L. Cooper™, Korg™,™ Lowrey™, Oberheim™, PPG™, Roland™, Sequential Circuits™, Siel™, and Yamaha™. The authors point out that "in some cases, the System Exclusive commands have been included in the owner's manual, but usually not." (Introduction) There is no index or bibliography.

161. De Furia, Steve & Joe Scacciaferro. **The MIDI Book: Using MIDI and Related Interfaces.** Rutherford, NJ: Third Earth Production, Inc., 1986. 95p. illus. ISBN 0-88188-514-2.

The MIDI Book: Using MIDI and Related Interfaces begins with a definition of the MIDI protocol and how it relates to various MIDI interface devices. The book is intended to be a small reference work to be used when establishing various combinations of MIDI equipment. Information is provided for specific devices, computers, and other electronic instruments.

162. De Furia, Steve & Joe Scacciaferro. **The MIDI Implementation Book.** Pompton Lakes, NJ: Third Earth Publishing, Inc., 1986. 216p. illus. ISBN 0-88188-558-4.

In this book the authors provide "implementation charts" for over 200 digital synthesizers, hybrid synthesizers, samplers, pianos, preset instruments, organs, accordions, performance controllers, sequencers, drum machines, audio processors, interfaces, and other devices. Each chart provides information on channel, mode, note number, velocity, touch, pitch blender, control change, program change, system exclusive, system common, system real time, and additional notes. All major electronic instrument manufacturers are represented. There is no bibliography or index.

163. Donaldson, Peter. **A Guide to Computer Music: An Introductory Resource.** Peabody, MA: Sound Management Productions, 1988. 88p. illus. LCCN 88-92700. ISBN 0-9621514-0-8.

"This guide is an introductory resource to help you identify and understand the components used for controlling sound and music with a computer-based music workstation." (Introduction). The work is

divided into six chapters: Chapter One introduces the goals of the guide
and discusses recent developments in the field of musical electronics,
Chapter Two provides buying tips, planning forms for MIDI systems,
and illustrations about MIDI connections, Chapter Three explains what
parts are needed to organize the Apple IIGS™ as a computer-based
music system and identifies the components of a computer-based MIDI
system with illustrations of popular MIDI configurations. Chapter Five
contains a collection of product information for the Apple II GS™ and
Macintosh™ products. Chapter Six is a comprehensive listing of purchasing contacts and resources for MIDI dealers, how to books, catalogs,
videos, magazines, MIDI associations, and modern bulletin boards. The
work is clearly illustrated with diagrams and patching diagnoses to support the text. A glossary of computer and electronic music terms is also
provided.

164.   Dorfman, Len & Dennis Young. **Atari ST: Introduction to MIDI
       Programming.** Grand Rapids, MI: Abacus Software, Inc., 1986. 256p.
       illus. ISBN 0-916439-77-1.

       The authors point out that "the Atari ST™ is a powerful computer line
       allowing both the creative programmer and the musically inclined a
       multitude of opportunities. One of the many fascinating features of the
       ST's architecture is the built-in MIDI interface and the MIDI INPUT and
       MIDI OUTPUT ports on the back of the computer. This book is
       intended to explain what the MIDI experience is, and how the reader
       may use the ST to access these MIDI ports to communicate with com-
       mercially available synthesizers." (Preface) Sections include "MIDI and
       your ST," "The MIDI Language," "Programming your Atari ST," and
       "ST Music Box Auto-player."   The work includes the complete
       computer code in "c" to a program called the *ST Music Box* which was
       created to demonstrate the capabilities of the Atari ST™ and to serve as
       a mechanism to automatically play pieces. There is no index or bibliog-
       raphy.

165.   Eiche, Jon F. **What's MIDI? : Making Musical Instruments Work
       Together.** Milwaukee, WI: Hal Leonard Pub. Corp., 1990. 62p. illus.
       ISBN 0-7935-0082-6.

       This little pamphlet is for the complete MIDI novice. It begins with a
       rather humorous introduction where MIDI is explained in very simple
       terms and then proceeds to cover what MIDI does, how MIDI interfaces
       with systems, and how to troubleshoot systems and connections. The
       book includes a useful troubleshooting chart that allows the user to look

up the symptom in the left-hand column and then find a cause and solution in other columns. An interesting feature of this book is how it explains what MIDI is and what it isn't. There is an index.

166.   Grigger, David. **Making MIDI Work by Someone Who Does.** Newbury Park, CA: Alexander Publishing, 1987. iii. 22p. illus.

This little volume attempts to answer basic questions a novice may have concerning MIDI. Chapter I consists of brief questions and answers about MIDI including "What MIDI is Not," "How Do You Use MIDI?," and "What's the Difference Between a MIDI Cord and a Five Pin DIN Cord?" Chapter II covers hooking up two synthesizers with MIDI, Chapter III details the use of one synthesizer, & one sequencer, Chapter IV shows setup for one synthesizer, one sequencer and a drum machine, Chapter V adds two or more synthesizers together, and Chapter VI covers hearing the MIDI setup. The work is simply written in outline form and contains good illustrations of wiring schematics. There is no index or bibliography.

167.   Hill, Brad. **MIDI for Musicians: Buying, Installing, and Using Today's Electronic Music-Making Equipment.** Chicago, IL: Cappella Books, 1994. 202p. illus. LCCN 94-9133. ISBN 1-55652-221-5.

Mr. Hill points out that his work is "a guidebook to the marvels and mysteries of modern music technology. It is part tutor, part workbook, part reference source, and part buyer's guide." (How to Use This Book) The work is intended for the beginner or near beginner who has some basic understanding of the MIDI system specifically and electronic music in general. It may be approached in three basic ways: 1) as a tutorial to help establish a friendly working relationship with MIDI equipment already owned, and to further understand the capabilities of this equipment, or 2) to gain a more theoretical understanding of MIDI and how it connects musical devices, and finally, 3) as a purchasing guide for setting up a MIDI system for musicians who have had some experience. Sections include: "The Basics," "Pieces of the Puzzle," "Putting it Together," "MIDI Topics," and "Shopping for MIDI Equipment." Appendices include a glossary of MIDI and general electronic music terms, and a resource list of journals and software houses (18 items - 6 journals & 12 software houses). There is also a detailed index.

168.   Honeybone, Andy. **What's MIDI.** London, England: Track Record Publishing, 1990. 139p. illus. ISBN 1-872601-11-1.

This book is written more for the musician than the composer. It explains the basics of MIDI on a simple level and then proceeds to explain how the protocol works with synthesizers, sequencers, drum machines, and how the systems are set up and used. The final section of the work provides short chapters on the history of MIDI, MIDI and expanders, MIDI and sequencers, MIDI and master keyboards, MIDI and computers, MIDI and routing, MIDI live, MIDI and recording, MIDI files, MIDI and system exclusive, MIDI implementation, and MIDI technicalities. Each chapter includes the basics of the concept being discussed, and then provides information and tips for the musician using the system or instrument. The "technicalities" chapter includes information on binary, hexadecimal/binary tables, MSB/LSB (most significant bit/least significant bit), the shape of a status byte, and what system exclusive data means. There is also a useful glossary of terms but no bibliography or index.

169.   Huber, David Miles. **The MIDI Manual.** Carmel, IN: SAMS (Macmillan Computer Pub.), 1991. xviii, 269p. illus. ISBN 0-672227-57-6.

Mr. Huber's work provides an excellent introduction to the basics of MIDI. It provides detailed information on the features and functions of current electronic equipment and software. It includes clear, up-to-date coverage of topics including optical drives, standard MIDI files and MIDI time code as well as a MIDI software section. The work is specifically designed for the entry-level electronic musician who wishes to obtain a basic understanding of synthesizers and MIDI.

170.   Jacobs, Gabriel and Panicos Georghiades. **Music and New Technology: The MIDI Connection.** Wilmslow, England: Sigma Press, 1991. vii. 292p. illus. ISBN 1-85058-231-9.

This book provides a comprehensive look at the art of creating music through electronic means. The work is aimed at electronic musicians who wish to develop their own studios for composing, recording, and producing their music. The author explains that "using a studio means acquiring skills which until recently would have been considered peripheral to composition, if not irrelevant, including some knowledge of the physics of sound and of the way in which computers work. Trained musicians who have little understanding of electronic technology will have to come to terms with some unfamiliar concepts." (Preface, vi.) Readers with little knowledge of music, but some knowledge of computers will find this book an interesting explanation of how the two are combined to produce musical compositions. Also, the musician who wishes to get started with a basic electronic studio will find the work a good starting point. The book includes chapters on the MIDI studio, how computers work with music, the theory behind MIDI, MIDI interfaces, sequencers, MIDI instruments and other input devices, MIDI output, creative sound, practical sound, adding acoustic sounds, aids to composition, music notation software, a section on basic musical education, and selling music. Appendices include MIDI message specification tables, channel messages, system messages, and a list of equipment addresses and additional publications. A glossary and an index are also provided.

171.   Keyboard Magazine. **MIDI Sequencing for Musicians.** Cupertino, CA: GPI Publication, 1989. v. 138p. illus. ISBN 0-88188-911-3.

MIDI Sequencing for Musicians is part of the Keyboard Magazine Synthesizer Library and contains articles by the editors of *Keyboard* Magazine. The work is divided into two sections: Theory And Application and, Product Reviews. The articles in the first section include "MIDI Sequencing," by Jim Aikin, "Mechanical Analog, Digital--Sequencer History in a Nutshell," by Jim Aikin, "Sequencer Features," by Jim Aikin, "Bugs, Crashes, and Revs," by Jim Aikin, "MIDI Basics," by Jim Aikin, "The Sequencer in a Music System," by Jim Aikin "Beyond Sequencing," by Jim Aikin. The second part provides product reviews for "C-Lab Creator: Sequencer Software for the Atari ST™" by Jim Aikin, the "Voyetra Sequencer Plus Mark III: IBM™ Sequencer Software," by Michael Marans, the "Iawai Q-80: MIDI Sequencer" by Michael Marans, the "Yamaha QK5™: MIDI Sequence Recorder," by Dominic Milano, the "Q-Sheet:Event Sequencer and MIDI Automation Mac™ Software," by Dominic Milano, the "Coda Finale: Music Notation and Transcription Software for the Mac™," by Dominic Milano, and "Ludwig: Algorithmic Composition for the Atari ST™," by Jim Aikin. There is no index or bibliography.

172.   Kozak, Donald P. **Guide to Computer Music: An Electronic Music Resource.** Peabody, MA: Sound Management Productions, 1992. 125p. illus. LCCN 90-91959. ISBN 0-9621514-2-4.

The primary goal of this book is to introduce the basics of musical electronics, to enhance the creative process and the understanding of basic computer-MIDI systems, to provide information and insight into the wide variety of music software and hardware, to provide information concerning sequencing & notation software, to provide user set-up information for organizing a computer music system, and to provide reading and purchasing resources for continued development and cost considerations for most computers. Mr. Kozak introduces the topic with a background chapter entitled "Musical Electronics 101: A Technology of Creativity and Productivity," where he covers basic electronics, MIDI, and computers. Additional chapters provide information concerning "MIDI Basics: Understanding Channels, Tracks & Sequencers," "Organizing a Computer-MIDI System," "MIDI Connections," and "45 Helpful Guidelines & Buying Tips." Chapter 4 of the book is an essay by Henry W. Peters entitled "An Introduction To Using The Apple IIGS™ for Sequencing With Passport Design's MasterTracks Pro™." A large portion of the book is concerned with recent innovations in MIDI, computers, and new product descriptions. Other sections include a list of resources for development & purchasing computer and MIDI systems, MIDI videos, periodicals that feature articles on MIDI, and MIDI associations & on-line user groups. There is also a list of books (55 items), magazine articles (52 items), and CD-Roms & multimedia sources (31 items.) The work ends with a list of computer & electronic music terms. One interesting feature of this book is that it provides forms for making up lists of needed equipment, and for designing system layouts. A problem with many of the lists of books and articles is that they lack complete bibliographic information; sometimes even the dates of the publications are missing.

173.   Lister, Craig. **The Musical Microcomputer: A Resource Guide.** Hamden, CN: Garland Publications, 1988. 192p. ISBN 0-8240-8442-X.

This work attempts to locate most important information concerning the MIDI (Musical Instrument Digital Interface) standard and its application to microcomputers. *The Musical Microcomputer: A Resource Guide* provides an annotated list of over 300 items on MIDI which covers anthologies, books, dissertations, journal articles, and music software in a subject arrangement. The work is also indexed by author and title. While a number of important titles are missing, e.g., *Music, Computers & Software* , *Music & Technology* (see item 89), and *Electronic Musician* , the work contains a very useful list of materials on the subject. Sections often combine software, articles, and books making it difficult to distinguish them by type.

174.   Mann, Marc. **Making the Most of MIDI.** Los Angeles, CA: HPI Home Video, 1988. (VHS Video HPIM 1. 28 min.)

Marc Mann has put together this video program for the beginning electronic musician who wants an introduction to MIDI. The tape begins with an example of MIDI music played in a studio and then proceeds to explain how the tape will be of use to the viewer. He points out that an outline card is provided with the tape which serves as a table of contents, and that the divisions of the tape will be easily found. The sections include "The Devices of MIDI," "Using MIDI," and "The Language of MIDI." Included with the tape is a MIDI technical reference chart, a troubleshooting tip sheet, and a MIDI implementation chart. While this tape is extremely elementary in its approach, it does provide a good look at the equipment of MIDI, and allows the beginning electronic musician to actually hear the sounds of the MIDI devices. Several guests appear on the tape to explain how they use MIDI in their home studios and to play examples. They include Stanley Clarke (bassist, artist and producer), Christopher Cross (recording artist), Larry Williams (session artist and sound designer), and Michael Bernard (synthesist & composers). The tape is exclusively distributed by Silver Eagle, Inc.

175. Massey, Howard. **Compact Guide to MIDI Software for the Commodore 64/128.** New York, NY:Amsco/Music Sales Corp., 1988. 72p. illus. ISBN 0-8256-1141-5.

The author points out that "The Commodore 64™ and later the 128 computers were among the first truly affordable home computers and still present an inexpensive though powerful way for musicians to enter the world of MIDI." (Introduction, p.4) The book contains thirty programs including sequencers, notation and transcription programs, patch editors, librarians, waveshape editors, compositional aids, scoring aids, and signal processing routines. Each program listing provides the title, the manufacturer, the author, the computer (generally the Commodore™), the MIDI interface, the note capacity, and any special features. Most programs listed require the Commodore™ computer and a Casio™ synthesizer. There is no index or bibliography.

176. Massey, Howard. **Compact Guide to MIDI Software for the Macintosh.** New York, NY: Amsco Publications Inc., 1988. 64p. illus. ISBN 0-8256-1140-7.

This guide lists a number of MIDI software programs for the Macintosh™ computer including sequencers, notation programs, scoring aids & event generators, patch editors & librarians, waveshape editors, synthesis aids, ear training aids, and compositional & improvisational aids. The programs discussed include: Keyboard Controlled Sequencer (Dr. T's Music Software), Master Tracks Pro (Passport Designs), MIDI-mac Sequencer (Opcode Systems), MIDI Paint (Southworth Music

Systems), Performer (Mark of the Unicorn), Concertware + MIDI (Great Wave Software), Deluxe Music Construction Set (Electronic Arts), Professional Composer (Mark of the Unicorn), Cue (Opcode Systems), Q-Sheet (DigiDesign), MIDIMac DX/TX Editor/Librarian (Opcode Systems), MIDIMac DX7II/TX802 Editor/Librarian (Opcode Systems), TX81Z Pro (Digital Music Services), FB Pro (Digital Music Services), MIDIMac CZ Editor/ Librarian (Opcode Systems), DMP7 Pro (Digital Music Services), Sound Designer (DigiDesign), SoftSynth (DigiDesign), Listen (Resonate), Jam Factory (Intelligent Music), M (Intelligent Music), Music Mouse (Opcode Systems), and Upbeat (Intelligent Music). Each entry includes program type, manufacturer, author, system requirements, MIDI interface required, version tested, suggested retail price, special features, and a section called "a final word" that provides tips and comments on the effectiveness of the program and other special considerations. All programs are written for the Macintosh™ computer. The manual is not indexed.

177.   Massey, Howard, et al **The Complete Guide to MIDI Software.** New York, NY: Amsco Publications, 1987. 252p. illus. ISBN 0-8256-1088-5.

This book was written by the staff of the Public Access Synthesizer Studio (PASS) in New York City.   PASS is a non-profit organization dedicated to providing information concerning state-of-the-art audio and synthesizer equipment. More than 30 MIDI programs are presented for the IBM PC™ and compatibles, the Apple Macintosh™, the Apple II™, the Atari ST™, the Commodore 64 & 128™, and the TI99/4A™. Each program is provided with a list of basic information including type, manufacturer, author, MIDI interface, price, special features, and limitations. This is followed by an illustrated discussion of the operation of the program. An introduction to MIDI is also included. There is no index or bibliography.

178.   Massey, Howard et al. **The Compact Guide to MIDI Software for the Commodore 64/128.** New York, NY: Amsco Publications, 1988. 72p. ISBN 0-8256-1141-5.

This brief work attempts to list most of the current (1988) software programs for Commodore™ computers. Mr. Massey points out in his introduction that "the Commodore 64 and later the 128 computers were among the first truly affordable home computers and still present an inexpensive though powerful way for musicians to enter the world of MIDI...[and] the thirty programs surveyed in this book represent quite a span: from sequencers to notation programs to patch editor/librarians to waveform editors to compositional and scoring aids to signal processors. Taken together, they represent an impressive body of work for a computer which is still of great value to musicians everywhere." (Introduction p. 4) Each program is listed with title, program type, sequencer, patch editors & librarians, notation & transcription programs, wave shape editors, compositional aids, scoring aids, or signal processing, manufacturer, author, MIDI interface, versions tested, suggested retail price, and special features. In addition, any special limitations or problems with the program are explained in special notes sections.

179.   Massey, Howard. **The MIDI Home Studio.** New York, NY: Amsco Publications, 1988. 77p. illus. ISBN 0-8256-1127-X.

Howard Massey explains in his Introduction that *The MIDI Home Studio* is "designed to show you how to get the most out of the MIDI equipment you own or plan to buy--whether it's obsolete by next Tuesday or not. It will also explain what you need to do in order to create a sensible and smoothly functioning MIDI system--big or small." The book begins with an explanation of MIDI basics, and then continues to describe how home systems are set up and operated. Chapter three entitled "Components of the Home MIDI Studio," provides a detailed overview of all aspects of setting up a home MIDI studio including samplers, drum machines, MIDI controllers, keyboard controllers, guitar controllers, drum controllers, real-time control devices, sequencers, and MIDI peripherals. In addition there is a discussion of synchronization (e.g. digital and analog timing signals), and step-by-step system design for both basic and advanced systems. The work is well illustrated and the explanations are easily read and understood. Also there is a brief bibliography (9 items) and a list of electronic music periodicals (9 items) at the end.

180.   Milano, Dominic, ed. **Mind Over MIDI.** Milwaukee, WI: Hal Leonard Books, 1987. vi. 117p. illus. ISBN 0-88188-551-7.

"*Mind Over MIDI* presents a comprehensive and practical introduction to this crucial new technology. A collection of seminal articles reprinted from the pages of *Keyboard* magazine, *Mind Over MIDI* is a valuable reference for beginning or advanced users of MIDI. The work...offers specific lessons and technical tips from leading writers, designers, and performing artists." (Introduction, v.) Chapters include "Beginnings: A Little History," "MIDI Basics: What MIDI Does," "Data Transmission Tutorial," "Channels," "MIDI Modes," "Mixing and Merging," "Beyond Basics: Bit and Bytes, A Data Analyzer Program," "The Song Position

Pointer," "System-Exclusive Formats," "Reading MIDI Implementation Charts," "SMPTE Time Code and MIDI," "Clearing the Air Surrounding the MIDI Spec," "Circuit Checkers," "Code Cracking, & "Continuous Clock," "The Gear: Keyboard Controllers, Computers," and "Computer-To-MIDI Interfaces, Software, Systems, Accessories." Appendices include a glossary, the MIDI 1.0 specifications, MIDI resources, an index, and a list of recommended reading (30 items).

181.   Otsuka, Akira & Akihiko Nakajima. **MIDI Basics.** Tokyo, Japan: Amsco Publications, 1987. 58p. illus. ISBN 0-7119-0952-0.

MIDI Basics explains the theory and basic practice of MIDI to both the person entering the field for the first time and to the more advanced user, and also serves as a guide to the basic workings of MIDI. The work is divided into two sections: "The World of MIDI" which includes MIDI cabling, connection of terminals, channels, modes, channel information, and basic system information, and "MIDI in Practice," including hardware, an implementation chart, specifications, control change, and software. *MIDI Basics* is written with the novice in mind and presents the MIDI protocol in extremely basic terms. The work is clearly written and illustrated and includes an index but no bibliography.

182.   Penfold, R. A. **Advanced MIDI Users Guide.** Tonbridge, England: PC Publishing, 1991. vi. 179p. illus. ISBN 1-870775-18-X.

As with other books on electronic music and MIDI Mr. Penfold has written (see items 46, 115, 116, 142, 183), this work provides a good explanation of all MIDI messages, the routing of MIDI signals in both advanced and more simple applications, and explains how to troubleshoot systems when there are problems. Mr. Penfold points out that "this book is aimed at those who have some previous knowledge of MIDI and electronic instruments, or perhaps little knowledge of MIDI but some previous experience with computers and music. It is designed to give readers a detailed knowledge of most aspects of MIDI, so that they are aware of MIDI's capabilities and limitations." (Preface, vi.) The chapters include "Getting the message," "MIDI routing," "MIDI troubleshooting," "MIDI gadgets," "Synchronization," "MIDI programming," and "System exclusive." There are several informative appendices containing information on MIDI hardware specifications and basic circuits, the MIDI specification 1.0 with explanations on conventions and hardware, multi outputs and choke information, a MIDI checklist that covers information to work with when developing a system, and a glossary of terms. There is also a final passage that points out recent additions to MIDI, and the most significant changes that need to be taken into account. This book provides reliable, up-to-date information on MIDI and the development of MIDI systems. There is a index but no bibliography.

183.   Penfold, R. A. **Practical MIDI Handbook.** 2d ed. Tonbridge, England: PC Publishing, 1990. [iv.] 152p. illus. ISBN 1-870775-13-9.

While not substantially changed, this second edition of the *Practical MIDI Handbook* provides basic information about MIDI for the musician, the electronic enthusiast, and studio technicians. The author points out that "the basics of MIDI are explained, including such things as interconnecting a system, and just why MIDI is needed at all. However, the majority of the book is devoted to an explanation of just what MIDI can do, and how to exploit it to the full...[including] fundamentals of control codes, details of the types of equipment and software that are currently available, and how systems can be tailored to suit individual requirements." (Preface, [iii.]) The book begins with a history of the problem electronic musicians had before the MIDI protocol was established, and continues with discussions of the limitation of MIDI, synchronization, serial interface, musical digits, the right connections, and the possibilities of MIDI. Additional chapters cover the MIDI modes, MIDI transmission, MIDI control specification, and how MIDI works with microprocessors. Chapter 5 entitled "MIDI equipment," focuses on the various devices the electronic musician generally works with including MIDI instruments in general, MIDI keyboards, MIDI guitars, MIDI drum machines, and MIDI effects units. Appendices include information on "MIDI modes," a "Hexadecimal number table," "Useful addresses" (generally for the United Kingdom), and a glossary of terms used in the book. This is probably one of the better introductions to MIDI in that it provides basic information without becoming too technical. An index is provided.

184.   Rona, Jeff. **MIDI: The Ins, Outs & Thrus...** Milwaukee, WI: Hal Leonard Pub Corp., 1987. 96p. illus. LCCN 86-27746. ISBN 0-88188-560-6.

Mr. Rona's book is designed for the beginning electronic musician who wishes to understand the basics of the MIDI protocol and how MIDI instruments are used in performance and recording. The work begins with a brief history of electronic music and continues through MIDI application. Also included is a rudimentary explanation of computers and their use in electronic music. Chapters include: "1) Beginnings," 2)

Sending Information," "3) What MIDI Sends - A Musical Breakdown," "4) From Bits to Bach," "5) The Basics of MIDI," "6) An Overview of MIDI," "7) Channel Voice Messages," "8) MIDI Controllers," "9) Mode Messages," "10) Real Time Messages," "11) System Common Messages," "12) The Mysteries of System Exclusive," "13) Putting It All Together," "14) Buying MIDI Instruments," and "15) Problem Solving." The work also includes a glossary of MIDI and electronic music terms, and a short bibliography (3 items).

185.   Rothstein, Joseph. **MIDI: A Comprehensive Introduction.** Madison, WI: A-R Editions, 1992. xi, 226p. (The Computer Music and Digital Audio Series: v. 7.) LCCN 91-39701. ISBN 0-89579-258-3.

Mr. Rothstein's book is written for both the beginner and the advanced electronic musician. It includes a lot of introductory information on MIDI, but also includes ample information on a more advanced level. Nearly all important information concerning MIDI is included. Chapters covering how to choose MIDI hardware and software are extremely useful. Also, important information concerning retail stores and obtaining information, useful publications, and on-line bulletin boards and user groups is included. The work is well written, but contains a number of terms not explained in the text and no glossary is provided.

186.   Rumsey, Francis. **MIDI Systems and Control.** London, England: Focal Press, 1990, 1994. xi, 131p. illus. LCCN 90-3304. ISBN 0-240-51300-2.

Written for the professional electronic musician or an advanced amateur, this work covers all aspects of MIDI implementation in a very complete fashion. The work is technical and provides complete instruction in MIDI systems and control. Information concerning computer systems and terminology, implementing MIDI in musical instruments, implementing MIDI in studio and lighting equipment, and practical MIDI system design is included. Appendices include contact information for standards and documentation of the MIDI protocol, information on PAN (the Performing Arts Network on-line data service), and a selected bibliography (29 items). The writing is concise and detailed and requires close attention to the technical explanations. The second edition, 1994, is almost completely rewritten and the subject has been brought up to date. More information has been added concerning ways in which MIDI may be integrated with digital audio and video systems.

187.   Rychner, Lorenz M. & Dan Walker. **The Next MIDI Book: Starting with the Numbers.** Newbury Park, CA: Alexander Publishing, 1991.

147p. illus.

Mr. Rychner explains that "this book covers the numbers of MIDI. What they are, and what they mean. No more mysteries. No glossy vagueness, just plain language explaining what's what. And before I get into the number, I deal with the various ways of hooking up MIDI equipment. If your system is in place and working, skip the first section." (Foreword, p. 1) The work begins with an explanation of the MIDI protocol and how it is used, and then proceeds to an explanation of how MIDI is used in practical applications including general hookups, distribution of MIDI data, the language of MIDI, the binary numbering system, the hexadecimal numbering system, status bytes and data bytes, the note on status byte, the note off status byte, etc.. This book is extremely useful and popular with electronic musicians who wish to have specific information concerning MIDI hookups. It works well as a troubleshooting manual in addition to its intended use as a guide for setting up MIDI systems. Most of the examples are given for use on Yamaha™ synthesizers, especially the DX7. An epilogue at the end of the book provides the address of the International MIDI association and explains why it is important for MIDI users to join this organization.

188.   Sanchez, Rey. **MIDI Guitar: A Complete Applications Directory for the Modern Guitarist.** Miami, FL: Columbia Pictures Publications /Belwin, Inc., 1988. 116p. illus.

"This book was born out of the desperate need for guitar players to understand the technology and possibilities of MIDI Guitar. A guitar controller/synth package is not a 'plug-in-and-go' proposition...leave that to your metal pedal. MIDI Guitar is sophisticated, digital technology pushed to the limit. Its creative possibilities are endless but only for those who are ready to accept a whole new way of thinking." (Introduction, p. 7) The work begins with an explanation of the rudiments of MIDI and continues with an explanation of MIDI guitar controllers, synthesizer basics, and a discussion of other MIDI devices including signal processors, amplifiers, sequencers, and accessories. The chapter on computers provides information on the best computers to use with guitars including Amiga™, Apple™, Atari ST™, Commodore 64/128™, IMB PC™, and Macintosh™. Appendices include an explanation of MIDI for the guitar, MIDI specification tables, and a MIDI format chart. There is no bibliography or index.

189.   Trubitt, David (Rudy). **Managing MIDI Basics: A Guide to MIDI Basics...Including Wiring, Merging and Troubleshooting.** Van Nuys,

CA: Alfred Publishing Co., 1993. 48p. illus. ISBN 0-38081-119-6.

This little book is directed at songwriters, electronic composers, or musicians who wish to have a basic introduction to MIDI. The work begins with a brief explanation of MIDI and how it works, and then continues with sections on MIDI for guitarists, MIDI wind controllers, MIDI for drummers, and MIDI for keyboards and computers. The work is very well illustrated and clearly written. There is an interesting chapter on troubleshooting MIDI systems and their connections. A brief index is included.

190.   Turkel, Eric. **MIDI Gadgets.** London, England: Amsco Publications, 1988. 56p. illus. ISBN 0-8256-1130-X.

The establishment of the MIDI protocol has spawned a whole industry of support products. There are hundreds of MIDI-equipped synthesizers, samplers, drum machines, and sequencers currently on the market. Eric Turkel defines a MIDI gadget as "any kind of device that has a MIDI jack or two on board, yet isn't a synthesizer, sampler, drum machine, or sequencer. For the sake of brevity, this book does not include a discussion of MIDI interfaces and MIDI-capable computers. These items are discussed in detail in *The Compact Guide to MIDI Software* series, also written by CEM staff and published by Amsco Publications." (Forward, p. 4) The book is divided into five chapters: "Chapter One, MIDI Display, Routing, Processing, Mapping, and Storage Devices"; "Chapter Two, MIDI Controllers"; "Chapter Three, SMPTE and MIDI Sync Boxes"; "Chapter Four, MIDI-Controlled Signal Processing"; and "Chapter Five, MIDI-Controlled Automated Mixing." Each chapter provides an introduction to the type of devices being discussed, along with pictures and specifications. An appendix provides a complete list of manufacturers' addresses for the equipment being discussed. There is no index or bibliography.

191.   Wait, Bradley, ed. **Guitar Synth and MIDI.** Milwaukee, WI: Hal Leonard Books, 1988. vi. 135p. illus. ISBN 0-88188-593-2.

This is another volume in the *Guitar Player Magazine* Basic Library series. *Guitar Synth and MIDI* contains both original articles and material reprinted from *Guitar Player Magazine, Keyboard* Magazine, and GPI Books. The articles are collected into six chapters entitled "Part I: Beginnings," "Part II: Learning Basics," "Part III: Getting Started," "Part IV: Performing and Recording," "Part V: Learning from the Pros," and "Part VI: Product Information." The articles include "Guitar and the

MIDI Revolution," by Tom Wheeler, "High-Tech Guitar: What's in it for You?" by Paul LaRose, "History and Development," by Tom Mulhern, "MIDI Spoken Here," by Robert Moog, "What MIDI Does," by Robert Moog, "Channels," by Dominic Milano, "MIDI modes," by Dominic Milano, "Guitar Meets MIDI," by Warren Sirota, "Approaches to Digital Synthesis," by Robert Moog & Brent Hurtig, "Digital Sound Sampling," by Robert Moog, "Digital Audio Basics: A Basic Tutorial," by Craig Anderton, "Buying a MIDI Guitar Controller," by Bradley Wait, "Buying a Synthesizer," by Jim Aikin, "Reading MIDI Implementation Charts," by Helen Casabona & Dave Frederick, "Sequencers," by Ted Greenwald, "Digital Delays and Reverbs," by Brent Hurtig, "Choosing a Computer," by Peter Gotcher & Steve Cummings, "Accessories," by Ted Greenwald. "Setting up for a Performance," by Warren Sirota, "Performance Tips," by Warren Sirota, "Making Interesting Sounds," by Warren Sirota, "Using Delays Rhythmically," by Warren Sirota, "Pitch-Bending with Guitar Synthesizers," by Warren Sirota, "Using Velocity Information Synthesizers," by Warren Sirota, "Solo Guitar Synth in Concert," by Warren Sirota, "Putting MIDI to Work," by Warren Sirota, "Putting Digital Tools to Work," by Paul LaRose, "Getting the Most from Compressors and Noise Gates," by Warren Sirota. Part V includes personal accounts written by or told to the writers, of using guitar synthesizers and MIDI by a number of performers including Carlos Alomar, Steve Morse, Andy Summers, Al Di Meola, John MacLaughlin, Frank Zappa, Allan Holdsworth, and Lee Ritenour. The final chapter provides product reviews for a number of guitars, MIDI controllers, guitar-to-MIDI converters, MIDI converter pedals, and unisynths. The brands reviewed include the Beetle Quantar™, all Casio™ guitars, the Ibanez' MC1 System™, IVL Products™, K-Muse Photon™ controller, New England Digital's Synclavier™, Passac Senteint Six™, Roland™ guitars & controllers, Shadow Products™, Stepp DGX™ guitar controller, Suzuki Uni-synths™, the Synthaxe™, and Zeta Systems Products™. This is probably the best book for information on guitar synthesizers and controllers. Appendices include a glossary of terminology, a list of manufacturers, and brief biographical sketches of the authors. There is no index or bibliography.

192.   Yelton, Geary. **Music and the Macintosh.** Atlanta, GA: MIDI America, 1989. 199p. illus. ISBN 0-962339-76-8.

Mr. Yelton provides a complete guided tour for making music with a Macintosh™ computer in *Music and the Macintosh*. The work is very easily read and offers techniques for producing music for musicians on every level. Information is also provided on techniques for digitizing musical sounds and using them to create electronic compositions which can be performed electronically or printed. While not specifically called a textbook by the author, this work will work well in a music program in high school or college. In addition, the book provides introductory information on synthesizers, samplers, and synchronization.

193.   Zaza, Tony. **Mechanics of Sound Recording.** New York, NY: Prentice-Hall, 1991. 455p. ISBN 0-13-567660-6.

This work provides information on most aspects of sound recording pertaining mainly to film and video media. Subjects covered include computer-based audio recording, editing, and SMPTE audio recording and editing. There is a short section on the use of MIDI interfaces and MIDI equipped audio consoles. The author points out that with the advent of "multi-media" systems a rudimentary knowledge of MIDI is necessary for anyone working in the audio field. The work is clearly written and well illustrated. An index is provided.

Teaching Electronic and Computer Music

Electronic music experimentation began in the schools very early in the century, but few works were available specifically for the classroom until Brian Dennis published *Experimental Music in Schools: Towards a New World of Sound* in 1970 (see item 198). His little book was widely used in British, and to some extent American, schools. As the price of synthesizers came down in the 1970s (due mainly to the development of integrated circuits), the popularity of using them for music instruction in schools increased. These devices could produce the tones and textures necessary for instruction, and at a lesser cost than the piano-equipped classrooms that had been used historically.

As the colleges began developing courses based on the use of synthesizers, several textbooks became very popular. Jon Appleton and Ronald Perea put together a very popular volume entitled *The Development and Practice of Electronic Music* (1975) (see item 194) which was designed for the individual or for use in the classroom using what had become known as the 'standard' approach in that it provided a series of chapters on various electronic music topics by different authors. This approach made it possible to learn from the experts.

As synthesizers were developed which could interface with small computers, a number of works were written to provide instruction for specific computers, e.g., Thomas Rudolph's *Music and the Apple II™: Applications for Music Education, Composition, and Performance* (not included). After the development of the MIDI (Musical Instrument Digital Interface) protocol, numerous books were written for various computers including the Atari™, the IBM PC™, the Commodore 64 & 128™, the Apple II™, and others. Many of these guides were not written specifically for classroom use and are included in other chapters of this bibliography.

More recently a number of books have been written for classroom use. David Mash produced his *Computers and the Music Educator: A Curriculum and Resource Guide* (1991) (see item 205) to be used as a resource for music educators who want to integrate the latest computer technology in their classrooms using the Apple Macintosh™ operating system, and in 1993 Sam Holland published his *Teaching Toward Tomorrow: A Music Teacher's Primer for Using Electronic Keyboards, Computers, and MIDI in the Studio* (see item 202), which is a practical guide for teachers who wish to present music technology along with more traditional teaching techniques.

The following works are representative of textbooks either written for individual instruction, early experimentation with tape recorders, or for use in classrooms equipped with electronic instruments and computers.

194.   Appleton, Jon & Ronald Perea, eds. **The Development and Practice of Electronic Music.** Englewood Cliffs, NJ: Prentice Hall, 1975. vii. 288p. illus. LCCN 74-12478. ISBN 0-13-207605-5.

This work is intended for the "layman with an interest in electronic music, the student working in the field, and the musician who wishes to broaden his knowledge of the art outside his own speciality..." (Preface vii). Often used as a textbook, *The Development and Practice of Electronic Music* has become a standard for electronic music students. The book, known as a "standard" approach, is made up of a series of separate chapters by different authors: "Sound, Electronics, and Hearing," by Wayne Stawson, "The Tape Studio," by Gustav Ciamaga, "The Voltage Controlled Synthesizer," by Joel Chadabe; "The Uses of Digital Computers in Electronic Music Generation," by John E. Rogers; and "Live-Electronic Music," by Gordon Mumma. In addition there is an interesting introduction entitled "Origins," by Otto Luening.

195.   Bartle, Barton K. **Computer Software in Music and Music Education; A Guide.** Metuchen, NJ: Scarecrow Press, 1987. xiv. 252p. LCCN 87-16532. ISBN 0-8108-2056-0.

Mr. Bartle points out that "microcomputer technology and the development of digital sound synthesis have provided the impetus for the development of music applications software in four main areas: composition (music editing), music printing (transcription), performance (both real time and recorded), and music education." (Introduction, v.) This work lists more than 50 software programs for application in music education and music in general. Each entry provides the title of the program, the author, the publisher, cost, date, what equipment is necessary to run the program, the publisher's suggested audience if provided, and a detailed description of how the program runs and what it will do. In some cases the documentation for the program is discussed. Some of the software described requires MIDI equipment, and other programs run on specific computers. Appendices include a list of computer manufacturers, a list of peripheral manufacturers, software publishers, and a bibliography. Also, the work provides an audience index (it is possible to identify an audience, e.g., elementary school, and identify software directed to this group), a computer index, and a subject index. Because many of the computers and programs listed in the work are no longer in production, the book is more useful as a historical record that a current software source. In some cases more recent editions of the software are still being used on updated computers, and it is interesting to compare the capabilities of such programs with the versions of 8 years ago.

196.   Carpenter, Robert A. **Technology in the Music Classroom.** Los Angeles, CA: Alfred Publishing Co., Inc., 1991. vi. 70p. illus. ISBN 0-88284-493-8.

"This book is meant to provide a source of basic information concerning the technology that is available, its capabilities and its potential uses in the teaching of music." (Introduction, vi.) The work is directed at the complete novice in the area of electronic and computer music. Chapters are included on audio equipment, MIDI, synthesizers, keyboards, samplers, drum machines, and the general use of computers in composing and performing music. In addition, there are sections on drill and practice software for music applications, management tools, peripheral devices, curriculum issues, and writing & obtaining grants to obtain equipment for educational use. Appendices include a glossary of terms, a bibliography (22 items), and a list of software companies which produce software for classroom applications.

197.   Cope, David. **New Music Composition.** New York, NY: Schirmer Books, 1977. xii. 351p. illus. ISBN 0-02-870630-7.

Designed as a class textbook, this work covers most aspects of music notation including techniques for musique concrète, synthesizers, and computers. The book is divided into 27 chapters with a list of works for analysis at the end of each. Appendices include "The Composer's Table" (a list of materials needed for music notation), "Further Reference

Materials," and a "Brief Glossary of Terms." All concepts present in the
book are well illustrated.

198.   Dennis, Brian. **Experimental Music in Schools: Towards a New World
        of Sound.** London, England: Oxford University Press, 1970. [iii.] 76p.
        illus. (Includes score). ISBN 0-1932-3195-6.

"This book is written to help teachers who would like to introduce truly
modern music in their classes." (Introduction) It is a step-by-step
approach to teaching the basic physics of sound, improvisation, development of musical instruments, and musical creativity. A large portion of
the book is devoted to "Electronic Music in the Classroom," and provides both a brief history of electronic music and detailed plans for
creating tape music using common instruments. No index or bibliography is provided.

199.   Dwyer, Terence. **Making Electronic Music: A Course for Schools.** 3
        vols. London, England: Oxford University Press, 1975. unpaged. illus.
        (includes 4-45 rpm recordings) ISBN 0-1932-1071-1.

These three little volumes are designed for electronic music students who
wish to compose music with a tape recorder. A set of records containing
electronic sounds made on a synthesizer are included to provide raw
materials. The volumes take the student through a step-by-step set of
exercises designed to display the many musical possibilities using a tape
recorder. Sections include shaping dynamics, speed changes, variable
speed & filtering, musique concrète, working techniques, equipment, and
space music. Each section explains equipment needed and provides
examples of sounds to be produced. Directions and illustrations are clear
and easily followed. Contents: books 1&2, 1 Book, 2 Source material,
1: incl. 2 - 45 rpm mono records. Source material 2: incl. 2 - 45 rpm
records.

200.   Friend, David, Alan R. Pearlman & Thomas D. Piggott. **Learning Music
        With Synthesizers.** Newton, MA: Hall Leonard Pub. Co., 1974. vii.
        213p. illus.

"This text is designed to serve as an introduction to electronic music synthesis." (Preface) Part I provides the basic theory needed for understanding sound synthesis, Part II provides hands-on instruction for mas-
tering the ARP Odyssey™ synthesizer, and Part III ties the ARP™
Synthesizer into traditional music concepts. The book is basically a
series of actual synthesizer experiments which teach both the use of the

synthesizer and fundamental music concepts. It is well illustrated and easy to read with clear instructions for using the ARP Synthesizer. Also provided is a glossary of terms used in the book.

201.   Friend, David, Alan R. Pearlman & Thomas D. Piggott. **Lessons in Electronic Music.** Newton, MA: Contemporary Education Publications, 1976. 155p. illus. LCCN 76-7024.

The authors of this volume point out that the book is "about music, sound, and synthesizers. It is an organized lesson plan approach that relates every new concept and skill to music." (Foreword, i.) The lessons are oriented toward the ARP™ AXXE synthesizer. Each lesson provides a basic explanation of the type of sounds to be produced, tips for understanding the patching, and various exercises that can be carried out to improve the end results. After a section on basic concepts and the use of the synthesizer to produce music, the lessons begin with one entitled "Let's Begin with Noise," which concentrates on making sounds on the ARP™ AXXE synthesizer. Additional lessons include 2: "Shaping Noise Timbres: Frequency & Resonance Control," 3: "Shaping Noise Sound Patterns: Surf, Steam Locomotive," 4: "Extracting Pitches from Noise," 5: "Shaping Noise Events: Pitched Woodblock & Cymbal Effects," 6: "Shaping Bass Drum & Snare Drum Effects," 7: "Shaping Random Sample & Hold Percussion Timbres," 8: "Pitched Sounds I: Sawtooth & Square Waveforms," 9: "Pitched Sounds II: Exploring Pulse Waves," 10: "Pitched Sounds III: The Sine Wave," 11: "Exploring Pitch Range," 12: "Overtones & Harmonies," 13: "Frequency Modulation: Vibrato, Trill," 14: "Pulse Width Modulation," 15: "The Voltage Controlled Filter: LFO & ADSR Envelope Effects," 16: "Pitch Change As An Element In Timbre," 17: "Changing Timbre Effects," and 18: "Synthesizing Traditional & Modern Electronic Musical Timbres." An appendix provides information on synthesizers and loudspeakers. There is no index or bibliography.

202.   Holland, Sam. **Teaching Toward Tomorrow: A Music Teacher's Primer for Using Electronic Keyboards, Computers, and MIDI in the Studio.** Loveland, OH: Debut Music Systems, 1993. xi. 113p. illus. LCCN 93-71723. ISBN 0-9639311-0-5.

This book is a practical guide for teachers who wish to present music technology along with the more traditional teaching techniques. The work begins with a chart providing examples of musical and technical objectives and continues with an "encyclopedia" which includes definitions and examples of various instruments including digital pianos, drum machines, and MIDI piano. Also, information on the use of the personal computer in teaching music is covered along with chapters on portable keyboards, and sound sampling. Other chapters present solo performance projects, ensemble performance projects, using a sequencer, using a drum machine, and how to develop an electronic music studio in a school setting. Appendices include a glossary and index combined, a bibliography (11 items), and a short biography of the author.

203.   Judd, Frederick Charles. **Electronics in Music.** London, England: Neville Spearman, 1972. 169p. illus. ISBN 0-685-21939-9.

Generally written for students, this work attempts to explain how electronics have influenced musical instruments and music reproduction. Basic information has been provided for the student of music to understand the basic circuits but a basic understanding of electronics is necessary to use the work. Also, some knowledge of basic electronic test equipment is recommended. Chapters include "Electronics in Music," "Electronic Musical Instruments," "Synthetic Sound," "Electronic Music," "The Tape Recorder in Music," and "Electronics in Music Reproduction." While now somewhat out of date, this work has historical value in that it provides photographs and descriptions of a number of electronic music instruments and studios in existence in 1972. Also, the chapter entitled "Electronics in Music" provides a fascinating insight into how the author viewed the use of electronics in the production of music at that time. Appendices include a bibliography (9 items), a list of electronics and electronic music periodicals (11 items), and a list of synthesizer manufacturers.

204.   Kettelkamp, Larry. **Electronic Musical Instruments: What They Do, How They Work.** New York, NY: William Morrow & Co., 1984. 122p. illus. LCCN 83-23819. ISBN 0-688-02781-4.

Larry Kettelkamp provides one of the best textbooks to introduce electronic instruments in this little volume. He explains how ordinary instruments were first electrified, how sounds are amplified by microphones and magnetic pickups, and how electronics have produced the revolutionary instruments in use today. Also, the basic workings of synthesizers, electronic organs, computer rhythm unites, sound processors, and other devices are explained. An Introduction, written by Herbert Deutsch, points out that "interested students can learn about the synthesis of electronic music right along with their study of music theory, harmony, and the other musical rudiments. Hundreds of colleges and universities have extensive studios for electronic and computer music studies." (Foreword, p. 3) *Electronic Musical Instruments...* is designed to be a textbook for secondary or college students, but will also be useful for obtaining a general introduction to the history, design, and use of electronic instruments. Sections include "Amplified Sounds," "Electric Pickups," "Developing Electronic Sound," "Oscillators," "Synthesizers," "Electronic Organs," "Sound Processors," "Composers-Performers Sound Studios," "Playing Electronic Instruments," and "Future Trends in Electronic Instruments and Music."

205.   Mash, David. **Computers and the Music Educator: a Curriculum and Resource Guide.** Menlo Park, CA: Digidesign Inc., 1991. iv. 91p. illus.

David Mash points out that this book is for you "if you teach theory, ear-training, counterpoint, jazz or classical performance, appreciation, orchestration or electronic music." (Preface, i.) The work is designed as a resource for music educators who want to integrate the latest computer technology in their classrooms. Explanations and examples are provided based on the Apple Macintosh™ operating system. Sections include "Background and Overview," which includes a brief background on computers & synthesizers, software, and curricular implications, "Integrating Technology into the Curriculum," which includes information on the future of classrooms, the electronic music lab of the future and curriculum for music technology, and "Reference," which covers choosing a Macintosh™, internal sound modules, digital audio recording and editing systems, and many other aspects of teaching electronic music. In addition there are useful lists of commercial digital audio recording and editing systems, recommended multitimbral synthesizers, computer music peripherals, MIDI controllers, and instrument and computer manufacturers. Finally, Mr. Mash provides a listing of computer and electronic music conferences and associations, schools that provide music educator seminars, and centers for advanced studies. An index is not provided.

206.   Naumann, Joel and James D. Wagoner. **Analog Electronic Music Techniques: In Tape, Electronic, and Voltage-Controlled Synthesizer Studios.** New York, NY: Schirmer Books, 1985. xxi. 448p. illus. LCCN 83-24809. ISBN 0-582-28281-0.

This work grew out of materials prepared for electronic music classes at the Catholic University of America and the University of Wisconsin at Madison, and may be used as a text for a year-long course in basic analog electronic music techniques. Part I, "Tape and Electronic Music Studios," introduces students to the equipment, techniques, and processes required to use a voltage-controlled synthesizer. Part II, "Voltage-Controlled Synthesizer Studios," examines the nature and operation of the voltage-controlled synthesizer, and Part III, "Electronic Music Composition," provides compositional concepts that most often confuse electronic music students. There are numerous illustrations throughout the work, and a list of listening examples at the end of each chapter. Chapter 16 provides 16 composition projects. The book also contains an index and short bibliography (9 items).

207.   Nelson, Robert & Carl J. Christensen. **Foundations of Music: A Computer-Assisted Introduction.** Belmont, CA: Wadsworth Pub. Co., 1987. xv. 221p. illus. (includes a 3 1/2" computer disk) LCCN 86-13193. ISBN 0-534-06894-4.

"This book is intended for use in music fundamentals classes for non-music majors at the college level, but could also be used successfully at the advanced high school level, or as a supplement to first year theory for college-level music majors." (Preface) The book comes with a floppy computer disk to be used on an Apple II™ computer which acts as a personal tutorial that customizes the students' learning sessions. Each section provides a log to keep track of lessons on line and a list of suggested listening sources. Lessons include "The Notational System," "Rhythm and Meter," "Sound," "Scales," "Intervals," "Chords and Harmony," "Single Forms," & "Looking at Music." Indexes include "Standard Chord Progressions," "Roman Numeral Chord Designations," "Glossary," and indexes by composer, classical songs, chorales & hymns, folk songs, popular songs, instrumental examples, simple piano pieces, and topics. Examples are clear and well-written and provide excellent tutorials for learning music basics.

208.   Orton, Richard, ed. **Electronic Music for the Schools.** New York, NY: Cambridge University Press, 1981. viii 200p. LCCN 81-3838. ISBN 0-521-22994-4.

This book draws together some of the pioneers of electronic music education in England. Richard Orton was a senior lecturer and the founder of the York University Electronic Music Studio. Other contributors include: Peter Warham, Headmaster of Barlbly Bridge Primary School, Selby, Yorkshire; Phil Ellis, Head of music at Natley High School, Braintree, Essex; Tom Wanless, Head of music at the Sheldon School, Chippenham, Wiltshire; Andrew Bently, Finnish Radio Electronic Music Studio; Trevor Wishart; and, Hugh Davies, Assistant to Karlheinz Stockhausen in Cologne from 1964-66. The chapters include information on hardware, software, primary & secondary school approaches, music montage, and electro-acoustic instruments. Appendices include a glossary, course outline, bibliography (40 items), a discography, and a list of manufacturers.

209.   Trythall, Gilbert. **Principles and Practice of Electronic Music.** New York, NY: Grosset & Dunlap, 1973. v. 214p. illus. ISBN 0-448-40003-8.

This book was reprinted by Grosset & Dunlap as a juvenile edition in 1974. Designed as an introductory textbook for use in electronic music classes, Mr. Tyrthall's book provides information on basic acoustics, principles of electronics, electronic circuits, electronic music modules, procedures for sound synthesis, tape recording, and tape editing & mixing. In addition the work includes a short history of electronic music which is illustrated with numerous photographs of synthesizers. Only a brief bibliography is provided (30 items), but the work is well indexed and illustrated, and includes a useful glossary. Two editions of the book were published: a library edition and a text edition (ISBN 0-448-40002-X). A recording was available for musical examples in the text edition. The introduction was written by Robert A. Moog.

210.   Wiggins, Jackie. **Synthesizers in the Elementary Music Classroom: An Integrated Approach.** Reston, VA: Music Educators National Conference, 1991. 55p. illus. ISBN 1-56545-005-1.

Jackie Wiggins points out "that the purpose of this book [is] to help teachers feel comfortable enough with the new technology to make their own decisions as to how it should be integrated into their programs. It is intended as a guide for using the new technology side by side with what teachers already do [and] as such, many of the lessons included could easily be carried out with or without synthesizers; these lessons are included here as models for integration." (Introduction, p. 2) The book is divided into several introductory chapters including information on equipment, using students' instruments, teaching musical concepts, and composition, and then proceeds to lay out five units with lesson plans for each. The units include 1) " Synthesis and amplification," 2) "First performance experiences," 3) "Synthesizers in work stations," 4) "Ground bass," and 5) "Working with a drum machine." Each lesson plan includes the objective, materials needed, and procedure. A final chapter discusses ideas for developing intermediate lessons. Appendices include a list of equipment (8 listed), support services, and a brief bibliography (6 items).

211.   Willman, Fred. **Electronic Music for Young People.** New York, NY:

Center for Applied Research in Education, Inc.,1974. 64p. illus. LCCN 74-5278. ISBN 0-87628-210-9.

Mr. Willman has designed this little volume as a textbook for younger children. The lessons are arranged in a developmental sequence, with each building on the previous experiments. Each lesson begins with a list of materials and equipment needed (ranging from rubber bands to tape recorders), and then continues with a listening assignment. Several experiments are then developed using the basic materials suggested. Throughout the lessons, additional information is introduced including basic electronics, the history of electronic music, and music terminology. The final lesson includes designs for making simple electronic instruments. The work is clearly written and contains well designed illustrations. There is no index or bibliography.

Bibliographies and Directories

Sometime before 1952, Vladimir Ussachevsky began compiling a list of books and articles on electronic music instruments. His list, *Electronic Musical Instruments: A Bibliography* was published by the Tottenham Public Libraries and Museum in England (see item 224). He was able to identify 13 books & pamphlets, 15 articles in books and encyclopedias, and 271 periodical articles published between 1900 and 1952. Over the years a number of larger bibliographies were published with ever increasing numbers of citations chronicling an explosion of publishing on electronic and computer music. In 1966 Henry Otto published a list of over 700 periodical articles in *A Preliminary Checklist: Books and Articles on Electronic Music* (see item 219). Later in 1968 Hugh Davies compiled the *International Electronic Music Catalog* in which he claims to have included "every single composition that could be traced." (see item 216) By 1970, Lowell Cross was able to identify more than 1500 items on electronic music in his book *A Bibliography of Electronic Music* published in Toronto (see item 215).

More recently several book-length bibliographies on electronic and computer music were published including *A Bibliography of Computer Applications in Music* (1974) by Stefan Kostka that lists more than 600 books and articles on the subject (see item 220), Battier & Veiller's *Musique et informatique: une bibliographie indexee* (see item 213) where they identify more than 800 items on computer applications to music, and Deta Davis' 1988 and 1992 revision of *Computer Applications in Music: A Bibliography* (see item 217) where more than 4500 items from earliest times are listed.

The following books represent the major bibliographies and directories on electronic and computer music.

212.   Basart, Ann Phillips. **Serial Music: A Classified Bibliography of Writings in Twelve-Tone and Electronic Music.** Berkeley, CA: University of California Press, 1961, 1976. 151p. LCCN 75-045460. ISBN 0-83718-753-2.

Reprinted in 1976, this work is largely devoted to twelve-tone music but it includes lists of electronic music sources. Also included are bibliographies of works on specific composers including Milton Babbitt, Luciano Berio, Pierre Boulez, John Cage, Giselher Klebe, Luigi Nano, and Karlheinz Stockhausen. The work is arranged by theme but provides author and subject indexes in the back. Also included is a section on European journals and articles published before the beginning of the *Music Index* in 1949.

213.   Battier, Marc & Jacques ar Veiller. **Musique et informatique: une bibliographie indexée.** Paris, France: Department Musique, Universite Paris, 1978. 178p. ISBN 2-902671-05-9.

This bibliography contains over 800 listings of articles, books, software programs, technical papers, and dissertations concerning computer applications in music. Each entry has four-letter codes along the right margin indicating the type of article, country of origin, software needed, etc.. The entries are not annotated. Appendices include an index by type of article, an index of computer languages represented, an index of specific programs, and a key to codes used in the text. The main body of the work is arranged alphabetically by author.

214.   Buxton, William. **Computer Music: A Directory of Current Work.** Ottawa, Canada: The Canadian Commission for Unesco, 1977. xvii. 239p.

"The prime motive in preparing this document was to facilitate access to information in the rapidly expanding field of 'computer music'." (Preface) The information contained in this directory was obtained through the distribution of a questionnaire (a copy of the questions is not included in the book) and compiled with no editing or verification. The research was done under the auspices of UNESCO at the Conference on Cultural Policies in Europe, Helsinki, 1972. Computer music labs, equipment, and other resources in 15 countries are listed. Also a personal name index is included.

215.   Cross, Lowell M. **A Bibliography of Electronic Music.** Toronto, Canada: University of Toronto Press, 1967, 1970. ix. 126p. LCCN 67-

2573. ISBN 0-196237-53-X.

First published in 1967 and again by Books Demand UMI in 1970, Lowell Cross's bibliography provides a list of writings on electronic music compiled for a graduate research project supervised by Dr. Myron Schaefer at the University of Toronto in the fall of 1964. The author claims that the "books, articles, monographs, and abstracts cited here represent an attempt to compile as exhaustive a bibliography as possible for 'musique concrète,' 'elektronische Musik,' 'tape music,' 'computer music,' and the closely related fields in experimental music." (Preface, vii.) This bibliography is arranged in a single alphabetical list and contains more than 1500 items. It is provided with an abbreviated index. The entries are not annotated.

216.   Davies, Hugh. ed. **International Electronic Music Catalog.** Cambridge, MA: MIT Press, 1968. xxx. 330p. LCCN 68-20151. ISBN 0-262-04012-3.

This catalog grew out of a study done in 1961 by the Groupe de Recherches Musicales and published under the title *Ripertoire des Musiques Experimentales* or *RIME.* The original work approached the study from the standpoint of studios, but the 1968 publication included "every single composition that could be traced." (Preface, xx.) The list is arranged by country, city, and composer. Information provided includes title, function, date, duration, tracks, and format such as disk, tape, etc.. Studio information includes whether the studio is official, private, permanent or improvised. In addition there is a discography, a list of works by synthesizer, a list of studios with addresses, and an index by composers name. The catalog is "designed to be of maximum clarity and usefulness for all possible reference purposes. Thus a program planner can see at a glance what works can be included in a public or broadcast concert..." (Preface, xx.)

217.   Davis, Deta S., ed. **Computer Applications in Music: A Bibliography.** Madison, WI: A-R Editions, Inc., 1988, 1992. 537p. ISBN 0-89579-225-7.

The Computer Music and Digital Audio Series, first published by William Kaufmann, began in 1985 and was designed to serve as a series of sources for books on electronically generated music and related subjects. Mr. Davis' bibliography provides the most comprehensive list of electronic music lists (over 4500) to date. The work includes items from the earliest times of electronic music to mid-1986, and is divided into 25 chapters covering subjects such as aesthetics, composition, computers in music education, conferences, digital signal processing, electronic & pipe organs, MIDI, music printing, musicological applications, and psychoacoustics. The work is very inclusive and has a clearly understood arrangement. No annotations or references to software are included.

218.   Edwards, J. Michele. **Literature for Voices in combination with Electronic and Tape Music: An Annotated Bibliography.** Ann Arbor, MI: Music Library Association, 1977. 194p. (MLA Index & Bibliography Series, No. 17) ISBN 0-91495-409-1.

"The purpose of [this] bibliography is two-fold. First, it seeks to be a complete historical listing of compositions written for voices in combination with electronic and tape music...from the earliest known works through 1975, a total of 400 entries. Second, and more important, the bibliography is a finding list of compositions currently available to performers." (Preface) The work is arranged alphabetically by composer, and each entry contains country, title, date, instrumentation, text, duration, studio, audio type, publisher, available from, performance premiere, and an annotation. The annotations tend to be brief, but generally useful. There are 400 compositions listed. Appendices include a list of publishers, non published score sources, hard-to-find record labels, studios, and a bibliography of sources. There is also an index arranged by medium.

219.   Henry, Otto W. **A Preliminary Checklist: Books and Articles on Electronic Music.** New Orleans, LA: Electronic Music Studio, Newcomb College, Tulane University, 1966. 33p.

This manuscript bibliography was compiled by Otto Henry in June of 1966 using seven standard bibliographies including the *Music Index, Applied Science and Technology Index, Essay and General Literature Index, Guide to the Musical Arts (1953-56), Guide to the Performing Arts, International Index,* and the *Readers Guide to Periodical Literature.* There are 709 items listed from 53 periodicals. No annotations are provided. There is no indexing. (Available from Tulane University Library, Call no. 016.78 T917p Music.)

220.   Kostka, Stefan M. **A Bibliography of Computer Applications in Music.** Hackensack, NJ: Joseph Boonin, Inc., 1974. iii. 58p. (Music Indexes and Bibliographies, No. 7.) ISBN 0-913574-07-4.

This bibliography provides a list of 641 books and articles on electronic music published by the summer of 1973. While no annotations are provided, there are notes and cross references for a number of entries. There are no appendices.

221. Martin, Vernon. **Bibliography of Writings on Electronic Music.** New York, NY: Columbia-Princeton Electronic Music Center, 1964, 1969. Unpaged, Mimeograph.

This bibliography is an attempt at a listing of all books and articles written on electronic music through 1963. There are 657 items. The scope is broad in that it contains works which have a more or less remote connection with the subject. The work is organized by entry number and country. It begins with Czech (3 items) and continues through Swedish (1 item). It is interesting to note that the largest number of articles on electronic music are in English (316 items) with German (206 items) and French (75 items) coming in second and third. Each entry includes the item number, title, name of journal with volume, date, and page, and often a call number for the Columbia University Music Library or the New York Public Library, Music Division--42nd. Street. The original (1964) bibliography has an index. Four supplements were published through November, 1969, which bring the bibliography up to that date.

222. Melby, Carol, comp. **Computer Music Compositions of the United States, 1976.** Urbana, IL: University Library, University of Illinois, 1975. 28p.

This catalog of computer music compositions was compiled for the First International Conference on Computer Music held at The Massachusetts Institute of Technology, October 28-31, 1976. The pieces listed represent only original compositions and not realizations of older music. Composers were asked to answer a questionnaire concerning their compositions in order to obtain the listing. Over 250 compositions are listed by 91 composers. A list of the individual composers is provided at the beginning of the publication. Each entry contains the name of the composer, the title, the type of scoring, the availability of the score if any, the availability of a recording if any, the availability of tape if any, the duration, and the computer, its location, and program used.

223. Tjepkema, Sandra L. **A Bibliography of Computer Music: A Reference for Composers.** Iowa City, IA: University of Iowa Press, 1981. xvii. 276p. LCCN 81-2967. ISBN 0-87745-110-9.

"This bibliography is intended to be a comprehensive listing of books, articles, dissertations, and papers relating to the use of computers by composers of music." (Preface) Mr. Tjepkema's bibliography is annotated and selections were made from the point of view of a composer interested in these developments. The list was compiled from the bibliographies of various works on the subject and standard reference sources. Over 500 items are listed. Additional sections include a list of commonly used acronyms, manufacturers of computers & computer components, and indexing by subject, names, & studios.

224.   Ussachevsky, Vladimir A. **Electronic Musical Instruments: A Bibliography.** 2nd. ed. London, England: Tottenham Public Libraries & Museum, 1952. ii. 27p.

This little bibliography is of interest mainly because it is one of the earliest published. "All the existing traceable bibliographies have been collated and individual items from various sources have been added. It may be, therefore, that this represents the most comprehensive single bibliography on the subject at the moment... (Introduction, ii.) The list covers materials in several languages including 13 books & pamphlets, 15 articles in books and encyclopedias, 271 periodical articles, and a list of nearly 100 references to patents and the names of the patent holders.

225.   Willman, Fred. **Electronic Music: Resources for Performance Groups and General Music Classes.** St. Louis, MO: Cross Creek Press, 1973, 1979. 95p.

Fred Willman compiled this list of electronic music materials while he was Coordinator of Music Education at the University of Missouri--St. Louis. It was first published by the University in 1973 and later enlarged and published by Cross Creek Press in 1979. Both popular and more classical electronic music is included. The list begins with a comprehensive discography which lists 720 items. Each entry provides the name of the composer, the title, the record label name and number, and some brief annotations which include dates, turntable speed, etc.. The second section provides a list of 630 electronic music scores for performance. Each entry lists the name of the composer, the title of the work, the medium required for performance (e.g., tape, orchestra with tape, electronics), and the source for the score. Addresses of the score publishers are provided at the end of the section. The final section is a bibliography of books (86 items), journal articles & papers (837 items), student textbook sources (8 items), and multi-media resources (27 items). Also included is a list of periodicals (22 items) in which electronic music articles frequently appear.

Dictionaries

The marriage of electronics and music has resulted in the development of a new lexicon. From the very earliest experiments in applying electronics to music there has been a need for glossaries of terms and dictionaries to help experimenters understand the technical manuals that accompanied equipment ranging from the Theremin to modern synthesizers. In addition, the many books and articles published on electronic music were filled with unfamiliar terms. To address this need, authors began including glossaries and lists of terminology used in their publications. By 1961 Andre Hodeir felt the need to explain the terminology used concerning electronics and other unfamiliar terms in his book *Since Debussy: A View of Contemporary Music*, New York, NY: Da Capo Press, 1961.

The problems related to use of technical terminology in the study of electronic and computer music eventually led to whole dictionaries to aid musicians in their understanding of the technology. One of the earliest publications solely devoted to the technical terminology of electronic music was the little pamphlet entitled *The Terminology of Electronic Music* (see item 232) published by the National Research Council of Canada in 1956. Compiled by Werner Meyer-Eppler, this publication is an interesting look at the terminology being used in connection with the early instruments, e.g., touch-sensitive organs, multi-track tape recorders, and voltage-controlled synthesizers in studios.

One of the first large dictionaries of electronic music terminology was published by Herbert Eimert & Hans Humpert in 1973. *Das Lexikon der Elektronischen Music* (see item 230) became the major source for understanding terminology until Craig Anderton published *The Electronic Musician's Dictionary* in 1988 (see item 226).

The following works provide a list of the major dictionaries of terminology related to electronic and computer music. Only larger works devoted to this subject have been included. In addition to these works a number of books listed in other chapters contain large lists of electronic music terminology and can be found by consulting the Subject Index.

226.   Anderton, Craig. **The Electronic Musician's Dictionary.** New York, NY: Music Sales Corporation, 1988. 120p. illus. ISBN 0-8256-1125-3.

Mr. Anderton explains that he has "tried to match the definition to the assumed level of expertise of the person looking up the word. Some esoteric concepts need a long explanation (beyond the scope of this book) in order for beginners to understand what's going on, but often the same terms can be explained fairly easily to those who already know a bit about of the subject." (How to Use This Book, p. 7) The book is arranged as a dictionary with illustrations. More than 1000 terms are defined. Definitions are generally brief and easily understood. Words used in definitions which appear as terms in the dictionary are indicated by an asterisk.

227.   Cary, Tristram. **Dictionary of Musical Technology.** Westport, CN: Greenwood Pub. Group, 1992. 576p. LCCN 92-14583. ISBN 0-313-29694-9.

Mr. Cary's *Dictionary of Musical Technology* begins with an historical overview of the development of technology as it has been applied to music. He begins with Pythagoras who more than 2500 years ago "showed the relationship between pitch intervals and number ratios," (Introduction, xi) and continues through the development of synthesizers, and computer applications. His Introduction is chatty and auto-biographical but generally informative, and provides an excellent beginning to the dictionary. While Mr. Cary's definition of most terms is brief and to the point, he writes complete essays on amplifiers, synthesis, computer composition techniques, MIDI, and sound samplers. The book has a select bibliography which lists many of the important books and journal articles on electronic and computer music.

228.   Devito, Albert. **Computer MIDI Desktop Publishing Dictionary.** Milwaukee, WI: Kenyon Publications (Hal Leonard Pub. Corp.), 1991. viii. 228p. illus. ISBN 0-934286-67-1.

The *Computer MIDI Desktop Publishing Dictionary* provides more than 2500 definitions of words used in electronic technology with an emphasis on MIDI devices, electronic and computer music applications, and other electronic technology. The definitions are generally brief but to the point and useful. This is a handy resource for understanding terminology associated with music, film, video cameras, computers, and much more.

229.   Dobson, Richard. **A Dictionary of Electronic and Computer Music Technology, Instruments, Terms, Techniques.** New York: Oxford University Press, 1992. x. 224p. ISBN 0-1931-1344-9.

This work surveys the entire field of electronic and computer music with entries on major commercial instruments, synthesizers, sound samplers, sequencers, signal processors, MIDI, and computers. Much historical information is included. The author assumes no technical knowledge on the part of the reader and entries are clear and comprehensive. Specific products are referred to as examples allowing an explanation of links between instruments such as the sampler, synthesizer, etc.. While the work is obviously directed at the novice, the examples are of interest to anyone in the field. Appendices include a binary and hexadecimal conversion table, a list of MIDI commands, scale and frequency tables, an index of products, an index of names, and a general index.

230.   Eimert, Herbert & Hans Ulrich Humpert. **Das Lexikon der Elektronischen Musik.** **[The Dictionary of Electronic Music]** New York, NY: European American Music Distributors Corporation, 1973, 1988. ixx. 426p. ISBN 3-764920-83-1

The authors point out in their forward that this work grew out of their frustration that definitions of terms used in electronic music were often contradictory and confusing. This work may be the first full-length dictionary of electronic music. Definitions are very complete and often exceed 200 words. Illustrations are used when necessary. Whenever possible definitions are provided from a musical standpoint instead of electronic, and the work attempts to follow a "middle ground" between technical language and more common terminology. Professor Stroh points out in his *Zur Soziologie der Elektronischen Musik*, (Zurich, 1975) that this dictionary is a major accomplishment in the area of electronic music studies. Appendices include an index of personal names, a list of encyclopedias and periodicals concerning electronic music, a general bibliography (242 items), an afterword by Hans Humpert on technology & electronic music, synthesizers and computers, an index of names cited, and short biographies of the authors.

231.   Enders, Bernd. **Lexikon Musik-Elektronik. [Encyclopedia of Electronic Music].** Mainz, Germany: Wilhelm Goldmann Verlag, 1981. 283p.

This little encyclopedia is written for anyone who deals with electronic music, both professional and armature. While the work is written in German, there are some dual entries providing Japanese and English translations. Each entry includes the term or phrase, pronunciation when necessary, and a brief definition of the concept. Many entries include illustrations. The work is written for popular musicians, music teachers, composers, music scholars, electronic music equipment builders, radio & sound technicians, equipment dealers, etc.. No composers or titles are included. This encyclopedia is strong on equipment functions and the theory behind them.

232.   Meyer-Eppler, Werner. **The Terminology of Electronic Music.** Ottawa, Canada: National Research Council of Canada, 1956. 9p.

This little pamphlet is one of the first attempts to define the terminology of electronic music. It was produced for a conference sponsored by the Canadian National Research Council. More than 100 terms used to explain music as it was applied to electronics at the time are defined. The majority of the terms relate to musique concrète and tape music.

233.   Petersen, David. **Electronic Musician's Tech Terms; A Practical Dictionary for Audio & Music Production.** Milwaukee, WI: Hal Leonard Corporation, 1992. 56p., illus. (Reprinted with by EM-Books, 1993).

This little dictionary provides terminology relating mostly to audio and music production.

234.   Petersen, George and Steve Oppenheimer. **Tech Terms: A Practical Dictionary for Audio and Music Production.** Emeryville, CA: EM-Books, 1993. iii. 50p. illus. LCCN 92-075168. ISBN 0-793519-89-6.

This little dictionary, written by George Petersen, products editor for *Mix* magazine, and *Electronic Musician* editor Steve Oppenheimer, provides a basic source for defining terms and phrases of the electronic music world. Mr. Petersen points out in his Preface that "today's electronic musician has the ability to create any type of music, ranging from pop, rock, jazz, R & B, and new age to large orchestral pieces and film scores, on a desktop system. Yet beyond the retail sticker shock, a steep learning curve is another price to be paid for all the power (and the fun) that musical technology offers...[and, because of this] an understanding of the basic terminology is an essential part of literacy in music synthesis and MIDI." The dictionary explains more than 300 of the most commonly misunderstood words and phrases in the field of studio recording, digital audio, and electronic music. The definitions are generally detailed and provide illustrations where necessary.

235. Tomlyn, Bo & Steve Leonard. **Electronic Music Dictionary.** Milwaukee, WI: Hall Leonard Pub. Corp., 1988. 80p. LCCN 88-614. ISBN 0-88188-904-0

This little manual is intended to be a practical glossary to the basic concepts of synthesizers, amplification, MIDI, computers and the physics of sound. The list contains more than 300 terms. Each entry contains a general category term to the right of the entry which identifies the item as a synthesizer, computer, amplification, signal processing, etc.. Also there are ample "see also" indicators to provide cross references for terms that require them.

Electronic Music Conferences

One of the first music conferences that included discussions of electronic music was the International Conference of Composers held at the Stratford Festival, Stratford, Ontario, during the summer of 1960. (See item 236) A number of papers presented discussed the present use and future of electronically created music. Six years later the West Virginia University Conference on Computer Applications in Music was held on April 29 and 30, 1966, and the significance of computer applications in music was the main consideration. In 1974 the International Computer Music Association (ICMA) was established and the first conference was held at Michigan State University, East Lansing, Michigan, that same year. Conferences of the International Computer Music Association have been held most years since 1974.

The following works are proceedings which record the activities of the International Computer Music Association Conferences (ICMA) and other groups. In most cases the sessions listed represent only part of those presented at a specific conference. Emphasis has been placed on sessions that are concerned with computer music production, the use of synthesizers, and computer music in general. The works are arranged by date of conference.

236. **The Modern Composer and His World: A report from the International Conference of Composers, held at the Stratford Festival, Stratford, Ontario, Canada, August, 1960.** John Beckwith and Udo Kasements, eds. Toronto, Canada: University of Toronto Press, c1961, 1962. xi. 170p. illus. ISBN 0-8020-7090-6.

This book is a report of the International Conference of Composers held at the Stratford Festival, Stratford, Canada, in the late summer of 1960. Leading composers officially represented a large number of countries, e.g., United States, Great Britain, Canada, U.S.S.R, Sweden, Poland, Mexico, Denmark, and Israel, to name only a few. Both the papers and the discussion following each is reported here. A fascinating picture of the state of contemporary music is presented. A number of papers discussed the present use and future of electronically created music.

237. **Papers from the West Virginia University Conference on Computer Applications in Music.** Lefkoff, Gerald, ed. Morgantown, WV: West Virginia University Foundation, 1967. 105p. illus. LCCN 67-24519. ISBN 0-318-36153-1.

This volume consists of five papers presented at the West Virginia University Conference on Computer Applications in Music on April 29 and 30, 1966. Mr. Lefkoff points out in his Introduction that "it is hoped that these papers may, in addition to the message which each conveys, combine to suggest the significance of computer applications for the advancement of musical art and scholarship." (Introduction, p.7) The papers presented included "Music Bibliography and the Computer," by Barry S. Brook, "Computer-Implemented Analysis of Musical Structure," by Allen Forte, "Computers and the Study of Musical Style," by Gerald Lefkoff, "Programming a Computer for Musical Composition," by Lejaren A. Hiller, and "An Introduction to the Information Processing Capabilities of the Computer," by Charles C. Cook.

238. **Proceedings of the International Computer Music Conference. 1977. ICMC 1977.** Curtis Roads, Comp. La Jolla, CA: University of California, San Diego, 1977. v. 196p. illus. (xeroxed)

The 1977 International Computer Music Conference was held at the University of California, San Diego, October 26-30. The event was sponsored by the University of California, San Diego, and the National Endowment of the Arts. The proceedings published in this volume are only a partial record of the papers presented. The compiler points out in the Preface that "some of the papers presented...have already been published, and therefore they are not included here." A bibliography of the published papers is included. The papers reproduced in the Proceedings include "Digital Synthesis of Complex Spectra by Means of Non-Linear Distortion of Sine Waves and Amplitude Modulation," by Daniel Arfib, "Towards Improved Analysis-Synthesis Using Cepstral and Pole-Zero Techniques," by Richard Cann & Kenneth Steiglitz, "Envelope Control with an Optical Keyboard," by Paul E. Dworak & Alice C. Parker,

"Nuances in the Synthesis of 'Live Sounds'," by Ercolino Ferretti, "Computer Facilities for Music at IRCAM," by John K. Gardner, Brian Harvey, James R. Lawson & Jean-Claude Risset, "Interactive Compositional Algorithms," by Emmanuel Ghent, "Computer Music Studies and Research at CNUCE, Institute of the National Research Council (CNR), Pisa," by P. Grossi, "A Technique for Time-Variant Filter Design," by James H. Justice, "The Carnegie-Mellon Computer Music System Digital Hardware," by Alice C. Parker, Richard D. Blum & Paul E. Dworak, "The Composer as Surgeon: Performing Phase Transplants," by Tracy Lind Petersen, "Composing Grammars," by Curtis Roads, "A Fuzzy Hierarchical Systems Model for Real-Time Visual Interpretation in Musical Experiences," by Gary W. Schwede, "New Developments in Stochastic Computer Music," by Jon C. Siddall & James N. Siddall, "Design Considerations for Computer Music Systems," by John P. Walsh, "Psychoacoustic Aids for the Musician's Exploration of New Material," by David L.Wessel & Bennett Smith, and "A Microprocessor-Based Live Performance Instrument," by Michael A. Yantis.

239. **Proceedings of the 1978 International Computer Music Conference. ICMC 1978.** 2 vols. Curtis Roads, Comp. Menlo Park, CA: Computer Music Journal, 1979. 872p. illus. ISBN 0-8101-0539-X.

These two volumes are the record of the fifth International Computer Music Conference held at Northwestern University, Evanston, Ill., November, 1978. The volumes contain 45 unedited papers presented by as many participants on topics related to the use of computers in all aspects of music. The papers are organized under the following general groups: "Synthesis Hardware," "Computer Graphics and Music," "Studio Reports and Systems Overviews," "Music Encoding and Notation," and "Computer-Aided Analysis and Musicology." The opening address concerning the history of electronic music was given by Iannis Xenakis. Some of the papers presented include "A Microcomputer-Controlled Synthesis System for Live Performance," by Martin Bartlett, "A Low-Cost, Real-Time, Frequency Modulation Hardware Module for Mini and Micro Computers," by Richard Blum, "An Introduction to the SSSP Digital Synthesizer," by William Buxton, et al., "The DMX-1000 Signal Processing Computer," by Dean Walraff, "Digital Synthesis of Complex Spectra by Means of Multiplication of Non-Linear Distorted Sine Waves," by Daniel Arfib, "Brass Tone Synthesis by Spectrum Evolution Matching with Non-Linear Functions," by James Beauchamp, "Interactive Synthesis Without Obscure Diagnostics," by Nelson Bridwell, "The Use of Hierarchy and Instance in a Data Structure for Music," by William Buxton, et al, "A Musical View of

Analysis-Synthesis," By Richard Cann, "Nuance Blending for the Synthesis of a Brass Choir," by Ercolino Ferretti, "Using the Plato/TI980A Music Synthesis System: The PLACOMP Language," by David Murray, et al., "Interactive Digital Composition," by Trace Lind Petersen, "A Composer's Notes on the Development and Implementation of Software for a Digital Synthesizer," by Neil Rolnick, "Further Studies in Compositional Algorithms," by Emmanuel Ghent, "Phrase Structure in Computer Music," by Lejaren Hiller, "Timbral Structures for Computer Music," by Hubert Howe, Jr., "Tuned Cyclic Tone Systems," by Gerald Lefkoff, "MUSIC 3150, A Fortran Program for Composing Music for Conventional Instruments," by Justus Matthews, "Some Simplifications and Improvements in the Stochastic Music Program," by John Myhill, "Reflections on My Use of Computers in Composition 1970-1975," by Gary Nelson, "Score-Time and Real-Time," by John Rogers & John Rockstroh, "Polyphonic Timbral Construction in *Androgeny*, " by Barry Truax, and "Plucking-One Aspect of Plucked String Synthesis and Its Realization by Computer and a Musical Application," by Maurice Wright.

240. **Proceedings of the 1980 International Computer Music Conference. ICMC 1980.** Hubert S. Howe, Comp. New York, NY: Queens College of the City University of New York, 1980. v. 824p. illus.

The 1980 International Computer Music Conference was the sixth Conference devoted to computer music, and the fourth international conference. It was held at Queens College on November 13 - 15, 1980. The Computer Music Society was established at this conference which has sponsored all Computer Conferences since that time. The papers presented are arranged in the following subject divisions: "Computer-Assisted Composition," "Educational Applications," "The Structured Sound Synthesis Project," "Sound Analysis and Signal Processing," "Studio Reports," "Musical Data Structures and Input Languages," "Software for Interactive Synthesis," "Music Printing," "Microcomputers," "Synthesis Hardware," "Compositional Approaches," "Generative Modeling of Music," "Sound Synthesis," "Theory and Philosophy of Music," "Digital Synthesizers," and "Addendum." The articles reproduced in this volume include "Subscore Manipulation as a Tool for Compositional and Sonic Design," by Otto Laske, "A Space Grammar for the Stochastic Generation of Multi-Dimensional Structures," by Kevin Jones, "Timbral Construction as a Stochastic Process," by Barry Truax, "'OBJED' and the Design of Timbral Resources," by W. Buxton et al., "On the Specification of Scope in Interactive Score Editors," by W. Buxton et al., "A Microprocessor Controlled Clavier," by G. Federkow et al., "A Microprocessor-based Conducting System," by W. Buxton et al., "PROD: A Grammar Based Computer Composition System," by M. Green, "Using the SSSP System: Reflections on One Composer's Experience," by James Montgomery, "The 'SCORE' Program for Musical Input to Computers," by Leland Smith, "Musical Data Structures in a Multi-Use Environment," by Peter J. Clements, "A Binomial Representation of the Pitch Parameter for Computer Processing of Music Data," by Alexander R. Brinkman, "The Design of a Portable Translator for DARMS," by Bruce McLean, "Musicbox in C: An Interactive, Graphic Digital Sound Editor," by Andrew S. Glassner, "The 4CED Program," by Curtis Abbott, "VLSI and the Design of Real-Time Digital Sound Processors," by Mark Kahrs, "Imagination and Linear Prediction," by Paul Lansky, "Composing from a Geometric Model: *Five-Leaf Rose* ," by Gary S. Kendall, "Sound Image Synthesis," by Tamas Ungvary, "The Musical Use of Non Linear Distortion," by Daniel Arfib, "The Fairlight Computer Musical Instrument," by Steve Levine & J. William Mauchly, "SBASS-1 Features," by Michael Yantis, and "The ADS 200 Advanced Digital Synthesizer," by Don Lieberman. This book also contains a very large (1202 items) bibliography of books and journal articles entitled "Computer Applications in Music: A Bibliography," by Deta S. Davis, 1980. There is also a name index for the volume.

241. **Proceedings of the 1981 International Computer Music Conference. ICMC 1981.** Larry Austin, Director, Thomas Clark, Assoc. Director. Denton, TX: North Texas State University, 1981. iv. 423p. illus.

The 1981 International Computer Music Conference was held at North Texas State University, Denton, Texas, November 5 - 8. The conference was sponsored by the School of Music, the Union Program Council, and the National Endowment for the Arts. The sessions included "Tutorials," by Lejaren Hiller, James Beauchamp, & Charles Dodge, "Compositional Approaches," by David Keane, Joel Chadabe & Tod Machover, "Compositional Philosophy," by Otto Laske & Malgorzata Mikulska, "Studio Reports," by Brad Albers, Alan Schindler, Bruce W. Pennycook & Wayne Slawson, "Computer-Assisted Composition," by Sever Tipei, Michael Matthews, John Meinecke, Charles Ames, John Abel & Paul Barth, "Musical Data Structures," by Bruce McLean, Philip Baczewski, Dan W. Scott, Alexander Brinkman, Colin Banger & Bruce Pennycook, "Computer-Assisted Instruction," by Paul E. Dworak, Ikuo Kitagaki & Bruce Pennycook, "Computer-Assisted Instruction," by Paul E. Dworak, Ikuo Kitagaki & Kunihiro Suetake, "Synthesis Hardware and Signal Processing," by James A. Moorer, John Snell, Curtis Abbott, John Stautner, Barry Vercoe, Miller Puckette, Alexandre Parodi, G. DiGiugno, Jean

Kott, Andrew Gerzo, J. B. Barrier, J. Holleville, Y. Potard & X. Rodet, "Real-Time Synthesis," by Barton McLean, Neil B. Rolnick, Jeffery S. Risberg, M. V. Mathews, J. Pasquale, Stanley Haynes, Miller Puckette, Barry Vercoe, John Stautner, L. Sasaki, G. Fedorkow, W. Buxton, C. Retterath, & K. C. Smith, "Psychoacoustics and Sound Analysis," by Martin Piszczalski, B. A. Galler, Stephen McAdams, David Wessel, David N. Stewart, Dexter Morrill & James W. Beauchamp, "Computer-Assisted Analysis," by J. Timothy Kolosick, William F. Blair, John H. Chalmers & Denise A. Lagasse, "Music Notation and Printing," by David Crawford & John Maxwell. Also a number of tutorials were presented included "Development of Computer Music," by Lejaren Hiller, "Review of Acoustics Research and Sound Analysis/Synthesis Technique," by James Beauchamp, and "Theory and Technique of Computer Sound Synthesis," by Charles Dodge. In addition to the sessions and tutorials, five concerts of electronic and computer music were given during the conference.

242.   **Musical Grammars and Computer Analysis: Atti del Convegno (Modera 4-6 Ottobre 1982).** Mario Baroni & Laura Callegari, eds. Florence, Italy: L. S. Olschki Editore, 1984. 374p. illus. ISBN 8-82223-229-1.

This book is a collection of essays on the application of computers to the analysis of musical styles which were delivered at a conference in Florence, Italy, October 4th through 6th, 1984. Curtis Roads (who was at M. I. T. at that time) provided an introductory lecture for the conference which he called "An Overview of Music Representations," in which he defines "music representations" as referring to "formal symbolic specifications used within computers for capturing musical structure and meaning. A main goal of developing more effective representations for music is to improve musician-machine communication, replacing the current rigid protocols and shallow user-interfaces with deeper and richer dialogues. Another goal is more scientific--to develop better models of human musical cognition." (Introduction) Mr. Roads continues with discussions of "Precomputer Formalisms," "Predicate Calculus," "Set Theory," "Modal Logic," "Semiotic Representations," "Simple Encoding: Music V, Mustran, And Score," "Stochastic Processes," "Systems Theory: Linked Automata," "Grammars," "Extended Grammars," "Procedural Representations for Music," etc.. Other addresses collected in the book include "Teorie su alcuni mottetti dell'ars antiqua, con relative considerazioni metodolgistiche," by John Rahn, "A Pattern recognition system in the study of Cantigas de Santa Maria," by Leo J. Plenckers, "Some unsolved problems in Schenkerian theory," by Célestin Deliège, "Toward an analytical symbology: the melodic harmonic and durational functions of implication and realization," by Eugene Narmour, "Per una teoria generale del linguaggio musicale," by Franco Oppo, "From traditional to formalized analysis; in memoriam Jean Barraqué." by André Riotte, "How saussurian is a music?" by Shuhei Hosokawa, "Keith: a rule-system for making music-analytical discoveries," by Otto Laske, "A grammar for melody. Relationships between melody and harmony," by Mario Baroni et al., "Musical competence, analysis and grammar," by Gino Stefani, "A grammar of the melodies of Schubert's Lieder," by Gino Stefani, and others. This work, while not specifically related to electronic music, presents important articles concerning the use of computers in musical analysis in general. There is a list of the lectures at the end of the volume, but no index or bibliography.

243. **Proceedings of the International Computer Music Conference (ICMC). Venice 1982.** Thomas Blum & John Strawn, Comp. Venice, Italy: Computer Music Association, 1982. iv. 749p. illus.

The ICMC Computer Music Conference, 1982, was held in Venice, Italy, on September 27, 28, 29, 30 & October 1. This volume contains copies of all of the materials generated by the conference including music scores, papers, and presentations. Included are *Studio Reports*: "The New Electronic and Computer Music Studio at Simon Fraser University," by Barry Truax, "Computer Audio Research Laboratory Studio Report," by F. Richard Moore & D. Gareth Loy, "The GRM Digital Studio for Treating Natural Sounds," by Bénédict Maillard & Jeab-Francois Allouis, "Real-Time Synthesis at the University of Victoria," by John Celona & Michael Longton, "Studio Report S. I. M./Rome," by Stefano Petrarca & Nicola Sani, "Un Progetto Dello Iasm Per La Costituzione Di Un 'Centro Di Informatica Musicale'," by Nel Turco: *Computer Music Systems:* "Phthong: An Interactive System for Music Composition," by Thomas Blum, "Use of Microprocessor in Real-Time Synthesis of Sounds," by Sylviane Sapir & Richard Kronland-Martinet, "The Control Channels of Instrumental Playing in Computer-Music-Real Time in Computer Music Incidence on the Choice of the Basic Models," by Claude Cadoz & Annie Luciani, "A Generalized Orchestra Compiler for Z80 Microprocessor," by Leslie Kleen, "Alternative Software for DMX-1000," by Alan Marr & Bruce W. J. Pennycook, "A Portable 'Walsh' Synthesizer," by Goffredo Haus & Mario Malcangi, "An Efficient Method to Implement Amplitude Modulation in Hardware," by Sergio Cavaliere & Immacolata Ortosecco; *Computer Music Systems with Emphasis on UNIX:* "A Microprocessor-Based System for Music Production," by Leonello Tarabella, "A Sound File System for UNIX," by Gareth Loy, "The Arts Digital DSY8201 Polyphonic Digital Music

Synthesizer," by Vito Asta & Adrian Freed, "Introduction to the Mshell," by Stephen T. Pope, "The Audio Composition System of the Defense and Civil Institute for Environmental Medicine," by Bruce W. Pennycook; *Synthesis Hardware:* "A Multi-Microprocessor System for Real-Time Music Synthesis: Design and Implementation," by Andrew S. Noetzel, "Architecture for a Digital Sound Synthesis Processor," by Giovanni B. Debiasi & Maurizio Rubbazzer, "The SYTER Project: Sound Processor Design and Software Overview," by Jean-François Allouis & Jean-Yves Bernier, "Real-Time Control System for Digital Synthesizer," by Martin de Loye; *Languages and Input Data Structures:* (sessions not listed here); *Analysis and Synthesis Techniques:* "Synthesis of Bowed Strings," by Julius Orion Smith III, "Is MUSIC V a Real Time Program?" by Daniel Arfib, "Computer Synthesis of Sound Applied to Composition with Sonic Processes," by Jean-Claude Risset, "The Computer Orchestra," by James Beauchamp: *Analysis and Synthesis Techniques:* "Digital Simulation of the Piano," by J. Rogers, "A Microprocessor Oriented Toward the Frequency Synthesis," by Antonio de Santis, "The Simulation and Extrapolation of Instrumental Sounds Using Direct Synthesis at IRCAM," by M. Battier & T. Lancino, "A Flexible Acoustic Ambience Simulator," by John P. Stautner, "The CHANT Project...," by X. Rodet & J-B Barriere. Additional section titles included *Psychoacoustics, Computer-Assisted Instruction, Computer-Assisted Research in Theory and Musicology, Tools for Live Performance, Composition and Live Performance, Computer Composition I & II.* There is a list of contributors at the end of the volume but no index.

244.   **Program for the 1983 International Computer Music Conference. ICMC 1983.** Allan Schindler, Director.   Rochester, NY: Computer Music Association, 1983. (unpaged)

The 1983 International Computer Music Conference was sponsored by the Eastman School of Music, Rochester, New York, Oct. 7-10, 1983. This work presents the program of the conference along with detailed descriptions of each session, a list of the composers attending (34 individuals), and a list of the 36 papers presented and their authors. There is a synopsis of each paper presented.   Also, short biographies of each presentor and/or composer are included. Some of the more prominent composers who attended   were   Larry Austin,   Don Buchla,   John Chowning, James Dashow, Charles Dodge, Paul Lansky, John Melby, Dexter Morrill, Jean-Claude Risset, and Trevor Wishart. There is no index or bibliography.

245.   **Proceedings of the International Computer Music Conference 1984.**

IRCAM, Paris, France. 1984. David Wessel, Director. San Francisco, CA: Computer Music Association, 1984. viii. 318p. illus.

The 1984 International Computer Music Conference was held in Paris, October 19 - 23, 1984 and directed by David Wessel. The papers presented were organized into seven general categories including "Software," "Signal Processing," "Composition and Research," "Expressive Control," "Control in Live Performance," "Music Printing and Data Structures," and "Studio Reports." Some of the articles include "A Procedural Control Language for a Digital Signal Processor," by Paul Berg, "A Functional Approach to Real-Time Control," by Roger B. Dannenberg & Paul McAvinney, "Recur: Composition and Synthesis," by Robert Rowe, "Score and/or Gesture - The System RT141 for Real Time Control of the Digital Processor 41," by Franco Azzolini & Sylviane Sepir, "The VLSI Approach to Sound Synthesis," by John Wawrzynek et al., "Refinements in Phase-Vocoder-Based Modification of Music," by Mark Dolson, "Frequency Dependent Waveshaping," by Giovanni De Poli, "An Allpass Approach to Digital Phasing and Flanging," by Julius O. Smith, "Shaping A Compositional Network with Computer," by Kaija Saariaho, "Operations on Timbre: Perspectives and Problems," by Wayne Slawson, "Models of Interactive Composition with the DMX-1000 [Wallraff 1979] Digital Signal Processor," by Barry Truax, "Ensemble Timing in Computer Music," by David A. Jaffe, "Hugh Le Caine's 1948 Sackbut Synthesizer Performance Mode of Electronic Instruments," by Gayle Young, "The Digital Piano and the Patch Control Language System," by Richard Teitelbaum, "MOXIE: A Language for Computer Music Performance," by D. J. Collinge, "Secrets of Life in Music: Musicality Realised by Computer," by Manfred Clynes, "A Data Structure for Computer Analysis of Musical Scores," by Alexander R. Brinkman, "A Modular Approach to Sound Synthesis Software," by Shawn L. Decker & Gary Kendall, "Toward a Device Independent Representation of Music," by Lounette M. Dyer, "Music Editing and Graphics (MEG 1.00): A Personal Computer Based Operative System for Editing and Printing Musical Scores," by Minciacchi Marco & Minciacchi Diego, and "Carnegie-Mellon University Studio Report," by Roger B. Dannenberg et al.. The book also includes an author index.

246. **Proceedings of the International Computer Music Conference. 1985. ICMC 1985.** Barry Truax, Conference Director. San Francisco, CA: Computer Music Association, 1985. x. 429p. illus.

The 1985 ICMC International Computer Music Conference was held at the Centre for the Arts, Simon Fraser University, Burnaby, British

Columbia, Canada, August 19 - 22, 1985. A Keynote Paper entitled "The Premise is That There Be Music" was presented by Herbert Brün. Papers presented include "The CARL Computer Music Workstation -- An Overview," by F. Richard Moore, "Designing an Operating Environment for a Realtime Performance Processing System," by D. Gareth Loy, "A Cost-Effective Input Processor - Pitch Detector for Electronic Violin," by A. Voelkel, "User Software for Realtime Input by a Musical Instrument," by X. Chabot, "Data Reduction of Musical Signals," by T. A. Wilson, "Sound Synthesis by Hierarchic Sampling," by G. Schwartz, "Alias-Free Synthesis by Stochastic Sampling," by E. Wold & M. A. Z. Dippe, "A New Approach to Digital Reverberation Using Waveguide Networks," by J. O. Smith, "Recent Advances in Musique Concrète at CARL," by Mark Dolson, "A Network Sound System for UNIX," by J. M. Roth, Gary S. Kendall, & Shawn L. Decker, "A Unified Approach to the Editing of Time-Ordered Events," by Shawn L. Decker & Gary S. Kendall, "The Synthesis of Complex Audio Spectra by Cheating Quite a Lot," by I. Bowler, "Physicals Models of Instruments: A Modular Approach, Application to Strings," by Jean-Marie Adrien & Xavier Rodet, "High Quality Synthesis-by-Rule of Consonants," by Xavier Rodet, & P. Depalle, "Identity and Ambiguity: The Construction and Use of Timbral Transitions and Hybrids," by J. Vanderheede & Jonathan Harvey, "A Low-Cost Development System for Digital Audio Signal Processing," by S. F. Hoge & A. Agnello, "The Emulator II Computer Music Environment," by D. Massie, "Some Aspects of Sample Rate Conversion," by D. Rossum, "A Machine-Independent Sound Conversion/Storage System," by Kurt J. Hebel, "The Use of Interpolating Memories for Music Processing by Microcomputer," by A. S. Noetzel, "A Computer-Based Harmonic Analysis/Additive Synthesis System," by L. Chouinard, L. N. Bélanger, & H. T. Huynh, "Sound Kit -- A Sound Manipulator," by M. Lentczner, "The Image and Audio Systems Audio Workstation," by Bruce Pennycook, J. Kulick, and D. Dove, "A New Architecture for a Digital Sound Synthesizer," by M. Rubbazzer, M. Santoiemma, & G. A. Patella, "Music Synthesis by Simulation Using a General-Purpose Signal Processing System," by J. Kitamura, et al., "Music Applications for the MSSP System," by J. Gordon, "A Sine Generation Algorithm for VLSI Applications," by J. Gordon & J. O. Smith. There is also an index by subject and contributor.

247. **Proceedings of the 1986 International Computer Music Conference. ICMC 1986.** Paul Berg, Director. San Francisco, CA: Computer Music Association, Inc., 1986. x. 463p. illus.

The 1986 International Computer Music Conference was held at the

Royal Conservatory, The Hague, Netherlands, October 20 - 24, 1986. The sessions presented include (General Presentations: Composition and Research) "A Lisp Environment for Creating and Applying Rules for Musical Performance," by Anders Friberg & Johan Sundberg, "Musical Experiments with Prolog II," by Jan Vandenheed, "Developing a Knowledge-Based System for Timbral Design," by Richard D. Ashley, (General Presentations: Real-Time Applications and Small Systems) "What Ever Happened to SSSP?" by John Free & Paul Vytas, "The Impact of MIDI upon Compositional Methodology," by Christopher Yavelow, "A Performance Literature for Computer Music: Some Problems from Personal Experience," by Neil B. Rolnick, "A Model of Real-Time Computation for Computer Music," by David P. Anderson & Ron Kuivila, "Interprocess Communication and Timing in Real-Time Computer Music," by Miller Puckette, (Lecture/demonstrations) "Space Perception in the Computer Age," by Leo Küpper, "Renaissance and Baroque Microtonal Music Research in Computer Real Time Performance," by Patrizio Barbieri & Lindoro Del Duca, "A Workstation in Live Performance: Composed Improvisation," by Xavier Chabot, Roger Dannenberg & Georges Bloch, "The Biniou Real-Time Music System," by P. Barbaud, F. Brown & R. Lengagne, (General Presentations: Approaches to Input Languages) "Adding a Graphical User Interface to FORMES," by Lee Boynton, Jacques Duthen, Yves Potard & X. Rodet, "LOCO: Composition Microworlds in Logo," by Peter Desain, Henkjan Honing, "A Natural Language System for Music," by Brian L. Schmidt, "MacMix: Mixing with a Mouse," by Adrian Freed, "The Development of an Intelligent Composers's Assistant Interactive Graphics Tools and Knowledge Representation for Music," by Stephen T. Pope, (General Presentations: Synthesis Models)"Techniques for Timbral Interpolation," by Yee-On Lo, "MIDIM Sound-Duplications and Their Applications," by H. Kaegi, J. Janssen, & P. Goodman, "A Computer Model for Bar Percussion Instruments," by Xavier Serra, "Modeling Piano Tones," by Joseph Marks & John Polito, "Experimenting with Models of Resonance Produced by a New Technique for the Analysis of Impulsive Sounds," by Y. Potard, P. F. Baisnèe & J. B. Barrière, "Efficient Simulation of the Reed-Bore and Bow-String Mechanisms," by Julius O. Smith, (Special Presentations) "The Computer and Live Musical Performance," by Jon H. Appleton, "Timing Accuracy and Response Time in Interactive Systems," by Ron Kuivila & David P. Anderson, "A Unified Set of Software Tools for Computer-Assisted Set-Theoretic and Serial Analysis of Contemporary Music," by Craig Harris & Alexander Brinkman, "Computer-Assisted Musical Analysis: A Question of Validity," by John Morehan, "Computer and Music Software in an Educative-Formative Role in Italy," by G. Codeluppi & E. Iannuccelli, "A System of Rules for

Computer Improvisation," by Marco Ligabue, and "Computers and Music Education: A Compositional Approach," by Gary Greenberg. There is also an index of authors.

248.   **Proceedings of the 1987 International Computer Music Conference. ICMC 1987.** James Beauchamp & Sever Tipei, Directors. San Francisco, CA: Computer Music Association, 1987. ix. 373p. illus.

This is the second International Computer Music Conference which was held at the University of Illinois, August 23 - 26, 1987.   James Beauchamp, the chair of the conference committee, points out in his Foreword that "the number of conferees has increased from 130 to 450 (at the 1986 ICMC), the technical papers presented from 27 to 55 (out of 116 submitted), and the number of concert programs from 2 to 9." The papers reproduced in this proceedings book are arranged in 13 broad subjects including "Tutorial Talks," "Computer-Assisted Composition," "Studio Reports," "Sound Synthesizers and Processing Techniques," "Real Time Systems: New Techniques," "Music Workstations: Software and Hardware," "Understanding and Assisting Musical Thinking," "Cybernetics in Composition," "MIDI Performance Systems...," "Sound Analysis, Synthesis and Perception," "Music Notation Encoding and Printing," "Computers and Learning," and "Special Session: Composers' Talk." Some of the papers presented include "Integration of Music and Graphics through Algorithmic Congruence," by Brian Evans, "Procedural Composition," by Gary Greenberg, "Composition Design System...," by Keith Hamel et al., "The P-G-G Environment for Music Composition," by Daniel V. Oppenheim, "Kyma: An Object-Oriented Language for Music Composition," by Carla Scaletti, "Musical Information from a Narrowed Autocorrelation Function," by Judith C. Brown, "Modeling Piano Sound Using Waveguide Digital Filtering Techniques," by Guy E. Garnett, "Elthar-A Signal Processing Expert that Learns," by Brad Garton, "Javeline: A Environment for the Development of Software for Digital Signal Processing," by Kurt J. Hebel, "Control of Phrasing and Articulation in Synthesis," by David Wessell, "On the Scheduling of Multiple Parallel Processors Executing Synchronously," by D. Garath Loy, "Real Time Synthesis of Bowed String Timbres," by Charlie Robinson, "General-Purpose Hi-Fidelity Affordable Real-Time Computer Music System," by John M. Snell, "Real-Time Granulation of Sampled Sound with the DMX-1000," by Barry Truax, "The Composers' Desktop Project," by Martin Atkins, "Le_Loup, and Object-Oriented Extension of Le_Lisp for an Integrated Computer Music Environment," by Jacques Duthen, "A Sun-Mercury Music Workstation," by Gerhard Eckel, "A Smalltalk-80-Based Music Toolkit," by Stephen T. Pope,

"Synthesizer Management Based on Note Priorities," by David P. Anderson, "MIDI Synthesizers in Performance: Realtime Dynamic Timbre Production," by Jean-Charles Francois, "Following an Improvisation in Real Time," by Roger B. Dannenberg, "Personal-Computer Microworlds for Learning About Signals and Sound," by Mark Dolson, "PRECOMP/GT - A Graphic Tool for Learning Topics in Computer-Assisted Composition," by Richard Kufrin, "Design of an Intelligent Tutoring System in Harmony," by Linda B. Sorisio, and "Computer Music and Human Engineering: The Making of Labyrinth," by David Keane. Many of the papers included are illustrated and most have brief bibliographies at the end. There is also an index of authors.

249.   **The Proceedings of the AES 5th International Conference: Music and Digital Technology.** John Strawn, Conference Chair. New York, NY: Audio Engineering Society, 1987. 248p. illus. ISBN 0-937803-11-1.

The AES International Conference on Music and Digital Technology was held in Los Angeles, California, May 1 - 3, 1987. John Strawn points out in his Introduction to the Proceedings that "the papers here are arranged in the order in which they were given at the conference. The opening session served to lay a historical framework for the conference, and to point out the current trends that are guiding the developments of the near and far future...[and in the second session] the speakers [emphasized] their personal experience in coming to grips with real-world problems in designing digital music synthesizers." (Introduction} Some of the papers presented include "An Armchair Analysis of Electronic Music's Current State-of-the-Art," by Dominic Milano, "Digital Musical Instrument Design: The Art of Compromise," by Dave Rossum, "Practical Considerations in the Design of Music Systems using VLSI," by J. William Mauchly & Albert J. Charpentier, "Multitasking Operation System Design for Electronic Music," by Steve M. Misek & Dana C. Massie, "What is a Computer Music Workstation?" by F. Richard Moore, "Music Workstations: Real-Time Subsystem Design," by Bruce Pennycook, Jeffrey Kulick, & Dave Dove, "Linear Prediction: The Hard, but Interesting Way to do Things," by Paul Lansky, "Composition or Improvisation? Only the Computer Knows," by Christopher Yavelow, "The MIDI Protocol," by Craig Anderton, "MIDI by Modem: The Future is Now," by Perry Leopold, "Computer Tools for Engraving-Quality Notation," by Kimball P. Stickney, "Software in the Studio," by Evan Brooks, "Recording, Mixing, and Signal Processing on a Personal Computer," by Adrian Freed, "MIDI-LISP: A LISP-Based Programming Environment for MIDI and the Macintosh," by David Wessel, et al., "Natural Language Interfaces and Their Application to Music Synthesis," by Brian L.

Schmidt, and "Masters and Slaves Versus Democracy: MIDI and Local Area Networks," by Bill Buxton. A list of participants is also provided.

250.   **Proceedings of the 14th International Computer Music Conference, Cologne, September 20-25, 1988.** Clarence Barlow, Director. Genter Straffe, West Germany: Feedback Studio Verlag, 1988. vi. 436p. illus.

The 14th Annual Computer Music Conference held in Cologne in 1988, and was organized around ten broad subject areas including: "Musician-Machine Interaction," "Music Workstations," "Computers & Composition," "Music Representation," "Machine Perception," "Real-Time Performance," "Digital Audio (Theory)," "Digital Audio (Applications)," "Composition & Research," and "Miscellaneous." Forty-nine papers or presentations were delivered during the week-long conference by almost as many presentors. Many of the papers presented include illustrations, brief programs, and in-depth bibliographies. Some of the papers presented include "A Database Environment for Musician-Machine Interaction Experimentation," by Sylvie Gibet & Jean-Loup Florens, "A Music Workstation Based on Multiple Hierarchical Views of Music," by Mira Balaban, "Dynamic Patches: Implementation and Control in the SUN-Mercury Workstation," by Rodet Xavier & Gerhard Eckel, "ESQUISSE: A Compositional Environment," by Pierre-Francois Baisnée et al., "Key-Music: An Expert System Environment for Music Composition," by A. Camurri et al., "The CAMP Music Configuration Database," by John Free & Paul Vytas, "Performance with Performer Objects," by Gary Greenberg, "Toward a Theory of Formal Musical Languages," by Marc Ghemillier & Klaus Balzer, "TTrees: An Active Data Structure for Computer Music," by Glendon Diener, "Connection Machine Tracking of Polyphonic Audio," by Barry Vercoe & David Cumming, "Introducing Oscar," by Peter Beyls, "A Real Time Scheduler/Dispatcher," by Roger Dannenberg, "New Techniques for Enhanced-Quality of Computer Accompaniment," by Roger Dannenberg, "Dynamic Modeling of Stringed and Wind Instruments, Sound Synthesis by Physical Models," by Jean Marie Adrien et al., "A Survey of Users' Experience with Digital Audio Synthesis," by Peter Castine, "Diphone Sound Synthesis Based on Spectral Envelopes and Harmonic/Noise Excitation Function," by Xavier Rodet, "Experiments in Computer Controlled Acoustic Modeling (A Step Backwards??)," by R. W. Berry, "A Real-Time Acoustic Processing Card for the Mac II," by Lee Boynton, "VOCEL: New Implementations of the FOF Synthesis Method," by John Michael Clarke, Peter Manning, Ron Berry & Alan Purvis, "PRAESCIO: Toward Dynamic Tapeless Performance," by Bruce Pennycook, "Sound Structure in Message: A Lecture with Sound Examples," by Curtis Roads, "Rapid Event Development in a MIDI Environment," by Rodney Waschka II & Tózé Ferreira, and "The Development of Context Sensitivity in the Midiforth Computer Music System," by Bruno Degazio. There is a brief name index.

Nielzen, Soren & Olle Olsson. **Structure and Perception of Electroacoustic Sound and Music: Proceedings of the Marcus Wallenberg Symposium Held in Lund, Sweden, on 21-28 August, 1988.** New York, NY: Excerpta Medica, 1989. 214p. illus. ISBN 0-444-81105-2.

See item number 43.

251. **Proceedings of the International Computer Music Conference. 1989. ICMC 1989.** David Butler & Thomas Wells, Directors. Ohio State Univ., Columbus, OH: Computer Music Association, 1989. 339p. illus.

The 1989 ICMC was hosted by the School of Music of The Ohio State University in Columbus, Ohio, November 2 - 5, 1989. The book begins with a facsimile reproduction of the program for the 1989 Conference and then continues with each of the papers presented. Some of the papers include "The Interactive Arts System: Introduction to a Real Time Performance Tool," by Kristi Allik & Robert Mulder, "A Computer System for Learning Analytic Listing," by Richard D. Ashley, "Computer-Based Learning: Models and Lessons for Computer Music Systems," by Richard D. Ashley, "The Artificially Intelligent Computer Performer on the Macintosh II™ and a Pattern Matching Algorithm for Real-Time Interactive Performance," by Bridget Baird et al., "A Digital Signal Multiprocessor and its Musical Application," by Jean-Baptiste Barrière et al., "The Computer Music Project at the University of Illinois at Urbana-Champaign: 1989," by James Beauchamp, "TRAILS: [Tempo Reale Audiomatica Interactive Location System] An Interactive System for Sound Location," by Nicola Bernardi & Peter Otto, "A Modular Approach to Excitator-Resonator Interaction in Physical Models Synthesis," by G. Borin, G. De Poli & A. Sarti, "Cellular Automation as a Means of High Level Compositional Control of Granular Synthesis," by Peter Bowcott, "Performance with Electronics: Gesture Interfaces and Software Toolkit," by Xavier Chabot, "Synthesis of the Singing Voice Using a Physically Parametrized Model of the Human Vocal Tract," by Perry R. Cook, "CONTOUR: A Real-Time MIDI System Based on Gestural Input," by Arne Eigenfeldt, "DMIX: An Environment for Composition," by Daniel V. Oppenheim, "MIDI SHARE: A Real-Time Multi-Tasks Software Module for MIDI Applications," by Yann Orlarey and Harvé Lequay, "Modeling Musical Structures as Even Generators," by Stephen Travis Pope, and "COMMON MUSIC: A Compositional

Language in Common Lisp and CLOS," by Heinrich Taube. A number of reports on the operations of various electronic music studios were also included. Most of the papers have bibliographies. There is no index.

252. **Proceedings of the International Computer Music Conference. ICMC 1991.** Bo Alphonce & Bruce Pennycook, eds. Montreal, Canada: McGill University, 1991. [xv.] 594p. illus.

The 1991 International Computer Music Conference was co-produced by the International Computer Music Association and the Réseaux des Arts Médiatiques. It was held at McGill University, Montreal, Canada, October 16 - 20. The keynote address, "Viewpoints on the History of Digital Synthesis," was given by Julius Orion Smith, III. This conference included 130 papers (all included in the Proceedings), two special panel sessions, nineteen demonstrations, and a Forum on the Preservation of Electro-Acoustic Music. The sessions are divided into subject areas with three to six papers each. Some of the papers presented include (Session 6: Composition Systems 2) "Sound Models: The Representation of Knowledge about Sound-Synthesis in the CPL Environment," by Peter Luden, "A Phase Vocoder Graphical Interface for Timbral Manipulation of Cellular Automata and Fractal Landscape Mappings," by A. I. Katrami, R. Kirk, & A. Mayatt, "Interactive Music Composition with a Minimum of Input States," by Justin R. Shuttleworth, & "PAT-PROC: An Interactive, Pattern-Process, Algorithmic Composition Program," by Phil Winsor; (Session 7: Sound Synthesis Techniques 1) "A Multiprocessor DSP System for Real-Time Interactive Sound Processing and Synthesis," by John A. Bates, "Additive Synthesis and Resynthesis: A Tentatively Objective Evaluation," by Louis N. Bélanger, "A MIDI Foot Controller - The Podoboard," by Eric Johnstone, & "Parametric Spectrumization" by Nil Parent; (Session 14: Sound Synthesis Systems 2) "Sine Circuit: 10,000 High Quality Sine Waves Without Detours," by Cor Jansen, "An Expandable Real-Time Transputer Sound Generator," by Avi Parash & Uri Shimony, "T-MAX: a Parallel Processing Development System for MAX," by Bruce Pennycook & Chris Lea, & "Morphological Mutation Functions: Applications to Motivic Transformation and to a New Class of Time Domain Cross-Synthesis Techniques," by Larry Polansky & Martin McKinney; (Session 25: Interactive Performance Systems 3) "MAX Objects for Media Integration," by Adrian Freed, David Wessel & David Zicarelli, "CASCADES: Interactive Algorithmic Performance," by George W. Logemann, "The Expanded Instrument Systems (EIS)," by Pauline Oliverous, & "Hierarchical Real Time Interapplication Communications," by Yann Orlarey; (Session 20: Composition Theory

1) "Deriving a Quarter-Tone Harmonic Language Using Harmonic Spectra and Their Formant Regions as a Model for Chord Voicings," by Ronald B. Smith, "The Architecture of a Musical Composition System Based on Constraint Resolution and Graph Rewriting," by Mynam Desainte-Catherine, "A Tool for Manipulating Expressive and Structural Hierarchies in Music," by Stephen Travis Pope, & "A Theory of Poetry as Music and Its Exploration through a Computer Aid to Composition," by Fred Lerdahl & Xavier Chabot; (Session 22: Sound Synthesis Techniques 3) "Generalized Time Functions," by Peter Desain & Henkjan Honing, "Further Experiments with Non-Linear Dynamic Systems: Composition and Digital Synthesis," by Agostino Di Scipio, "An Analysis-by-Synthesis Approach to Sinusoidal Modeling Applied to the Analysis and Synthesis of Musical Tones," by E. Bryan George & Mark J. T. Smith, & "Implementation of the KL Synthesis Algorithm Under Real-Time Control," by W. Brent Weeks, W. Andrew Schloss & R. Lynn Kirlin. An author index is also included.

253. **Proceedings of the International Computer Music Conference. 1992. ICMC 1992.** Alan Strange, Director. San Jose State Univ., San Jose, CA: Computer Music Association, 1992. xiii. 497p. illus.

The 1992 International Computer Music Conference was held in San Jose, California, October 14-18. In addition to San Jose State University, the event was sponsored by the Center for Computer Research in Music and Acoustics, Stanford University, and the Center for New Music and Audio Technologies of the University of California at Berkeley. The chairman of the event was Allen Strange. The keynote speaker was Max Mathews, Professor of Music Research at the Stanford University Center for Computer Research in Music and Acoustics (CCRMA). His address was entitled "My View of the Future of Real-Time Computer Music." Seven concerts of electronic music were given at the event. The sessions were divided into seventeen subject areas including "Analysis/ Synthesis," "Cognitive Science Approaches," "Physical Models," "Real-Time Software," "Controllers," "Music Representation," "Optical Recognition of Musical Symbols," "Specialization," "Synthesis Control," "Studio Reports," "Realizations," "Rhythm and Expression," "Software Environments," "The MARS Project At IRIS," "Poster Sessions," and "Demonstration Sessions." Some of the sessions included "Extended Nonlinear Waveshaping Analysis/Synthesis Technique," by James Beauchamp & Andrew Horner, "Timescale Modification and Wavelet Representations," by Daniel P. W. Ellis, "Additive Resynthesis of Sounds Using Continuous Time-Frequency Analysis Techniques," by Philippe Guillemain & R. Kronland-Martinet, "A Sinusoidal Synthesis

Algorithm for Generating Transitions Between Notes," by Bryan
Holloway & Lippold Haken, "Wavetable and FM Matching Synthesis
of Musical Instrument Tones," by Andrew Horner, James Beauchamp &
Lippold Haken, "The Musical Intrigue of Pole-Zero Pairs," by Dana C.
Massie & Virginia L. Stonick, "Implementation of An Analysis / Synthe-
sis System on a DSPG56001 for General Purpose Sound Processing," by
Rupert C. Nieberle & Michael Warstat, "Making Digital Filters Sound
'Analog'," by Dave Rossum, "Prototyping and Interpolation of Multiple
Musical Timbres Using Principle Component-Based Synthesis," by
Gregory J. Sandell & William L. Martens, "Toward a Unification of Al-
gorithmic Composition, Real-Time Software Synthesis, and Live Perfor-
mance Interaction," by Brian Belet, "DKompose: A Package for Inter-
active Composition in the Max Environment, Adapted To the Acoustic
MIDI Disklavier Piano," by Simon Bolzinger, "Iconic Programming for
HMSL," by Phil Burk & Robert Marsanyi, "Introduction to the Interactor
Language" by Mark Coniglio, "Real-Time Software Synthesis on
Superscaler Architectures," by Roger B. Dannenberg & Clifford W.
Mercer, "New Tools for Rapid Prototyping of Musical Sound Synthesis
Algorithms and Control Strategies," by Adrian Freed, "Score Following
in Practice," by Miller Puchette & Cort Lippe, "Parsing Real-Time Musi-
cal Inputs and Spontaneously Generating Musical Forms: Hierarchical
Form Generator (HFG)," by David Rosenboom, "Improvisation
Builder: Improvisation as Conversation," by William Walker, Kurt
Hebel, Salvatore Martirano & Carla Scaletti, "More on Morphological
Mutation Functions: Recent Techniques and Developments," by Larry
Polansky, "An AI Tool for the Analysis and Generation of Melodies," by
Matt Smith & Simon Holland, "A Connectionist System for Exploring
Melody Space," by Peter M. Todd, "Music Technology as a Form of
Parasite," by David Zicarelli, "The Light Baton: A System for Conduct-
ing Computer Music Performance," by Graziano Bertini & Paolo Carosi,
"Dynamical Modeling of the Grand Piano Action," by Brent Gillespie,
"The Continuum: A Continuous Music Keyboard," by Lippold Haken,
Radi Abdulla & Mark Smart, "Real Time Control of 3D Sound Space by
Gesture," by Tsutomu Harada, Akio Sato, Shuji Hashimoto & Sadamu
Ohteru, "A Programmable MIDI Instrument Controller Emulating a
Hammer Dulcimer," by Randy C. Marchany & Joseph G. Tront, "A Sys-
tem for Computer Assisted Gestural Improvisation," by Emile Tobenfeld,
"The Making of 'Wildlife': Species of Interaction," by David A. Jaffe &
W. Andrew Schloss, "A Meta-Wind-Instrument Physical Model, and a
Meta-Controller for Real-Time Performance Control," by Perry R. Cook,
and "Connectionist Models for Real-Time Control of Synthesis and
Compositional Algorithms," by Michael Lee & David Wessel. Also,
some of the studio reports included "The Activities of CRM (Centro

Ricerche Musicali)," by Alessandra de Vitis, "The Constance J. Upchurch Studio for Electro-Acoustic Music," by Gerald Gabel & Jay Upchurch, "The Center for Computer Music Research and Composition," by JoAnn Kuchera-Morin & Douglas Scott, "Studio Report from the KACOR Multimedia Lab," by Peter Lundén, Peter Rajka & Tamas Ungvary, "Studio Report: SUNY, Buffalo," by Peter Otto, "Musical Creation at Ateliers UPIC and CEMAMu," by Gerard Pape, Jean-Michel Raczinski, Gerard Marino & Marie Helene Serra, "The University of Texas Accelerando Project: An Update," by Russell Pinkston, and "Studio Report: Composition Studios, School of Music, University of Auckland, New Zealand," by John Rimmer & John Elmsly. The work also includes an author and subject index.

254. **Proceedings of the 1994 International Computer Music Conference. ICMC 1994.** Wayne Siegel, Chairman. San Francisco, CA: Internationalal Computer Music Association, 1994. xxi. 506p. illus.

The 1994 International Computer Music Conference was held at the Musikhuset in Aarhus, Denmark, September 12 - 17, 1994. The theme of the conference was "The Human Touch," and concentrated on the role of humans in computer music. The conference included poster sessions, concerts, demonstrations, workshops, and papers. The keynote address, "Touching the Public," was given by Trevor Wishart. More than 120 papers were presented over the 6 day period. Subjects of the papers included "Music Works," "Aesthetics, Philosophy, Criticism," "Psychoacoustics, Perception," "Machine Recognition of Music," "Machine Recognition of Music-Foot-Tapping," "Expressive Performance Analysis," "Neural Nets," "Genetic Algorithms," "Interactive Performance," "Composition, Composition Systems," "Music Workstations," "Music Languages," "Music Representation, Data Structures," "Music Graphics," "Music Notation," "Audio Signal Processing," "Audio Analysis and Re-Synthesis," "Sound Synthesis Techniques," "Audio Hardware, Networking," "Acoustics and Simulation," and "Education, Studio Reports." Some of the more unusual papers presented include the selections on machine recognition of music and included "Kant: a Critique of Pure Quantification," by Gerard Assayag et al., "Pattern Processing in Music," by Robert Towe & Tang-Chun Li, "Automating Ensemble Performance," by Lorin Grubb & Roger B. Dannenberg, and "Adaptive Karaoke System: Human Singing Accompaniment Based on Speech Recognition," by Wataru Inoue & Shuji Hashimoto. Papers on electronic music composition included "Formal Processes of Timbre Composition Challenging the Dualistic Paradigm of Computer Music," by Agostino Di Scipio, "Algorithms Adapted from Chaos Theory:

Compositional Considerations," by James Harley, "The Morpho Concepts: Trends in a Software for Acousmatic Music Composition," by Daniel Teruggi, "A Common Lisp Interface for Dynamic Patching with the IRCAM Signal Processing Workstation," by Thomas Hummel, "Design and Implementation of an Object-Oriented Media Composition Framework," by Philipp Ackermann, and "The Communal Groove Machine," by Amnon Wolman & Canton Becker. The proceedings also have an author and subject index.

255. **Proceedings of the International Computer Music Conference. ICMC, 1995.** Rich Bidlack, Chairman. San Francisco, CA: The International Computer Music Association, 1995. xvi. 605p. illus.

The 1995 International Computer Music Conference was held at the Banff Centre for the Arts, Banff, Alberta, Canada, September 3 - 7. More than 240 abstracts of papers, concerts, posters, demos and studio reports were presented in a number of subjects including "Esthetics and Criticism," "Studio Reports," "Chaos, theory and synthesis," "Architecture," "Approaches to Physical Modeling and Synthesis," "Computer music and media," "Issues in interactive performance," "Representations, Recognition and archives," "Motion detection and gesture analysis," "Pitch tracking and noise reduction," "Synthesis and processing tools," "Waveguide II: strings and piano," "Graphical interfaces," "Signal processing pot-pourri," "Neural networks and signal processing," "Algebras and algorithms," "Spectra and timbre," "Waveguide synthesis I: winds," "Grammars," and "Computer music and culture." This conference included an unusual number of posters in order to present many of the ideas, systems & concepts submitted by the more than 190 individuals. Also, many of the systems were demonstrated for an entire day. Studio reports include "CCRMA Studio Report," by Fernando Lopez-Lezcano, "The International Digital Electroacoustic Music Archive," by Marcia L. Bauman & Thomas Gerwin, "The Institute of Electroacoustics and Experimental Music at the Vienna University of Music," by Tamas Ungvary & Peter Mechtler, "The Electroacoustic Music Studio at the Royal Academy of Music, Copenhagen," by Ivar Frounberg, "Computer Music Studios at Michigan State University," by Mark Sullivan, and "Computer Music at the University of Bradford," by Anna I. Katrami, Peter J. Comerford & Barry M. Eaglestone. In addition to many papers on computer music systems and equipment there were papers presented on newer subjects such as motion detection, gestural analysis, and chaos theory & synthesis including "Interactive Dance/Music Systems," by Antonio Camurri, "The Sentograph: Input Devices and the Communication of Bodily Expression," by Roel

Vertegall & Tamas Ungvary, "Gesture Analysis Using 3D Acceleration Sensor for Music Control," by Hideyuki Sawada et al., "Making Motion Musical: Gesture Mapping Strategies for Interactive Computer Music," by Todd Winkler, "Sensor Integration for Interactive Digital Art," by Tsutomu Kanamori et al., "A Physical Model of Recorder-Like Instruments," by Marc-Pierre Verge, Rene Caussé & Avraham Hirschberg, "Experiments with Chaotic Oscillators," by Richard Dobson & John Fitch, "Chaotic Predictive Modeling of Sound," by Jonathan P. Mackenzie, and "Adding Vortex Noise to Wind Instrument Physical Models," by Chris Chafe. The proceedings volume also contains indexes by author and subject.

Appendix A:
Theses and Dissertations

The growth of interest in electronic and computer-generated music is reflected in the increasing number of theses and dissertations written on the subjects at universities and colleges. The *Comprehensive Dissertation Index,* [1] published by Xerox University Microfilms, lists most theses and dissertations written in American and Canadian colleges and universities (some European and Australian are also included) from 1861 to the present. A search of this index shows that more than 150 theses and dissertations have been written on topics related to electronic music during that time. Of these theses and dissertations a relatively large number (more than 50) are original compositions, and the rest are generally analyses of some aspect of electronic music. The growth of interest in the study of electronic music has increased dramatically through the years. From 1940 through 1969 seven theses or dissertations were written on the subject, but during the decade of the 1970s this number had increased to 27 items. During the decade of the 1980s more than 60 theses and dissertations were written on electronic and computer music. And this trend continues in the 1990s with 60 items listed from 1990 through the end of 1995.

Two of the early dissertations on the subject involve analysis of music using digital computers (see Harvey Roller & Robin Gatwood below), but in 1968 Ronald Pellegrino wrote an original electronic music composition at the University of Wisconsin-Madison as part of his Ph. D. dissertation. (see Pellegrino below) During that same year, Brian Fennelly wrote a dissertation at Yale University that explored a notation system for electronic music, and Thomas

---

[1] *Comprehensive Dissertation Index.* Ann Arbor, MI: Xerox University Microfilms, *1961-* . (annual)

Wells wrote *Systems of Electronic and Instrumental Music* which is an original composition and a commentary on electronic music. (see Brian Fennelly and Thomas Wells below) Another important early dissertation on the subject is David Jensen's *Basic Principles of Electronic Sound Synthesis* written for his Ph. D. at Florida State University. This is one of the first dissertations to explore the use of synthesizers for the production of music composition.

Listed below are most of the theses and dissertations found in the *Dissertation Abstracts Index* in the area of electronic and computer music. These items may be obtained in microform copy or in bound paper copy by writing, or calling Xerox University Microfilms at P. O. Box 1764, Ann Arbor, MI 48106-1764. 1-800-521-3042. (The Interlibrary Loan departments of most larger public or academic libraries will be able to assist in obtaining theses and dissertations from Xerox University Microfilms, but they are not generally available for loan from the universities where they were produced.) The accession number for Xerox University Microfilms has been listed in each citation. Brief explanations of the contents of the items are included when the title is not self explanatory.

Ackerman, Anthony. **A Collection of Environmental Compositions.** (Original Composition) The University of California, Santa Barbara, 1989. Ph. D. 69p. No. AAG9016134. This dissertation contains six compositions; two are in written score form, and four are on 1/4 inch tape.

Agbenyega, Stephen Tete. **Libation: Music Written for Two Pianos and Electronic Tape With Essay on Space-Time and Implications for African Music.** Columbia University Teachers College, 1983. Ed. D. 292p. No. AAG8322171.

Alewine, Murry Lee. **The Establishment and Utilization of an Electronic Music Studio in Small College and Universities.** University of Miami, 1973. Ph. D. 136p. No. AAG7403474.

Alvarez, Geoffrey Neil. **Folio of Compositions.** (Original Composition) University of York (England), 1989. D. Phil. 1p. No. AAGC185918. These compositions use live electronic modification of sound behind a screen for voice, bassoon, and synthesizer.

Anderson, John Davis. **The Influence of Scientific Concepts on the Music and Thought of Edgard Varèse.** (Aesthetic Approach) University of Northern Colorado, 1984. D. A. 143p. No. AAG8418115.

Austin, Leslie E. **Rock Music, The Microchip, and the Collaborative**

Performer: Issues Concerning Musical Performance, Electronics and the Recording Studio. New York University, 1993. Ph. D. 305p. No. AAG9333606.

Baitz, Richard Keith. **The Riverfisher, Part 1, [original composition] and, The Riverfisher, Part 1: A Written Analytical Commentary.** Columbia University, 1991. D. M. A. 179p. No. AAG9202651. This composition was realized using a Yamaha DX7™ digital synthesizer.

Benson, Mark Elling. **Fount: Chamber Music for Voices, Instruments and Loudspeakers.** (Original Composition) Michigan State University, 1987. Ph. D. 139p. No. AAG8801792.

Bernardin, Paul Andre. **To Maynard on the Long Road Home: For Mixed Ensemble, Vocalists, Narrator, and Electronic Tape.** (Original Composition) State University of New York at Buffalo, 1990. Ph. D. 223p. No. AAG9033684.

Blackinton, David P. **Lecture Recital: An Analysis of the Work "Something Else" for Solo Trumpet and Electronic Tape by Edward Diemente.** The Catholic University of America, 1974. D. M. A. 1p. No. AAG-0286836.

Blumenthal, Paul Steven. **P. T. Barnum: A Work for Dancers, Musicians and Electronic Tape.** (Original Composition) University of Maryland-College Park, 1978. D. M. A. 59p. No. AAG7905455.

Bonneau, Paul Gregory. **A Capella Electronnica.** (Original Composition) University of North Texas, 1995. M. Mus. No. AAI1375471. This thesis is a single movement work (14 min.) scored for vocal quartet (soprano, alto, tenor, bass) that was later electronically processed by two digital sound processors (Yamaha SPX1000™ multi-effects processor, and the Ensoniq DP/4™ parallel effects processor).

Brandenburg, Octavia Leigh. **Aspects of Performance in Three Works for Piano and Tape: Larry Austin's "Sonata Concertante," Thomas Clark's "Peninsula," and Phil Winsor's "Passages."** University of North Texas, 1993. D. M. A. 83p. No. AAG9326617. This dissertation describes performance aspects in compositions for piano and tape through the use of three works: *Sonata Concertante* by Larry Austin, *Peninsula* by Thomas Clark, and *Passages* by Phil Winsor.

Bridwell, Barry O. **The Multi-Percussion Writing of William Kraft in His**

"Encounters" Series with Three Recitals of Selected Works of Erb, Ptaszynska, Redel, Serry, and Others. University of North Texas, 1993. D. M. A. 116p. No. AAG- 9326618. This dissertation reports on a series of ten works that cover the years 1966 to 1992 which include chamber works, a solo with electronic tape, a solo with quartet accompaniment, and two unaccompanied solos.

Bullock, Barbara Joan. **A Comprehensive Performance Project in Clarinet Literature With a Thesis Consisting of an Original Composition: "Psalm 37" for Electronic Tape and Three Performers.** The University of Iowa., 1989. D. M. A. 96p. No. AAG9019991.

Burke, Barbara Patricia. **Electronic Detection of Nasality in the Singing Voice Using Waveshape Analysis.** The Florida State University, 1982. Ph. D. 205p. No. AAG8217968.

Butler, John Harrison. **Personality Factors as Correlates of Receptivity to Electronic Music.** University of Georgia, 1968. Ed. D. 150p. No. AAG6909474.

Byars, Janita Kay Ashby. **A Study and Recital of Selected Compositions for Clarinet and Electronic Music.** Columbia University, 1972. Ed. D. 175p. No. AAG7302582.

Byrd, Donaldson Toussaint L'Ouverture, II. **The Performance and Analysis of an Original Afro-American Musical Composition for Trumpet and Orchestra.** Columbia University Teachers College, 1983. Ed. D. 103p. No. AAG8403292. The purpose of this study was to create an original composition for trumpet and orchestra which also has a section for improvisation with a jazz rhythm section that includes electronic instruments.

Cann, Richard Louis. **Speech Analysis: Synthesis for Electronic Vocal Music.** Princeton University, 1978. Ph. D. 191p. No. AAG7823506.

Caplan, Stephen Frank. **Three Programs of Oboe Music.** (Performance) The University of Michigan, 1992. A. Mus. D. 1p. No. AAG0571975. This recital ended with *Sonic Landscapes* for Oboe and taped electronic music written by Mark Phillips.

Chabot, Xavier Luc. **Performance with Electronics: Gesture Interfaces and Software Toolkit.** University of California, San Diego, 1989. Ph. D. 69p. No. AAG9013655.

Chang, Juie-Wen. **Summary of Dissertation Recitals: Three Programs of Percussion Music.** (Performance) The University of Michigan, 1995. D. M. A. 1p. No. AAI0576570. The composer uses three recitals of percussion instruments including a solo mallet-keyboard, chamber music, solo multiple percussion, and percussion instruments with electronic tape.

Cooper, Robert Lee. **Streams.** (Original Composition-Computer Assisted, Orchestra, Tape) University of Missouri-Kansas City, 1992. D. M. A. 70p. No. AAG9239636.

Costinesco, George. **"The Musical Seminar": A Music-Theatre Piece for Electronic Organ, Trombone, Bass, Piano, Percussion, Two Additional Musicians, Actors, and Electronic Tape.** Columbia University, 1976. D. M. A. 561p. No. AAG7819320.

Criswell, James Alan. **The Horn in Mixed-Media Compositions Through 1991.** University of Maryland-College Park, 1995. D. M. A. 170p. No. AAI9539765. The purpose of this thesis is to "examine the extent which the horn has been utilized in juxtaposition with other audio and visual media. These mixed-media compositions combine musical parameters of timbre, texture and time relation with nontraditional devices ranging from electronic media to lighting and slides." (Abstract)

Crowe, Don Raymond. **Error Detection Abilities of Conducting Students Under Four Modes of Instrumental Score Study.** The University of Arizona, 1994. D. M. A. 186p. No. AAG9426218. Mr. Crowe uses students in beginning conducting classes to explore four score study styles: 1) no score study, 2) study with score alone, 3) study with score and a correct aural example, and 4) study at the electronic keyboard.

Davidson, George Rusty. **Music for Electric Guitar and String Quartet in Three Movements.** (Original Composition). San Jose State University, 1995. M. A. 31p. No. AAI1375680. Mr. Davidson's thesis is an original composition that combines the amplified sound of the electric guitar with the acoustic sound of the string quartet. He points out in his Abstract that "this thesis blends old and new with due respect for the continuum of Western music."

Davis, Jolene Rae. **A Survey of Music for Organ and Tape Published Prior to 1981.** University of Kansas, 1981. D. M. A. 94p. No. AAG8208074.

De Graaf, Thomas George. **St. John, Seventeen (A Twentieth-Century**

Oratorio) and Sanctuary of His Praise. (Original Composition) The Southern Baptist Theological Seminary, 1984. 379p. No. AAG8619029. This work is written for reinforcement electronic amplification and scored for electronic synthesizers as substitutes for the string instruments.

De Sena, Ferdinando V. **Requiem for the Living.** (Original Composition for Chorus and Electronic Music) University of Miami, 1994. D. M. A. 195p. No. AAI9519718. This composition is realized through chorus and electronic synthesizers, digital samplers, and digital audio processors under MIDI control.

Deal, William Scott. **Electronic Percussion Controllers: Their Application in Electronic Realization and Live Performance of "Embers," by John Van Der Slice and "A Change of Scenery," by Robin Cox.** University of Miami, 1994. D. M. R. 128p. No. AAI9519719. This dissertation is both an essay on percussion controllers and a live performance of two pieces for percussion.

Del Monaco, Alfredo. **"Electronic Study No. 3."** (Original Composition) Columbia University, 1975. D. M. A. 70p. No. AAG7527397.

Denton, David Bryan. **The Composition as Aesthetic Polemic: "December 1952" By Earle Brown.** The University of Iowa, 1992. Ph. D. 142p. No. AAG9235817.

Doerksen, David Paul. **Development of Individualized Electronic Rhythmic Instruction.** University of Oregon, 1972. D. M. A. 95p. No. AAG730-7881.

Duehlmeier, Susan Hunter. **Vladimir Ussachevsky: Life and Works with Emphasis on the Piano Compositions.** Boston University, 1985. Mus. A. D. 138p. No. AAG8522953.

Fabregas, Elisenda. **Designing and Implementing an Electronic Music Program in a Community Music School in New York City.** Columbia University Teachers College, 1992. Ed. D. 383p. No. AAG9228460.

Faulk, Harry Robert. **A Curriculum Guide Designed to Teach a Basic Knowledge of Electronic Music to Undergraduate Music Education Students.** Carnegie-Mellon University, 1978. D. A. 127p. No. AAG791-6175.

Faust, Randall Edward. **A Comprehensive Performance Project in Horn Literature with an Essay Consisting of Three Original Concertpieces for Horn and Electronic Media, an Explanation of Techniques Used, and a Listing of Relevant Literature.** The University of Iowa, 1980. D. M. A. 138p. No. AAG8114321.

Fennelly, Brian Leo. **A Descriptive Notation for Electronic Music.** Yale University, 1968. Ph. D. 169p. No. AAG6908343.

Fetterman, William Benson. **John Cage's Theatre Pieces: Notations and Performances.** New York University, 1992. Ph. D. 500p. No. AAG922-2877.

Frykberg, Susan. **Woman and House: The Creation of a Performance Work Combining Elements of Electronic Music, Vocal Work, Theatre, Storytelling and Ritual.** (Original Performance) Simon Fraser University, Canada, 1991. M. A. 119p. No. AAGMM69458.

Gabura, Andrew James. **An Analog/Hybrid Instrument for Electronic Music Synthesis.** University of Toronto, 1974. Ph. D. (np) No. AAG0506843.

Gamper, David Edwards. **Preliminaries to Electronic Music Studio Designing.** University of California, San Diego, 1973. M. A. (Not Available Through Xerox University Microfilms-Contact University Directly.)

Gardner, Burgess Lamarr. **The Development and Testing of a Basic Self-Instructional Program for the ARP 2600 Portable Electronic Synthesizer and Effects on Attitudes Toward Electronic Music.** Michigan State University, 1978. Ph. D. 102p. No. AAG7900693.

Gatwood, Robin Frederick. **The Application of Certain Types of Electronic Equipment to the Teaching of Music. Part I. (Part II: A Handbook for the Help and Guidance of Teachers of Applied Music.)** New York University, 1960. Ed. D. 307p. No. AAG6100364.

Gatzert, Eric William. **DMX-1000 User Guide and Tutorials.** (Computer Music) San Jose State University, 1989. M. S. 329p. No. AAG13378 03.

Glinsky, Albert Vincent. **The Theremin in the Emergence of Electronic Music.** (Soviet Union, Musical Instruments) New York University, 1992. Ph. D. 417p. No. AAG9237752.

Godvovitch, Standley I. **Philosophical Problems of Musical Performance.** The University of Maryland-College Park, 1990. Ph. D. 295p. No. AAG9030899. This dissertation explores, among other things, modern electronic technology and its tendency to make certain musical tasks vastly easier to accomplish with greatly reduced skill.

Goldman, Erica Hillary. **The Effect of Original and Electronically Altered Oboe, Clarinet, and French Horn Timbres on Absolute Pitch Judgments.** University of Oregon, 1984. D. M. A. 180p. No. AAG8422845.

Gross, Robert Wenzel. **A Comparison of Active Experience and Lecture-Discussion Methodology as Means for Developing Musical Knowledge, Musical Discrimination, and Musical Preference within an Electronic Music Course at the High School Level.** The Pennsylvania State University, 1984. D. Ed. 160p. No. AAG8429084.

Helfrich, Paul Michael. **Soundscapes for Orchestra and Tape: Considerations for Its Construction and a Brief Analysis of its Significant Structural Determinants.** (Original Composition) Temple University, 1987. D. M. A. 124p. No. AAG8711347.

Henry, Otto Walker. **The Evolution of Idiomatic and Psychoacoustical Resources as a Basis for Unity in Electronic Music.** Tulane University, 1970. Ph. D. 284p. No. AAG7024525.

Hinkle-Turner, Anna Elizabeth. **Daria Semegen: Her Life, Work, and Music.** University of Illinois at Urbana-Champaign, 1991. D. M. A. 169p. No. AAG9210837. Daria Semegen was director of electronic music studios at the State University of New York-Stony Brook.

Holmes, Reed Kelley. **Relation Systems and Process in Recent Works of Luciano Berio.** (V. 1: Concepts and Analysis. V. 2: Examples) The University of Texas at Austin, 1981. Ph. D. 349p. No. AAG8128638.

Holmes, William Dewey. **Style and Technique in Selected Works for Tuba and Electronic Prepared Tape: A Lecture Recital, Together with Three Recitals of Selected Works of V. Perschitti, A. Cappuzzi, E. Gregson, W. Ross, N. K. Brown, and Others.** University of North Texas, 1985. D. M. A. 58p. No. AAG8604555.

Irvin, Nathaniel, II. **A Voice Crying in the Wilderness: An Opera Based on the Life of John The Baptist.** (Original Opera) The University of North Texas, 1987. D. M. A. 655p. No. AAG8723764. This opera is scored for string orchestra, amplified solo viola, and two electronic digital keyboards.

Jacobs, Sara Johanna. **The Compositions of Hans Roosenschoon.** University of South Africa (South Africa), 1987. M. Mus. 1p. No. AAG0663384. Roosenschoon mainly composed traditional symphonic works but did distinguish himself as a composer of electronic music later in his career.

Jaffe, Peter. **Edgard Varèse's Orchestral and Ensemble Works: History, Theory and Conducting Analyses.** Stanford University, 1989. D. M. A. 274p. No. AAG8925813.

Jagosz, Kenneth Paul. **An Electronic Music Studio: Design and Construction.** California State University, Long Beach, 1979. M. A. 74p. No. AAG1313217.

James, Richard Schmidt. **Expansion of Sound Resources in France, 1913-1940, and Its Relationship to Electronic Music.** The University of Michigan, 1981. Ph. D. 345p. No. AAG8116258.

Jenkins, Kevin Joseph. **A Study of Seven Compositions for Tuba and Electronic Sound Source.** Arizona State University, 1994. D. M. A. 95p. No. AAG9500726. Mr. Jenkins' dissertation explores the solo repertoire of the tuba through the analysis of a number of compositions for tuba and electronic sound source.

Jensen, David E. **Basic Principles of Electronic Sound Synthesis.** The Florida State University, 1972. Ph. D. 251p. No. AAG7304204.

Johnson, Jeffrey Scott. **Waiting Looking Reflecting: A Journey Through Self.** (Original Compositions and Video) The University of Iowa, 1990. Ph. D. 96p. No. AAG9112436. Audio elements on tape for this dissertation were made at the University of Iowa Experimental Music Studio II.

Johnson, Kenneth Brettell. **"To The Young": An Examination of Vladimir Ussachevsky's Last Choral Composition.** California State University, Long Beach, 1995. M. M. 56p. No. AAI1362414. This thesis is a study of Vladimir Ussachevsky's last choral composition entitled *To The Young*. While the work is not concerned with Ussachevsky's electronic music, it does study the contribution Ussachevsky made to purely choral music.

Kim, Haeyon. **Concerto for Saxophone.** (Original Composition) The

University of Texas at Austin, 1991. D. M. A. 156p. No. AAG9200575. This work was realized on computer-generated electronic tape.

Klimko, Ronald James. **Echoes: A Dance Cantata for Mixed Chorus, Orchestra, and Electronic Sounds.** (Original Composition) The University of Wisconsin-Madison, 1968. Ph. D. 214p. No. AAG6809089.

Kneupper, David Joseph. **The Soundscape to "Heartbeat": A Narrative-Form Music Video.** Texas Tech. University, 1988. Ph. D. 48p. No. AAG8819406. This work combines the aesthetic potentials of telecommunications and digital synthesis technologies as a pioneering effort in electronic synthesis.

Kohl, Jerome Joseph. **Serial and Non-Serial Techniques in the Music of Karlheinz Stockhausen from 1962-1968.** University of Washington, 1981. Ph. D. 273p. No. AAG8212566.

Kuderna, Jerome George. **Analysis and Performance of Selected Piano Works of Milton Babbitt. (b. 1916)** New York University, 1982. Ph. D. 179p. No. AAG8226774.

Lee, Nohee Kwak. **The Representative Solo Piano Works of John Wilham Downey. (b. 1927)** The University of Wisconsin-Madison, 1993. D. M. A. 193p. No. AAG9318626. This thesis is an analysis of the solo piano works of John Wilham Downey, a leading American composer who experimented with music realized on electronic tape.

Lehr, Lester Eugene. **The Effect of an Instructional Unit of Electronic Music on the Musical Achievement of Students in College Basic Musicianship and Music Theory Classes.** University of Southern California, 1980. D. M. A. (np) No. AAG0533745.

Lieberman, Glenn. **A Discussion of Concertino.** (Original Composition and Thesis) Columbia University, 1989. D. M. A. 235p. No. AAG891-9167. This dissertation is a nineteen-minute, original composition for solo viola, 2 flutes/piccolos, bass clarinet, contrabass, piano, and Yamaha™ DX-7 synthesizer.

Little, Jeanie Rebecca. **Serial, Aleatoric, and Electronic Techniques in American Music Published Between 1960 and 1972.** The University of Iowa, 1975. Ph. D. 242p. No. AAG7613412.

Lovendusky, James Vincent. **Part I: Voices and Creatures** (Original

Composition)**; and, Part II: Subsets of the Eight Sound-Color Collection.** (Vocal music, Timbre, Electronic Music Composition) University of Pittsburgh, 1986. Ph. D. 163p. No. AAG8702013.

Maldonado, Carlos Daniel. **Keyboard Performance Techniques Required for Music Synthesizers. (Electronic).** University of Illinois at Urbana-Champaign, 1994. 313p. No. AAI9512475. In this dissertation Mr. Maldonado explores the questions: "What keyboard skills do expert synthesists consider important in the development of performance proficiency on the synthesizer." (Abstract)

Marin, Servio Tulio. **The Concept of the Visonual, Aural, and Visual Associations in Twentieth Century Music Theatre.** University of California, San Diego, 1994. Ph. D. 132p. "This work demonstrates with experiments on instrumental, electronic, and music theatre the Visonual metaphorical construction: music can be heard through the eyes and seen through the ears. According to Foucault's collateral, correlative, and complementary spaces (1969) and in correlative, and complementary spaces (1969) and in Deleuzian and Guattarian (1980) terms as well as in Emily Hicks' model of holography (1991) the visonual metaphor results [in] several aesthetical, psychoacoustical, and cultural factors from the deterritorialization of the aural and visual senses." (Abstract)

Maris, Barbara English. **American Compositions for Piano and Tape Recorded Sound.** (Volumes 1 and 2) Peabody Institute of the Johns Hopkins University, 1976. D. M. A. 565p. No. AAG8200450.

Matthews, Wade Albert. **Two Structures for Improvisation** (Original Composition) Columbia University, 1992. D. M. A. 149p. No. AAG9221187. "This dissertation explores music for magnetic tape, and the affect of electronic music on notation and the concept of 'the work'." (Abstract)

McCreary, Richard Deming, Jr. **Z. (Original Composition for a Combination of Taped Electronic and Concrete Sounds with Instrumental Sounds.)** The University of Iowa, 1974. Ph. D. 30p. No. AAG75012- 29.

McNeil, Joe Bailey. **"Sonic Images," "Light Years," and "Kaleidoscope."** (Original Compositions for Electronic Synthesizer & Tape) California State University, Long Beach, 1985. M. A. 92p. No. AAG1325764.

Meachem, Margaret McKeen Ramsey. **"Alice in Wonderland," A Chamber Opera in One Act.** (Original Composition) University of Maryland-

College Park, 1982. D. M. A. 88p. No. AAG8308757. The author of this dissertation claims that it uses "pure electronic sound" but no other details are provided in the Abstract.

Mecham, Mark Leonidas. **The Choral Music of Vladimir Ussachevsky.** University of Illinois at Urbana-Champaign, 1985. D. M. A. 195p. No. AAG8511641.

Miller, Scott Lawrence. **Angel of Progress II.** (Original Composition-Electronic Music). University of Minnesota, 1994. Ph. D. 123p. No. AAG- 9424325. *Angel of Progress II* was composed using a MIDI enabled clarinet with a Pitch Rider MIDI controller. The work was also realized using a Diskclavier™ Grand Piano, a Korg™ Wavestation synthesizer, and an Ensoniq™ ESQ-M synthesizer.

Molyneux, Garth Eckert. **"In Memoriam Kathryne": Five Essays on Madness.** (Original Composition-Electronic Music) The University of Texas at Austin, 1991. D. M. A. 182p. No. AAG9212476. This work was realized using two Yamaha SPX-90™ special effects processors and tape playback.

Montague, Stephen Rowley. **"Voussoirs" For Large Orchestra and Electronic Tapes.** (Original Composition) The Ohio State University, 1972. D. M. A. 63p. No. AAG7301922.

Montalto, Richard Michael. **...For the Time Is at Hand: An Original Musical Composition.** University of North Texas, 1982. D. M. A. 107p. No. AAG8307 903. This composition was realized using a stochastic composition program written in Hewlett-Packard BASIC.

Moylan, William David. **An Analytical System for Electronic Music.** Ball State University, 1983. D. A. 259p. No. AAG8401292.

Muennich, Rose Marie. **The Vocal Works of Jean Eichelberger Ivey.** Michigan State University, 1983. Michigan State University, 1983. Ph. D. 208p. No. AAG8324748. Jean Eichelberger Ivey has written for virtually every medium, and since 1970 her interest has focused on the composition of vocal works in combination with various media and electronic tape.

Muller, Giovanni. **Interaktiv Bearbeitung Konventioneller Musiknotation. [Interactive Editing of Conventional Music Notation]** Universitaet Zurich (Switzerland), 1991. Dr. Sc. Tech. 150p. No. AAGC186398. This study explores an electronic music notation system.

Oppenheim, Daniel Vincent. **Concerto in 'D' for 5 String MIDI Violin (or Cello) and MIX.** (Original Composition-Computer Music) Stanford University, 1993. D. M. A. 107p. No. AAG9414524. The *Concerto in 'D'* is scored for solo 5 string MIDI violin (or cello), three synthesizers, and three signal processors. The hardware is controlled in real-time by a computer program called MIX developed by the composer at the Stanford Center for Computer Research in Music and Acoustics (CCRMA).

Palkowski, Daniel Henry. **"Views of Time": An Analytical and Philosophical Commentary.** (Original Composition) Columbia University, 1992. D. M. A. 234p. No. AAG9232122.

Paredes, Robert Wesley. **"Speakers" As Is As About.** (Original Works) The University of Iowa, 1990. Ph. D. 285p. No. AAG9122096. This dissertation presents a 29 minute original work for sounds on magnetic tape and a written section of words, drawings, photographs, and scores in conventional notation.

Parkinson, William Michael. **An Analysis of the Wind and Jazz Ensemble Music of Donald Erb.** University of Cincinnati, 1991. D. M. A. 215p. No. AAG9215472. Electronic musicians including Varèse are discussed as they relate to Dr. Erb's compositions.

Paxton, Steven Errol. **Music for "Wings."** (Original Composition) Texas Tech University, 1981. Ph. D. 1p. No.AAG0535943. This dissertation describes a production which includes acoustic and electro-acoustic potentials and synthesizer.

Pellegrino, Ronald Anthony. **"The Tale of the Silver Saucer and the Transparent Apple," An Electronic Music Drama.** (Original Composition-with Electronic Studio Manual) The University of Wisconsin-Madison, 1968. Ph. D. 423p. No. AAG6900975.

Pellman, Samuel Frank. **An Overview of Current Practices Regarding the Performance of Electronic Music.** Cornell University, 1978. M. F. A. 160p. No. AAG1314081.

Pethel, Blair Woodruff. **Keith Emerson: The Emergence and Growth of Style: A Study of Selected Works.** Peabody Institute of the Johns Hopkins University, 1988. D. M. A. 132p. No. AAG8923- 915.

Petkus, Janetta. **The Songs of John Cage (1932-1970).** The University of Connecticut, 1986. Ph. D. 266p. No. AAG8622920.

Putnam, Mark Glenn. **B'Resheet--A Ballet Inspired by the Commentaries of Rashi.** (Original Composition) Memphis State University, 1989. D. M. A. 94p. No. AAG8922001. This work makes use of prerecorded electronic sounds played from a tape as part of the instrumental texture.

Radford, Ronald Laurie Charles. **Origophonie** (Original Composition, Percussion, Choir, Electronic Tape) McGill University (Canada), 1988. M. Mus. 196p. No. AAGMM64100.

Ray, Lee Gerry. **Some Technical Determinants of Composition and Performance Practice of Live Electronic Music.** University of California, San Diego, 1988. 1p. No. AAG0564514.

Rhea, Thomas Lamar. **The Evolution of Electronic Musical Instruments in the United States.** Peabody College for Teachers of Vanderbilt University, 1972. Ph. D. 255p. No. AAG7234209.

Rodriguez, Elvin Samuel. **The Use of Hypercard in the Development of Software for Creative Elementary Keyboard Activities.** (Music Software) Columbia University Teachers College, 1991. Ed. D. 143p. No. AAG9210553.

Rogers, Michael W. **The Effects of Aural and Tactual Feedback on Sightreading Music at an Electronic Piano.** Northwestern University, 1989. Ph. D. 403p. No. AAG9009683.

Roller, Gilbert Harvey. **The Development of the Methods for Analysis of Musical Compositions and for the Formation of a Symmetrical Twelve-Tone Row Using the Electronic Digital Computer.** Michigan State University, 1964. Ph. D. 487p. No. AAG6409750.

Rowan, Randy S. **"Sonic Sculptures" for Flute, Cello and Computer Processed Sounds.** (Original Composition) Western Michigan University, 1988. M. M. 34p. No. AAG1334187.

Sargent, David Henry. **Juan Carlos Paz, Self-Taught Twelve-Tonalist and Innovative Argentine Composer: "Apostasy and Restoration, for Orchestra, Choir, Solo Voices and Electronic Tape."** (Original Composition) University of Illinois at Urbana-Champaign, 1975. D. M. A. 258p. No. AAG7606941.

Schryer, Claude. **"A Kindred Spirit" (1985) For Ensemble and Tape.** McGill University (Canada), 1987. M. A. 231p. No. AAGMM75866.

Schwall, James. **Dierore: A Soap Opera, For Singer, Dancers, Players, Electronic Sounds and Projected Images.** (Original Opera) Western Michigan University, 1991. M. M. 139p. No. AAG1343632.

Shaw, Alison Ayers. **Three Programs of Percussion Music.** (Performance) The University of Michigan, 1994. 1p. No. AAG0574722. This is a dissertation recital given in 1993 at the McIntosh Theatre of the School of Music. The second program featured the Music of John Cage including *Sculptures Musicales, Amores, Five, Child of Tree,* and*Third Construction.*

Shaw, Gary Richard. **A Comprehensive Musicianship Approach to Applied Trombone Through Selected Music Literature.** (Performance) The University of Wisconsin-Madison, 1984. D. M. A. 106p. No. AAG-8428900. This dissertation includes a piece called *Animus I* for trombone and electronic tape by Jacob Druckman.

Shinn, Ronald Rulon. **The Mirror Inversion Piano Practice Method and the Mirror Music of Vincent Persichetti.** The University of Alabama, 1990. D. M. A. 123p. No. AAG9105968. The analysis in this dissertation was conducted using an electronic piano and a number of computer programs to assess MIDI information.

Shotola, Marilyn W. *Orfeo I* : **An Analytic Investigation of Thea Musgrave's Work for Flute and Tape, With Performance Guide.** The University of North Texas, 1989. D. M. A. 75p. No. AAG9005359. *Orfeo I* is a major work for flute and electronic tape using manipulated flute sounds.

Slater, Peter. **The Creation and Control of Digital Audio Waveforms: An Investigation into Techniques for the Creation and Real-Time Control of Audio Waveforms Using Data Representations Which Result in Timbral Flexibility and High Audio Quality.** University of Bradford (England), 1988. Ph. D. 241p. No. AAGDX86059.

Smith, Jeffrey B. **Parallels in the Development of Electronic and Percussion Music and an Examination of Performance Problems in Lejaren Hiller's "Machine Music" for Piano, Percussion and Two-Channel Tape Recorder with Three Recitals of Selected Works.** (Electronic Music, Lejaren Hiller, Iannis Xenakis, Neil B. Rolnick, Phil Winsor, Daniel Kessner, Tokuhide Niimi.) University of North Texas, 1992. D.

M. A. 115p. No. AAG9225013.

Smoot, Richard Jordan. **The Synthesis and Manipulation of Fused Ensemble Timbres and Sound Masses by Means of Digital Signal Processing.** (Electronic & Computer Music) The Ohio State University, 1986. D. M. A. 197p. No. AAG8618732. This dissertation includes sound masses and FETs created using digitally recorded instrument tone and derived sonorities found in the music of Edgard Varèse.

Solum, Stephen Edward. **Concerto for MIDI'D Grand Piano.** (Original Composition) (Electronic Music, Synthesis, Music Technology) University of Minnesota, 1994. Ph. D. 254p. No. AAG9433105.

Soule, Richard Lawrence. **"Synchronisms Nos. 1, 2, 3, 4, 5 and 6" of Mario Davidovsky: A Style Analysis.** Peabody Institute of the Johns Hopkins University, 1978. 304p. No. AAG8123525.

Stace, Stephen William. **"Axis": For Concert Band and Tape: An Analytical Study.** (Original Composition) Temple University, 1986. D. M. A. No. AAG8611935.

Stewart, James David. **Alias 610.** (Original Composition) San Jose State University, 1991. M. A. 45p. No. AAG1345824. *Alias 610* is a work for solo violin and tape using the Fibonacci sequence.

Stroope, Z. Randall. **Later Choral Works of Heinz Werner Zimmerman. (Germany)** Arizona State University, 1988. D. M. A. 232p. No. AAG-8907740. Later in his career Zimmerman incorporated improvisation and electronic sounds into his compositions.

Susser, Peter Matthew. **Attack, Sustain and Decay: An Analysis of "Synchronisms No. 3 for Cello and Electronic Sounds, [1964]" By Mario Davidovsky.** (With Original Composition) (Davidovsky, Mario, Chamber Music, Electronic Tape.) Columbia University, 1994. D. M. A. 154p. No. AAG9427146.

Sward, Rosalie La Crow. **An Examination of the Mathematical Systems Used in Selected Compositions of Milton Babbitt and Iannis Xenakis.** Northwestern University, 1981. Ph. D. 609p. No. AAG8125021.

Sylvander, Stefan Olof. **Electronic Musical Composition in Sweden, 1952-1970.** The University of Wisconsin-Madison, 1974. Ph. D. 250p. No.

AAG7510005.

Tamm, Eric Alexander. **Brian Eno, Electronic Musician: Progressive Rock and the Ambient Sound, 1973-1986.** University of California, Berkeley, 1987. Ph. D. 403p. No. AAG8726386.

Theberge, Paul. **Consumers of Technology: Musical Instrument Innovations and the Musicians' Market.** Concordia University (Canada), 1993. Ph. D. 364p. No. AAGNN87289. This dissertation begins with a look at the history of the piano and electronic keyboard industry, and continues by exploring the use of these instruments by musicians. The author points out that "with the shift to digital technologies, not only has the technical basis of musical instrument design changed but the organizational structure and marketing strategies of the instrument industry have also been transformed." (Abstract)

Thomas, Marilyn Taft. **Disparities for Ensemble and Electronic Tape.** (Original Composition) University of Pittsburgh, 1982. Ph. D. 137p. No. AAG-8312497.

Tolin, Craig Edmond. **A Spectral Analysis of Selected Vowels Sung By Bass and Baritone Student Singers. (Bass Singers, Singing)** The University of North Texas, 1990. Ph. D. 109p. No. AAG9105055.

Tomassetti, Emidio Benjamin. **"Image, Vision, and Celebration": For Flute, Clarinet, Alto Saxophone, Percussion, String Quartet, Piano, and Electronic Tape.** (Original Composition) University of Oregon, 1995. D. M. A. 237p. No. AAI9529065.

Torres-Santos, Raymond J. **Volume I: A Comparative Study of the Formal Structure in Music for an Ensemble and Tape. Volume II: Arevtos: A Symphonic Picture for Orchestra and Computer-Generated Sound.** (Original Composition) University of California-Los Angeles, 1986. Ph. D. 31p. No. AAG8621148.

Trainor, Christopher James. **A Macintosh Based Drum Simulator with 8-Bit Microcontroller Interface.** University of Lowell, 1995. M. S. C. P. 129p. No. AAI1362097. The system presented consists of sound libraries, software, and the hardware used.

Tredway, Curtis Brook. **A Curriculum for the Study of Audio, Video, Computer, and Electronic Music Technology for Undergraduate Music Education Majors Based on a Survey Among Members of the**

Florida Music Educators Association. The University of Southern Mississippi, 1994. Ph. D. 204p. No. AAI9509007.

Umble, James C. **Summary of Dissertation Recitals: Three Programs of Music for Saxophone.** (Performance.) The University of Michigan, 1995. D. M. A. 1p. No. AAI0576577. One selection of this recital was realized for saxophone and tape: Evan Chambers: *Rothko-Tobey Continuum for Saxophone and Tape.*

Van Scoyoc, Marilyn Linda. **The Development and Evaluation of Electronic Wind Controller Instructional Materials and Techniques for the Instrumental Music Educator. (Wind Instruments)** Columbia University Teachers College, 1991. Ed. D. 209p. No. AAG9136456. The materials were developed on a Yamaha WX11/WT11™ wind controller.

Verin, Micolas. **Two Musical Compositions: "Cirios" and "Le Spleen De Paris."** (Original work-Electronic) University of California-San Diego, 1986. Ph. D. 158p. No. AAG8622888.

Wells, Thomas Henry. **Systems of Electronic and Instrumental Music.** (Original Composition with Commentary.) The University of Texas at Austin, 1969. D. M. A. 55p. No. AAG7010742.

Wesner-Hoehn, Beverly A. **An Analysis of the Technical Development of the Salui Electronic Harp and an Exploration of Possible Performance Capabilities for Harpists and Composers.** Indiana University, 1989. D. Mus. (np) No. AAG0381044.

Wheeler, Raymond Irvin. **Lecture - Clarinet Performance in the Electronic Medium.** (Musical Performance) The University of Michigan, 1978. A. Mus. D. 1p. No. AAG0530250.

Winn, Kathleen A. **"Star RT. 2": A Study of Alternative Notation for a Chamber Ensemble.** California State University, Long Beach, 1989. M. M. 59p. No. AAG1339373. This thesis studies nontraditional notation and conducting for oboe, bassoon, violin, viola, percussion, and Yamaha™ DX7 synthesizer.

Yancey, Herbert R. **Electronic Music: An Essential Component in Secondary Music Education.** University of Sarasota, 1979. Ed. D. 115p. No. AAG8906812.

Yekovich, Robert Alan. **Some Remarks on "Duo."** (Original Composition-

Clarinet-Electronic Music) Columbia University, 1991. D. M. A. 143p. No. AAG9202776.

Young, Barbara G. **The Use of Computer and Keyboard Technology in Selected Independent Piano Studios.** The University of Oklahoma, 1990. D. M. A. 206p. No. AAG9029877.

Young, Mary Ellen. **Tashi Gomang. Pauline Oliveros: A Biography and Descriptive Catalog of Compositions.** University of Minnesota, 1991. Ph. D. 550p. No. AAG9112743. This dissertation includes an account of her electronic compositions.

Appendix B:
System Manuals

The following manuals are publications that have been written for use with specific electronic music instruments or related devices. These are generally works which were not shipped with the instruments at the time of purchase, but have been created to be supplemental guides. Many such guides have been published over the years but are mostly out of print at this time. The following list is of manuals which are still in print.

Most equipment manufacturers will be able to provide copies of the original manuals for specific equipment. To this end the following manuals are listed under the name of the company that produced the equipment being considered.

ALEXIS CORPORATION
Alexis Studio Electronics, 3630 Holdredge Avenue, Los Angeles, CA 90016. 213-467-8000.

Anderton, Craig. **The Complete Guide to the Alexis HR-16 & MMT-8.** New York, NY: Music Sales Corp., 1989. 192p. illus. ISBN 0-6856-5828-7.

ARP INSTRUMENTS
45 Hartwell Avenue, Lexington, MA 02173.

The ARP 2600 Patch Book. Lexington, MA: ARP Instruments, 1989.

Snow, Mary. **The Waveform Music Book.** (ARP 2600) Lubbock, TX: Lariken Press, 1977.

CASIO, INC.
Professional Music Products Division, 15 Gardner Road, Fairfield, NJ 07006.
201-361-5400.

Schlesinger, Andrew. **An Insider's Guide to Casio CZ Synthesizers: The Most Complete Hands-On Approach to Programming all CZ Synthes.** Los Angeles, CA: Alfred Publishing Co., 1988. viii. 95p. illus.

KAWAI AMERICA CORP.
2055 East University Drive, Campton, CA 90224.

Maestas, Bobby. **Kawai K-One Sound Making Book.** Newbury Park, CA: Alexander Publishing Co., 1988. 138p. illus. ISBN 0-939067-08-0.

Walker, Dan. **Kawai K-Five Making It Happen.** Newbury Park, CA: Alexander Publishing Co., 1988. 103p. illus. ISBN 0-939067-01-3.

_____. **K-1 Operations & Tweaking Sounds.** Newbury Park, CA: Alexander Publishing Co., 1988. 102p. illus. (Kawai K-One Support Series) ISBN 0-939067-07-2.

KORG, USA.
89 Frost Street, Westbury, NJ 11590.

Maestas, Bobby. **Korg M-One Sound Making Book: Level 1.** Newbury Park, CA: Alexander Publishing Co., 1989. 167p. illus. ISBN 0-93906-7039-0.

Rychner, Lorenz. **Korg DW Eight Thousand: Working Out with the Workhorse.** Newbury Park, CA: Alexander Publishing Co., 1987. 130p. illus. ISBN 0-939067-25-0.

Walker, Ron. **Korg M-One Drum Pattern Handbook.** Newbury Park, CA: Alexander Publishing Co., 1988. 92p. illus. (Korg M-One Support Series) ISBN 0-939067-40-4.

OBERHEIM CORP.
2015 Davie Avenue, Commerce, CA 90040.

Burger, Jeff. **Oberheim Matrix-Six: Getting the Most Out of Yours.** Newbury Park, CA: Alexander Publishing, Co., 1987. 102p. illus. ISBN 0-939067-17-X.

ROLAND CORPORATION/US.

7200 Dominion Circle, Los Angeles, CA 90040.

Rychner, Lorenz. **Roland Alpha Juno-One: Getting the Most Out of Yours.** Newbury Park, CA: Alexander Publishing Co., 1987. 65p. illus. ISBN 0-939067-11-0.

_____. **Roland Alpha Juno-Two: Getting the Most Out of Yours.** Newbury Park, CA: Alexander Publishing Co., 1987. 65p. illus. ISBN 0-939067-43-9.

Walker, Dan. **Roland PR100 Sequencing Handbook.** Newbury Park, CA: Alexander Publishing Co., 1988. 108p. illus. ISBN 0-939067-24-2.

_____. **Roland D10-20 Operations & Programming Guide.** Newbury Park, CA: Alexander Publishing Co., 1988. 251p. illus. ISBN 0-939067-60-9.

_____. **Roland D10-20 Drum Pattern Handbook.** Newbury Park, CA: Alexander Publishing Co., 1988. 60p. illus. ISBN 0-939067-61-7.

_____. **Roland D110 Programming & Basic Operations.** Newbury Park, CA: Alexander Publishing, 1988. 189p. illus. ISBN 0-939067-63-3.

_____. **Roland D-50: Sixty-Four New Sounds.** Newbury Park, CA: Alexander Publishing, 1987. 148p. illus. ISBN 0-939076-54-4.

_____. **Roland D-50 Vol. II: Sound Making & Programming.** Newbury Park, CA: Alexander Publishing, 1987. 250p. illus. ISBN 0-939067-53-6.

YAMAHA INTERNATIONAL CORP.
P. O. Box 6600, Buena Park, CA 90622.

Butler, Gabriel. **Fun With the Yamaha SHS-10.** New York, NY: Music Sales Corporation, nd. 48p. illus. ISBN 0-711913-92-7.

Massey, Howard. **The Complete DX711.** New York, NY: Music Sales Corp., 1987. 308p. illus. ISBN 0-825611-19-9.

_____. **The Complete DX7.** New York, NY: Music Sales Corp., 1986. 288p. illus. ISBN 0-711909-96-2.

Preskitt, Steve. **E1: Update for the Yamaha DX711.** Newbury Park, CA:

Alexander Publishing Co., 1989. 193p. illus. ISBN 0-939067-65-X.

Rychner, Lorenz. **Yamaha DX7 Patch Fake Book.** Newbury Park, CA: Alexander Publishing Co., 1987. 164p. illus. (Yamaha DX7 Support Series) ISBN 0-939067-75-7.

_____. **Yamaha TX81Z.** Newbury Park, CA: Alexander Publishing Co., 1987. 104p. illus. ISBN 0-939067-22-6.

_____. **Yamaha TX802.** Newbury Park, CA: Alexander Publishing Co., 1988. 110p. illus. ISBN 0-939067-23-4.

_____. **Yamaha MTIX.** Newbury Park, CA: Alexander Publishing Co., 1987. 72p. illus. ISBN 0-939067-74-9.

_____. **Yamaha DX100.** Newbury Park, CA: Alexander Publishing Co., 1987. 67p. illus. ISBN 0-939067-38-2.

_____. **Yamaha DX7IIFD: Vol. 1.** Newbury Park, CA: Alexander Publishing Co., 152p. illus. ISBN 0-939067-36-6.

_____. **Yamaha DX7 II.** Milwaukee, WI: Hal Leonard Corporation, 1987. 111p. illus. ISBN 0-88188-772-2.

_____. **Yamaha DX21: Getting the Most Out of Yours.** Newbury Park, CA: Alexander Publishing, 1987. 84p. illus. ISBN 0-939067-02-1.

_____. **The Classic Yamaha DX7.** Newbury Park, CA: Alexander Publishing Co., 1987. 93p. illus. ISBN 0-939067-05-6.

_____. **Yamaha DX21: Getting the Most Out of Yours.** Newbury Park, CA: Alexander Publishing Co., 1987. 84p. illus. ISBN 0-939067-02-1.

Six Hundred Voices for the DX7. New York, NY: Music Sales Corp., 1987. 206p. illus. ISBN 0-825624-99-1.

Appendix C:
On-line Sources

A number of online services have been established in recent years that concentrate on electronic and computer music. These World Wide Web sites, Discussion lists, Gophers, and other systems often change or move to new locations making it difficult to locate them easily on line. Often the sites provide links to other electronic music locations, or provide information on the relocation of on-line sites. Some of the sites are "under construction" while they are available on line, but still provide valuable information for the electronic music professional or experimenter.

In order to access the on-line sources listed below it is necessary to obtain a provider, either commercial or through an educational institution. Information on getting on line can be found at larger public and college libraries, or from computer outlets. Additional online music sites may be found using one of the many subject locator systems, e.g., Yahoo, Lycos, Excite, or the WebCrawler.

The information listed for the items below includes the name of the on-line site, the owner or provider of the site, the URL (Uniform Resource Locator), the Email address (if provided) to contact the online source system operator, and a brief explanation of the information provided on the site.

911 Gallery Home Page. 911 Gallery, Indianapolis, IN. World Wide Web Site. URL: http://www.iquest.net/911/iq_911.html Email: artgal@iquest.net (for information).

    The 911 Gallery specializes in digital media including art, computer graphics, video, and electronic music. Information on exhibits, shows, and video are provided.

Analogue Heaven. Mailing List Discussion Group. The Analogue Heaven Mailing List. Access: analogue-request@magnus.acs.ohio-state.edu.

This mailing list was founded in 1992 to serve the needs of musicians interested in vintage analogue electronic music equipment. It is unmoderated and features information on analogue synthesizers, sequencers, drum machines, and effects units. There is also a Gopher site for information on past discussions at [cs.uwp.edu].

Auricle Control Systems. World Wide Web Site. Auricle Control Systems. URL: http://www.webcom.com/~auricle/welcome.html Email: auricle@ix.netcom.com (for information).

This site introduces Auricle Control Systems (ACS), an interactive system for developing music for film, television, and multimedia presentations.

Bay Area Musicians' Forum. World Wide Web Site. Bay Area Musicians' Forum (BAMF) URL: http://bamf.org Email: sysop@bamf.org.

This is a Web site and a bulletin board for the San Francisco Bay Area's electronic musicians. The bulletin board is provided by Corporate Multimedia, Inc..

Bergman Electronic Music Studios at Dartmouth College. World Wide Web Site. Bergman Electronic Music Studio, Department of Music, Dartmouth College. URL: http://onyx.dartmouth.edu.

This Web site provides information on the Electro-Acoustic Music Program at Dartmouth College including requirements, seminars, and recent theses. Also links to other Web sites of interest to electronic musicians are provided.

The Buddy Project - A Music Clearinghouse. World Wide Web Site. Buddy Project URL: http://www.buddy.org Email: buddymeister@buddy.org (for information).

The Buddy Project is a clearinghouse for both electronic and acoustic music. This site also accepts original music electronically or on cassette.

Center for Computer Research in Music and Acoustics. (CCRMA) World Wide Web Site. Stanford University Center for Computer Research in Music and Acoustics. URL: http://ccrma-www.Stanford.edu Email:

webmaster@ccrma.Stanford.edu (for information).

The Center for Computer Research in Music researches composition, synthesis techniques, physical modeling, signal processing, digital re- cording, musical acoustics, psychoacoustics, and real-time applications & controllers. Links are provided to other sites of interest to electronic musicians.

Center for Electronic Art. (CEA) World Wide Web Site. URL: http://www .cea.edu/cea/about.us/history.html Email: info@cea.edu.

This Web sight explains the history of the Center for Electronic Art located in San Francisco. The subjects covered include computer graphics, video, and music.

Computer Music at the Laboratory of Integrated Systems. (LSI) World Wide Web Site. The Computer Music Group, Laboratory of Integrated Systems. (LSI) URL: http://www.lsi.usp.br/~musica/musica.html Email: roger@lsi.usp.br.

The Computer Music Group provides "an academic site where composers, electronic engineers, computer scientists and others can interact and share experiences in behalf of this subject." (Introduction) This site also provides links to home pages of the CERL Sound Group, The Csound Front Page, *Computer Music Journal,* and others.

Dartmouth College Bregman Electronic Music Studios. World Wide Web Site. Bregman Electronic Music Studios, Dartmouth College. URL: http: //music.dartmouth.edu.

This Web site introduces the Dartmouth College Bregman Electronic Music Studios at Dartmouth College and provides information concerning the electro-acoustic music program. Also, links are provided to related Web sites on electronic music.

Digital Village Exhibition. World Wide Web Site. Art Gallery, University of Maryland-College Park. URL: http://www.inform.umd.edu: 8080/EdRes/ Colleges/ARHU/ArtGal/.

This list describes the Digital Village Exhibition at the University of Maryland, Corcoran Gallery of Art in Washington, DC. The exhibition includes electronic art, music, and multimedia.

Dreampop. World Wide Web Site. E-Doc Front Door. URL: http://www. edoc. com/jrl-bin/wilma/mmu.806900582.html Email: ejournal@edoc.com (for information).

This site is devoted to "shoegazer" music described as "hazy, multi-layered guitars with vocals." (Introductory material.) Electroacoustic music is covered here, along with acoustic music, reviews, and essays.

Electronic Music from Surreal to Real. World Wide Web Site. Surreal To Real. URL: http://www.gold.net/users/dq03/ Email: surreal@cityscape. co.uk.

Surreal To Real is a record label in England which specializes in synthe-sizer music, and electronic music in general. This site provides links to other online electronic music sources.

EMUSIC-L. Mailing List Discussion Group. American University, Wash-ington, DC. Access: listserv@listserv.american.edu

This list is a discussion group for topics of electronic music including, technique, technology, composition, & equipment. (To join this list send a message to Listserv.American.Edu and put "subscribe EMUSIC-L your name" in body of message.)

Global Electronic Music Marketplace. World Wide Web Site. Global Elec-tronic Music Marketplace. URL: http://192.215.9.13/Flirt/GEMM/ gemm 2.html   Email: admin@gemm.com (for information).

The Global Electronic Music Marketplace provides listings on used CDs, LPs, and rare and out-of-print items. This is a good source for out-of-print recordings of electronic music.

Hal Leonard Online. World Wide Web Site. Hal Leonard Publishing Co., Winona, MI. URL: http://www.halleonard.com Email: hleonard@exec pc.com (for information).

This site provides information on publications by the Hal Leonard Pub. Co.. including a number of books including electronic keyboard manuals.

ICMA Software Library. World Wide Web Site. ICMA Software Library, The University of Leeds, England. URL: http://www.leeds.ac.uk/music/Net Info/ICMA/icma_cat.html   Email: ftpmail@Dartmouth.Edu   (for information).

This Web site provides information on the ICMA Software Library which collects information concerning software currently available for use by computer music researchers and composers.

Institute for Psychoacoustics and Electronic Music. (IPEM) World Wide Web Site. Institute for Psychoacoustics and Electronic Music (IPEM), Belgium. URL: http://next.rug.ac.be/EnglishHomepage.html Email: dirk. moelants@rug.ac.be. Also: http://next.rug.ac.be/Ipem30years.html.

This Web site provides information on the epistemological and methodological foundations of music and the perception of sound and the history of IPEM activity. Information can be found here on the *Journal of New Music Research* along with a short article entitled "Electronics and Music."

The Institute for Psychoacoustics and Electronic Music (IPEM) was founded in 1963 as a joint venture between the Belgian Radio and Television broadcasting company and the University of Ghent. The activities of the Institute include digital music research & multimedia focusing on the epistemological and methodological foundations of musicology based on the perception of sound.

Kraft Music. World Wide Web Site. Kraft Music, Milwaukee, WI. URL: http://www.execpc.com/~kraftmus/ Email: kraftmus@exe cpc.com.

Kraft Music sells software, MIDI keyboards, and other electronic music equipment. This site provides links to other online electronic music sources.

Kurzweil Music Systems. World Wide Web Site. Kurzweil Music Systems, Young Chang. URL:http://www.musicpro.com/kurzweil/ Email:kurzweil @aol.com (for information).

This site provides information on electronic instruments provided by Kurzweil including electronic keyboards and acoustic pianos.

Massachusetts Institute of Technology, Media Lab. World Wide Web Site. Media Lab, M. I. T. URL: http://spi.www.media.mit.edu Email: webmaster @media.mit.edu.

Founded in 1985, the Media Lab at MIT carries out research on all kinds of electronic technologies including computer music. This site provides links to other sources.

New Age / Electronic Music Links. World Wide Web Site. Chad Gould (editor) URL: http://www.webcom.com/~cgould/newage.html Email: cgould @gate.net (for information).

New Age provides a directory of new age sites on the Internet. Electronic music is included along with "space" music and the avant-garde. An annotated directory is provided.

Society for Music Theory. World Wide Web Site. Society for Music Theory. URL:http://boethius.music.ucsb.edu/smthome.html#about   Email: database@boethius.music.ucsb.edu.

This is the home page for the Society of Music Theory which provides information on all aspects of music theory.

Sonic Images Records Home Page. World Wide Web Site. Sonic Images Records. URL: http://www.sonicimages.com   Email: sales@higgs.com (for information).

Sonic Images Records is a commercial outlet for studio, soundtrack work, and electronic music.

Tangled Web. World Wide Web Site. Tangled Web. URL: http://www.edoc. com/jrl-bin/wilma/nws.807126415.html Email: ejournal@edoc.com (for information).

Tangled Web provides information on several journals including *Allegro Cambrio, The Harvard Square Literary Review,* and *Harvard Square Virtual* (art gallery). Articles on electronic and avant-garde music can be found here.

Wallingford Electronics Inc. World Wide Web Site. Wallingford Electronics, Inc. URL: http://www.wallingford.com Email: zardoz@colossus.com (for information).

This site provides information concerning the Wallingford Electronics company which produces electronic music equipment.

Weed Music. World Wide Web Site. Weed Music, Alberta, Canada. URL: http: //www.compusmart.ab.ca/weed Host site:http://www. compusmart. ab.ca

Email: weed@mail.compusmart.ab.ca (for information).

Weed Music specializes in music software and electronic instruments.
This site also provides an online discussion group in music education.

Appendix D:
Electronic and Computer Music
Periodicals

Over the years a number of periodical publications have been devoted, at least in part, to electronic and computer music. Some of these publications have lasted only a few years, but others have continued to publish articles concerned with electronic music up to the present time.

Artist/Musiker. Droste Verlag GmbH, Abt. Ed. Lintz Verlag, Pressehaus am Martin-Luther Platz, Postfach 11 22, D-4000 Dusseldorf 1, West Germany.

CLEM. (Contact List of Electronic Musicians) Alex Douglas, P. O. Box 86010. North Vancouver, British Columbia V7L 4J5, Canada. This newsletter was published for a number of years, and can be found in some library collections. It was a valuable directory of people in the world of music.

CMA/ARRAY. 1979- Quarterly. Array Association, San Francisco, CA. This is the newsletter of the Computer Music Association.

Computer Music Journal. 1977- Quarterly. P. O. Box E, Menlo Park, California 94025. This has ceased publication, but while it lasted it had very good articles on electronic music.

Cybernews. 1993- 6/year. Toulouse. This journal is devoted to the promotion of electronic music.

Die Reih. (see also item 22) (8 issues, 1955-1962). This famous journal on experimental and electronic music was established by Karlheinz

Stockhausen and Herbert Eimert and featured articles on early electronic music along with information on the avant garde.

Ear Magazine East. 1983- 5/year. New Wilderness Foundation, 325 Spring Street, New York, NY 10013. This tabloid style publication covers the avant-garde scene in the New York area.

Eighth Nerve, The. 1990- Quarterly. Symbolic Sound Corp., Champaign, IL. This journal covers general electronic music and computer composition.

Electro Acoustic Music. **(EAM)** 1984- Irregular. EAM London, England. This is the journal of the Electro-Acoustic Music Association of Great Britain.

Electronic Music Educator. 1988-1990. Quarterly. Instrumentalist Company, Northfield, IL. EMS featured articles on the use of electronic music in teaching.

Electronic Music Review. (7 issues were published, 1967-1969) The *Electronic Music Review* was a very scholarly journal that featured articles on electronic music and equipment.

Electronic Musician. 1985- Monthly. Mix Publications, Berkeley, CA. This is the standard source for current information on electronic music technology. It features product reviews, articles on hardware & software, and evaluations.

Eurock. 1976- Archie Patterson, P. O. Box 13718, Portland, Oregon 97213. This journal mainly covers rock and electronic music in Europe.

Future Music. Monthly. Future Publications, Inc., Somerton, Somerset, England.

High Fidelity. 1959-1989. Monthly. ABC Leisure Magazines, 825 7th Avenue, New York, NY 10019. *High Fidelity* is a very popular magazine which specializes in articles concerning audio equipment, and to some extent, reviews electronic music and equipment.

Home and Studio Recording. 1987- Monthly. Music Maker Publications, 7316 Topanga Canyon Blvd. Canoga Park, CA 91313. This is a favorite magazine for musicians who wish to have a home recording studio.

Home Recording. 1987- Bimonthly. GPI Communications, 20085 Stevens

Creek, Cupertino, CA 95014.

i/e: The Magazine of Progressive and Electronic Music. 1992- Quarterly. Think Tank Tomes, Chandler, AZ.

Interface: A Journal of the Arts. 1976- Mid-Atlantic Regional Media Center, University of Maryland.

International Musician. 1991-1992. Monthly. Northern & Shell, London, England. This monthly was concerned mainly with rock music and electronic instruments.

Journal of Electroacoustic Music. 1992- Annual. Sonic Arts Network, London, England. This annual publication reviews electronic composition and MIDI.

Keyboard Magazine. (officially *Keyboard*) 1939- Quarterly. GPI Publications, Cupertino, CA. *Keyboard* is a trade magazine for the commercial keyboard musician. Articles cover current issues in electronic music, techniques, new developments in technology, and advice. This journal is a good place to find the most recent equipment advertised.

Mix Bookshelf. 1974- 2/year. Whitehurst & Clark, Inc., 100 Newfield Ave., Edison, NJ 08837. *Mix Bookshelf* is a very popular semi-annual list for the music business. It features lists of books, recordings, and new equipment. Each issue features publications on electronic music.

Music, Computers and Software. (MCS) 1986- Bimonthly. MCS Publications, 190 East Main Street, Huntington, NY 11743. This journal is a great source for electronic musicians in that it covers all aspects of composition, synthesis, and MIDI.

Music Maker. 1966- Monthly. Central House, 42 Rayne Road, Braintree, Essex CM7 7QP, England.

Music Technology. 1986-1990. Monthly. Music Maker Publications, 2608 Ninth Street, Berkeley, CA 94710. This magazine is generally a source for MIDI information.

Music World. 1893- Quarterly. Central House, 42 Rayne Road, Braintree, Essex CM7 7QP, England. This is an early journal that included articles on early experiments in musique concrète and electronic music.

Musician. 1896-1948. Monthly. Amordian Press, Box 701, 31 Commercial Street, Gloucester, MA 01930. This is one of the best sources for information on early experiments in electronic music.

New Music Chicago. 1985- Monthly. Box 10742, Chicago, Illinois 60610. This little newsletter provided information on avant-garde concerts in the Chicago area. It can be found in some library collections.

Perspectives of New Music. 1962- Quarterly. Bard College, Annandale, New York 12504. This is a very well respected journal which concentrates on modern music, and includes articles and reviews of electronic music.

Piano and Keyboard. (Formerly *Piano Quarterly*) 1993- Bimonthly. The String Letter Press Publishers, San Anselmo, CA. This is more of a professional journal in that it features in-depth interviews with electronic musicians, teachers, and experimenters, and concentrates on technology.

Recordings of Experimental Music. 1979- Bimonthly. 104 Fern Avenue, Collingswood, New Jersey 18108. This journal publishes interviews and reviews on experimental and computer music.

Resonance. 1992- Irregular. Musicians' Collective, London, England. *Resonance* features articles on the history, criticism, and composition of electronic music.

Seamus Newsletter. 1988- Quarterly. Society for Electro-Acoustic Arts in the U. S. This work covers computer music in general.

Source: Music of the Avant-Garde. (published 9 issues, 1967-1971). This journal, which often provided recordings with issues, reviewed electronic music mainly in a rock vein.

Stereo Review. 1968- Monthly. Ziff Davis Pub. Co., One Park Avenue, New York, NY 10016. This is a very well known publication which reviews mainly rock and traditional classical music, but does review some electronic and computer music.

Village Voice. 1981- Weekly. 842 Broadway, New York, NY 10003. The *Village Voice* is well know for its reviews of avant-garde and experimental music.

Name Index

Numbers refer to item numbers except where a page number is indicated, e.g. (Pg. 33)

Subject Index

Numbers refer to item numbers except where a page number is indicated, e.g. (Pg. 2)

About the Author

ROBERT L. WICK is Assistant Professor and Fine Arts Bibliographer at the Auraria Library, University of Colorado at Denver. His interest in electronic and computer music bibliography grew as he developed a basic library collection for the Department of Music.

ISBN 0-313-30076-3

HARDCOVER BAR CODE